UOUS PASTS

AFRICAN PERSPECTIVES
Kelly Askew, Laura Fair, and Pamila Gupta
Series Editors

Continuous Pasts: Frictions of Memory in Postcolonial Africa
Sakiru Adebayo

*Writing on the Soil: Land and Landscape in Literature
from Eastern and Southern Africa*
Ng'ang'a Wahu-Muchiri

*Power / Knowledge / Land: Contested Ontologies of Land
and Its Governance in Africa*
Laura A. German

In Search of Tunga: *Prosperity, Almighty God,
and Lives in Motion in a Malian Provincial Town*
André Chappatte

*The Infrastructures of Security:
Technologies of Risk Management in Johannesburg*
Martin J. Murray

*There Used to Be Order:
Life on the Copperbelt after the Privatisation of the
Zambia Consolidated Copper Mines*
Patience Mususa

*Animated by Uncertainty: Rugby and the
Performance of History in South Africa*
Joshua D. Rubin

African Performance Arts and Political Acts
Naomi André, Yolanda Covington-Ward, and Jendele Hungbo, Editors

*Filtering Histories: The Photographic Bureaucracy
in Mozambique, 1960 to Recent Times*
Drew A. Thompson

A complete list of titles in the series can be found at www.press.umich.edu

Continuous Pasts

Frictions of Memory in Postcolonial Africa

Sakiru Adebayo

University of Michigan Press
Ann Arbor

Copyright © 2023 by Sakiru Adebayo

All rights reserved

For questions or permissions, please contact um.press.perms@umich.edu

Published in the United States of America by the
University of Michigan Press
Manufactured in the United States of America
Printed on acid-free paper
First published June 2023

A CIP catalog record for this book is available from the British Library.

Library of Congress Cataloging-in-Publication data has been applied for.

ISBN 978-0-472-07623-9 (hardcover : alk. paper)
ISBN 978-0-472-05623-1 (paper : alk. paper)
ISBN 978-0-472-22119-6 (e-book)

Publication of this volume has been partially funded by the African Studies Center, University of Michigan.

Cover image: Original Sankofa art painting by Donna-Lee Bolden-Kerr, used by permission. Courtesy of the artist and https://fineartamerica.com/featured/sankofa-donna-lee-bolden-kerr.html

This book will be made open access within three years of publication thanks to Path to Open, a program developed in partnership between JSTOR, the American Council of Learned Societies (ACLS), University of Michigan Press, and The University of North Carolina Press to bring about equitable access and impact for the entire scholarly community, including authors, researchers, libraries, and university presses around the world. Learn more at https://about.jstor.org/path-to-open/

*For Bhekizizwe Peterson (1961–2021),
a generous mentor of young Black scholars*

CONTENTS

Acknowledgments   ix

INTRODUCTION
The Past Is Full of Ruptures   1

    Memories of Conflict and Conflicts of Memory in Postcolonial Africa   1
    Postcolonial Memory Studies   6
    Frictions of Memory   13
    Fiction of Memory in Post-Conflict Africa   16
    Outline of the Book   18

CHAPTER 1
The Past Is a Contested Territory: *Half of a Yellow Sun* as a Postmemory Fiction   23

    The Shadow of Biafra   23
    Postmemory   26
    Chimamanda Adichie as a Vicarious Witness   28
    Aesthetics of Postmemory in *Half of a Yellow Sun*   31
    Remembering Back and Writing Back: The Nexus between Postmemory and Postcolonialism in *Half of a Yellow Sun*   36
    Remediation of Memory   40
    Postmemory and the Possibility of Justice for Biafra   43
    Concatenated Memories, Ancestral Memories   45

CHAPTER 2
The Past Continues in Silence: Memory, Complicity, and the Post-Conflict Timescapes in *The Memory of Love*   48

    Reading Silence   48
    A Sense of Something Unspoken: *The Memory of Love* as Textual Silence   52

Silence of Trauma	54
Silence of Oppression	56
A Culture of Silence	57
Silent and Silenced Memories	58
Silence of Complicity	64
Post-Conflict Timescapes in *The Memory of Love*	69

CHAPTER 3
The Past Continues in Another Country:
African Transnational Memory in a Migratory Setting … 74

Immigrant Melancholia	74
Memory, Translocalities, and Alternative Practices of Belonging in *Children of the Revolution*	83
In Search of an African Transnational Memory	89

CHAPTER 4
The Past Continues through Subject Positions:
Memory, Subjectivity, and Secondary Witnessing
in *The Shadow of Imana* … 96

African Transnational Memory and the Genocide against the Tutsi in Rwanda	96
Sites and Sutures of Memory: Véronique Tadjo's Affective Encounters	103
Memory and Positionality: Aesthetics of Secondary Witnessing in *The Shadow of Imana*	109

CHAPTER 5
The Past Continues in the Future … 117

Notes … 127

References … 153

Index … 173

ACKNOWLEDGMENTS

To say that the process of writing and completing *Continuous Pasts* was difficult is an understatement. While writing the book, I moved to a new country, started a new job, and was knocked down twice by COVID-19. But what made it worthwhile was the love and support I received from friends, colleagues, and mentors all over the world. My PhD supervisor, Bhekizizwe Peterson, who, sadly, passed away due to complications from COVID-19, was a firm believer in this project. I am grateful to him for preparing me for this complicated academic life and for always reminding me that the world is my oyster. I am also immensely thankful for Eric Worby's kindness and support over all of these years. Eric gave me the opportunity to pursue a PhD through his Mellon-funded THINK (Transforming Humanities through Interdisciplinary Thinking) initiative. He supported me while I was job hunting and continues to be there for me as I navigate the uncharted territory of the North American academy. I am indebted to Michael Rothberg for supporting this project right from when it was still a PhD proposal to this point. I also appreciate Michael for the professional support he has given me, especially since the passing of my PhD supervisor.

I am grateful to Jeffrey Olick for the opportunity to participate in the University of Virginia/Memory Studies Association (UVA/MSA) graduate seminar in 2020. That seminar helped me to rethink the trajectory of this book; it also exposed me to many important works in memory studies, some of which are cited in this book. I am grateful to the coordinators of the MSA mentorship program for doctoral researchers—a program through which I had the privilege of working with Stef Craps in the capacity of a mentee. I appreciate Stef for our many Skype calls and email exchanges over the years—some of the ideas that emerged from our numerous conversations are incorporated into this book. I am grateful to Hanna Teichler for her friendship and for introducing me to the MSA back in 2016. I also appreciate Ann Rigney for inviting me to present a part of this book at the Utrecht Forum Memory Studies in 2021.

I am grateful to all of the lecturers and staff members in the Department of African Literature at the University of the Witwatersrand for making that department the most intellectually exciting place in the world to teach and research African literature. I am particularly thankful to Isabel Hofmeyr, Dan Ojwang, Grace Musila, Danai Mupotsa, Khwezi Mkhize, and Merle Govind for the moral and intellectual support they gave me while I was a doctoral fellow there. I appreciate Chris Ouma for the support he gave (even when he did not have to) while I was doing my PhD and for the support he continues to give even now that I am far away from South Africa.

I had an amazing one year of postdoctoral fellowship (funded, again, by Eric's THINK initiative) at the Wits Institute of Social and Economic Research (WISER). Thanks to my host, Sarah Nuttall, for giving me the space and liberty to do the kind of research I wanted to do. At WISER, I met and interacted with many brilliant scholars and colleagues who inspired me— and continue to do so. For all of the exchanges of ideas and cross-pollination of thoughts at weekly seminars, workshops, and symposiums at WISER, I appreciate Achille Mbembe, Melanie Boehi, Charne Lavery, Keith Breckenridge, Pamila Gupta, Hlonipha Mokoena, Tinashe Mushakavanhu, Sizwe Mpofu-Walsh, Louise Bethlehem, Najibha Deshmukh, Christa Kuljian, Nolwazi Mkhwanazi, and Richard Rottenburg, among others. I am particularly grateful to Pamila Gupta for showing interest in this book and for helping to ensure that it found a publisher.

I am grateful to my colleagues who read bits and pieces of this book and offered insightful suggestions on how and where to make the book better. Thanks to Mihaela Mihai for reading the introduction and suggesting ways to tighten the arguments. Thanks to Gbenga Adeoba and Andreas Schmid for pointing out instances of sentential, punctuation, and argumentative ambiguities in chapter 1. I appreciate Olanrewaju Lasisi for reading and commenting on chapter 2, and Chigbo Arthur Anyaduba for reading and thoroughly editing chapter 3. Thanks to James Yeku and Ayorinde Oladele for reading and offering useful comments on the introduction and chapter 4. If readers enjoy this book, it is because I incorporated the comments and suggestions of these aforementioned colleagues. If readers do not enjoy this book, it is because I failed to incorporate the comments and suggestions of these aforementioned colleagues. I would also like to give a special shout-out to Nancy Hunt for closely reading chapter 1 (as a respondent to the "New Approaches to Memory" panel at the 2021 ASA conference) and for offering so many insightful suggestions that went into the revision of that chapter.

Over the years, I have benefited immensely from formal and informal conversations with amazing colleagues, and some of those conversations have shaped the way I think and do research. In light of that, I extend my appreciation to the following colleagues for allowing me to tap into their intellectual energies and vibes: Palesa Nqambaza, Manosa Nthunya, Mpho Matheolane, Dylan Valley, Refiloe Lepere, Femi Eromosele, Moshibudi Motimele, Hlengiwe Ndlovu, Adam Levine, Emery Kalema, Fabian Krautwald, Nancy Rushohora, Mpho Mathebula, Edwin Tallam, Eddie Ombagi, Naomi Ostwald Kawamura, Tracy Adams, Richard Benda, Shir'a Jeenah, Tasneem Essop, Job Zwane, Lindiwe Malindi, Zinhle Mkhabela, and Gorata Chengeta. I am also grateful to the following senior colleagues who inspire me either through their works or through the one-on-one conversations I have had the privilege of having with them: Pumla Gobodo-Madikizela, Astrid Erll, Rosanne Kennedy, Hugo Canham, Ato Quayson, Jill Bradbury, Senayon Olaoluwa, Kazeem Adebiyi, and Emmanuel Omobowale. I am grateful to the University of Michigan Press team for their support from the beginning to the end of this project. Special thanks and shout out to Ellen Bauerle and Kevin Rennells for their relentless support throughout the entire process.

It has been over a year since I joined the Department of English and Cultural Studies at the University of British Columbia (Okanagan campus), and I could not have asked for a better environment to work in. I am grateful to all my colleagues at UBCO for being so warm, understanding, and inspiring. I also appreciate the following friends who asked—and endured the torture of listening to my explanation of—what this book is about: George Holland, Joan Proudfoot, Jin Choi, Vera Makamu, Mulalo Mapfumo, Chijioke Ona, Theophilus Okunlola, Todd Statham, Niyi Asiyanbi, Madeline Donald, Umar Turaki, Robin Metcalfe, Ilya Parkins, Joanna Cockerline, George Grinnell, David Jefferess, and David Adepoju. Finally, I appreciate my family (my mum, sisters, and brother) and my best friends, Drs. Femi Dada and Victor Ogunlola, for being my greatest cheerleaders.

An earlier version of chapter 1 appeared in *Research in African Literatures* (52, no. 1), and a very small fraction of chapter 3 appeared in *Kairos: A Journal of Critical Symposium* (4, no. 1). I am grateful to the editors of both journals for granting permission to repurpose the articles in this book.

Introduction

The Past Is Full of Ruptures

The crimes that the African continent commits against her kind are of a dimension and, unfortunately, of a nature that appears to constantly provoke memories of the historic wrongs inflicted on that continent by others. There are moments when it almost appears as if there is a diabolical continuity to it all.
—Wole Soyinka, *The Burden of Memory, The Muse of Forgiveness*

The postcolonial bespeaks not just an ideological or intellectual rupture but a historical, political and economic rupture.
—Adebayo Williams, "The Postcolonial Flaneur"

The quest for historical understanding "aims at calming the dead who still haunt the present, and at offering them scriptural tombs."
—Michel de Certeau, *The Writing of History*

MEMORIES OF CONFLICT AND CONFLICTS OF MEMORY IN POSTCOLONIAL AFRICA

Europe's colonial rule in Africa was a distinct kind of tyranny that had—and still has—no genuine intention of producing autonomous postcolonial states. It left institutional loopholes that predisposed the postcolony to some of the civil and political conflicts that we see today. That said, should there be a limit to the over-belaboring of the legacies of colonialism? If so, what other explanations can be given for the problem of recurring political violence in the postcolony? Since the independence of Ghana in 1957, the African continent has had over a thousand armed conflicts ranging from genocide to secessionist and sectarian violence, state terror, religious terrorism, and vicious dictatorships. Additionally, the continent, since the second half of the twentieth century, has become a site of perpetual humanitarian emergencies for Western philanthrocapitalism. In fact, in the Western geography of reason, Africa remains synonymous with war and rumors of war.

The continent, without doubt, struggles with the challenges of neoliberal democracy and nation-building in the twenty-first century. On top of that are the unexpiated memories of slavery and colonialism that not only haunt the present but also are imbricated in—and superimposed on—current and ongoing sociopolitical conflicts. The past has not only become coeval with the present;[1] it has also continued in the present in a manner that leaves the continent with vulnerable futures. Instead of a "past perfected," what we see in many post-conflict African countries is a "past continuous." Put differently, the postcolony's distant and not-so-distant pasts constitute a major source of its continuous political conflicts. Many post-independence African countries are still metaphorically—if not literally—at war; they are still (not) dealing with the raw and open wounds of history.

Whether as a result of institutionalized amnesia or state repression, many post-conflict African countries do not show the political will needed to confront their difficult pasts. Even in places where confronting the past is considered a political exigency (Rwanda and South Africa, for example), memory's complicated relationship with political power and agency becomes a stumbling block to reconciliation. This is why Richard Werbner, in *Memory and the Postcolony*, avows that memory as a public practice is increasingly in crisis in postcolonial Africa.[2] My intention in this book is to investigate this crisis—or what I prefer to describe as *friction*—of memory in postcolonial Africa. I am interested in how memory has (or has not) been instrumentalized for nation-building, and, in view of that, I examine various memory politics, economies, and frictions in post-conflict situations across Africa. I investigate occasions of elitist memorialism as well as instances where memory becomes a subversive tool in the hand of subalterns asserting themselves against a repressive state.

Continuous Pasts essentially brings memory studies and African studies into dialogue. As I will show, these two fields of study seem—on the surface—like two parallel lines that can never meet, but in fact they have overlapping concerns. Despite the realities of political conflict and its attendant memory politics on the continent, the study of postcolonial African memories has long occupied the margins of mainstream memory discourses that often bestow a canonical status on the Holocaust memory. Most of what is known about contemporary memory theories and philosophies emanates from engagements with the Holocaust and a few other Euro-American historical events. *Continuous Pasts*, therefore, investigates the representations of memory in African texts and contexts to see what could be thought differently from the master narratives of memory. At the same time, it identifies instances where established memory theories illuminate certain aspects of the sociopolitical, cultural, and historical structures of African postcoloniality.

In the face of traumatic silences, archival elusiveness, official censorship, and mnemocide[3] in many post-conflict situations in Africa, *Continuous Pasts* brings together insights from memory studies and African literature in order to examine how the past is constructed, confronted, and contested. It asks, what happens when conflicting memories collide within the imaginative space of fiction? That is, how does African fiction deal with or, in some cases, become the source of memory friction? In a sense, this book is an attempt at deconstructing the complex interplay of literature, history, politics, and nation-statehood in order to generate a better African polemology. In another sense, it uses a method of critical reading to tease out different ways of thinking about conflicted pasts in postcolonial Africa. In essence, *Continuous Pasts* introduces a relatively new way of reading African literature through—and against—the lens of critical memory studies. In some instances, in the analyses of African literary texts in the book, I experiment with conceptual models generated from studies on the Holocaust in order to establish their in/applicability in African contexts. In other instances, I look for the ways in which the texts generate alter/native configurations of memory that challenge hegemonic understandings. This means that I do not simply place the selected texts in a range of theoretical engagements but that I also investigate the potential theorizations that emerge from a close and symptomatic reading of the texts themselves.

In *Continuous Pasts*, I examine literary texts that depict post-conflict situations in Sierra Leone, Nigeria, Ethiopia, and Rwanda as a way of making room for a balanced representation and an exploration of what Werbner describes as the "diversity of postcolonial memory practice."[4] I read literary texts that mirror the four aforementioned post-conflict African countries because of their thematic affinities and because they are particularly rich and insightful when placed in dialogue with critical writings on memory. Some of these texts include Chimamanda Adichie's *Half of a Yellow Sun*, Aminatta Forna's *The Memory of Love*, Dinaw Mengestu's *Children of the Revolution*, and Véronique Tadjo's *The Shadow of Imana*. As I will explain, these novels can be described as post-conflict fictions of memory in Africa. While Adichie's *Half of a Yellow Sun* narrates the traumatic experiences of the Igbo people during the Nigeria-Biafra War (1967–1970) and is gradually becoming an important *lieux de memoire* of the war, Forna's *The Memory of Love* chronicles the traumatic silences of Sierra Leoneans during an authoritarian regime that culminated into the eleven years of civil war (1991–2002) that the country is yet to fully recover from. Tadjo's *The Shadow of Imana* tells of the acute aliveness of the genocidal past in Rwanda and how the country's sites of memory reactivate the past in uncanny ways, even to secondary witnesses. Lastly, Mengestu's *Children of the Revolution* details the traumatic memories of the communist revolution that spread through Ethiopia in the 1970s and '80s. It depicts how the Ethiopians who fled to America during this period are still haunted by the (traumatic) memories even when America's capitalist culture relentlessly pushes for the suppression of those memories.

In view of the foregoing, this book claims that the post-conflict fiction of memory in Africa demonstrates how the past is etched on bodies and topographies, resonant in silences and memorials, and continuous even in experiences as well as structures of migration. It argues that the aforementioned literary texts invite critical deliberations on the continuity of the past within the realm of positionality and the domain of subjectivity—that is to say, the past is not merely present; instead, it survives, lives on, and is mediated through the subject positions of victims, perpetrators, and implicated subjects[5] as well as secondary and transgenerational witnesses. The texts illustrate how the unfinished business of the past produces fragile regimes of peace and asynchronous temporalities that challenge progressive historicism. Because of this continuous presence of the past, coupled with lingering injustices in the present, the post-conflict fiction of memory in Africa presents a kind of future that is under siege. In other words, victims and survivors of political violence in the postcolony are often unable to aspire to a desirable future because of the overbearing weight of the past and the ungraspable nature of the present. In most cases, the post-conflict present is beset with a tight political economy wherein the scramble for survival trumps the ability to imagine a just future among survivors. It is precisely this despairing disposition toward the future that the writers of the selected texts attempt to confront. To put it another way, while the selected texts depict individuals struggling to embrace the promise of a livable future, the artists write with the hope that their works will open up conversations about, and possibilities for, a reparative future. By and large, *Continuous Pasts* shows how post-conflict fictions of memory in Africa recalibrate discourses of futurity, solidarity, responsibility, justice, survival, and reconciliation. It also contends that post-conflict fictions of memory in Africa provide the tools for imagining and theorizing a collective African memory. Each text analyzed in the book provides, in very interesting ways, an imaginative possibility and template for how post-independence African countries can "remember together" in what I describe later in this chapter—and in greater detail in chapters 3 and 4—as an African transnational memory framework.

It is pertinent at this point to provide some conceptual, terminological, and analytical clarifications. In *Continuous Pasts,* you will come across the term "post-conflict" more often than "postwar." This is primarily because some of the violent histories I investigate may not be regarded as a "war" in the very conventional sense of the term. For instance, Mengestu's *Children of the Revolution* invites reflections on the aftermaths of a communist revolution that imploded Ethiopia while Tadjo's *The Shadow of Imana* speaks to the aftermaths of a genocide. In addition, while Adichie's *Half of a Yellow Sun* portrays the complexity of a civil war that involved state-sponsored violence, Forna's *The Memory of Love* depicts the intricacy of a war at the heart of which is political corruption and the struggle to control the diamond industry in Sierra Leone. Therefore, "post-conflict" is a more encompassing term that captures the complex network of conflicts that beset the African continent from the mid-twentieth century to the present. In addition, I use the word "conflict" more often because of the stereotypical baggage that "war" in relation to Africa has come to hold in the Western imagination. Despite ample evidence[6] showing that African countries are more susceptible to civil conflicts because of the continuing legacies of colonialism, and because of economic—rather than cultural or ethnic—reasons, the Western media still employ mostly simplistic narratives of ethnic wars and barbaric cultures to explain these conflicts. Achille Mbembe sheds light on the logic underlying this barbarization of postcolonial African conflicts as he writes, "Africa as an idea, a concept, has historically served, and continues to serve, as a polemical argument for the West's desperate desire to assert its difference from the rest of the world."[7] This is why there is a pressing need for a postcolonial African approach to conflict studies that is not reliant on Western frames of reference.

Furthermore, it is important to note that the "post" in "post-conflict," just as the "post" in "postcolonial," does not connote terminality because, as already mentioned, some of the conflicts in these African countries remain unfinished and are sometimes still unfolding in the present. The term "post-conflict" is a shorthand and a deliberate analytic choice that caters to geohistorical and aesthetic specificities that are likely to be glossed over in the broad category of postcolonialism. This, however, does not imply that the term "post-conflict" is outside the boundary of postcolonial imaginings. Rather, as I hope to show, the term coincides with, and illuminates, the category of the "postcolonial." Put differently, in the context of this book, the "postcolonial" is also "post-conflict," and as Terry Eagleton makes clear, "the term 'post,' if it has any meaning at all, means business as usual."[8]

It is also important to clarify that choosing to investigate Africa's traumatic histories and turbulent memories as depicted in its literatures is not an Afropessimist attempt at positioning the continent as an island of suffering caught in the trappings of victimhood. Rather, not talking about trauma in Africa might be a "neo-colonial mistake" and "another silencing of suffering."[9] Recently, the African literary market has been flooded with gripping stories of trauma, violence, and mourning. Instead of explaining these stories away as a romanticization of violence or as "poverty porn,"[10] I argue that they function as a testimony to the belatedness of collective, historical, and continental traumas. These stories help us to work through the violent histories that have spread through the continent since the mid-twentieth century. Therefore, as many African writers continue to gain recognition and clinch literary prizes all over the world,[11] there is a need for more theoretically informed dissections of their works. It is also noteworthy that post-conflict fiction is just one of the many genres of fiction coming out of Africa today. African writers often take up a diverse range of subjects in their works, and the subject of war or civil conflict constitutes just a tiny fraction of those works. For the purpose of this book, I am engaging specifically with post-conflict fictions of memory in Africa with the hope of contributing to existing knowledge on the workings of the memory of conflicts and conflicts of memory in postcolonial Africa.

POSTCOLONIAL MEMORY STUDIES

This book falls within the ambits of postcolonial memory studies, and in this section I elaborate on what that means. However, it is imperative to begin with an exploration of the rudiments of memory studies itself. Memory, Andreas Huyssen suggests, is difficult to define; it "is one of those elusive topics we all think we have a handle on. But as soon as we try to define it, it starts slipping and sliding, eluding attempts to grasp it either culturally, sociologically or scientifically."[12] Jeffrey Olick even goes as far as describing the study of memory as a "nonparadigmatic, centerless enterprise."[13] For the purpose of this book, memory is simply an act or a process of remembering—and forgetting—violent histories at individual and collective levels. Over the years, scholars have approached the subject from various theoretical, disciplinary, and methodological lenses. One could think of the works of Maurice Halbwachs, Pierre Nora, Aleida Assmann, and Jan Assmann which many memory scholars consider to be foundational to contemporary memory studies. Halbwachs, a student of Émile Durkheim, popularized the concept of "collective memory," which he describes as a collectively shared and societal representation of the past. Contrary to Sigmund Freud's and Henri Bergson's approaches to memory as an individual process, Halbwachs believes that what is known as an individual memory is actually based on social structures.[14] Pierre Nora, on the other hand, popularized the concept of *lieux de memoire* (site of memory) as any place, object, or concept vested with historical significance in the popular, collective memory. In Nora's quite nationalistic framing, a site of memory includes a monument, museum, memorial, symbol, flag, and so on.[15] Jan Assmann builds on the works of Nora and Halbwachs to elaborate on the idea of cultural memory, which he describes as an externalization and objectivation of memory that is found in symbols such as texts, images, landmarks, and other sites of memory.[16] Today we are witnessing a proliferation of memory concepts and theories such as "cosmopolitan memory,"[17] "prosthetic memory,"[18] "multidirectional memory,"[19] "travelling memory,"[20] "palimpsestic memory,"[21] "transnational memory,"[22] "agonistic memory,"[23] "globital memory,"[24] "planetary memory,"[25] and so on. These recent memory theories, although still quite Holocaust-centric, are more transcultural and even global in their orientation.[26]

Michael Rothberg—whose theory of multidirectional memory is one of the most influential of all these relatively new theories of memory—is among the few memory scholars who have engaged closely with the question of colonialism, especially in relation to the Holocaust. Rothberg, reflecting on the ironical avoidance of the subject of colonialism in the works of early European memory scholars, writes, "Halbwachs's organicism, Nora's purified national frame and Assmann's preponderant focus on canonical archives suggest that throughout the 20th century—the era of colonialism's apotheosis, collapse and reconfiguration in neo- and postcolonial guises—cultural memory studies may have inadvertently done as much to reproduce colonial mentalities as to challenge them."[27] This is even more striking when one considers the fact that the colonial enterprise, in and of itself, is a memory enterprise. After all,

Frantz Fanon notes that colonialism is not merely satisfied with "emptying the native's brain of all form and content" but that it also "turns to the past of oppressed people and distorts it, disfigures it, and destroys it."[28] In short, colonialism, among many other things, is an attempt to destroy and wipe out a people's memory.

It is in view of circumventing the coloniality of memory[29] that a turn to African studies becomes necessary. Given the history of violence on the continent ranging from slavery, colonialism, apartheid, postcolonial civil wars, military dictatorship, and genocide, Africanists have explored issues such as the memory of slavery in Africa,[30] the memory of precolonial Africa,[31] the disruption of the precolonial past by colonialism,[32] the reclaiming of Africa's past through anticolonial struggles,[33] the rereading of colonial archives,[34] and the cultural legacies of the colonial past in the postcolonial present.[35] In other words, Africanists have always been doing memory work, although they might have used vocabularies, methodological tools, and theoretical approaches different from the ones already established within mainstream memory studies. That said, the recent transnational and transcultural turn in memory studies[36] has necessitated more research forays into the memory of the empire as well as the entangled histories of the colonizer and the colonized. I will go as far as arguing that postcolonial studies actually had an unpronounced influence on transnational memory studies that only began to gain traction in the 1980s and '90s. The interest in postcolonial studies in academia was heralded by the decolonization clamors that emerged in the wake of the First and Second World Wars. It could also be traced back to the publication of seminal works such as Aimé Césaire's *Discourse on Colonialism* (1950), Frantz Fanon's *The Wretched of the Earth* (1961), and, later, Edward Said's *Orientalism* (1978), among many others. Furthermore, the mass exodus of people from the colonies to the colonial metropoles (beginning with the Windrush in 1948 to the years of massive brain drain in 1980s Africa[37]) made the question of migration become even more vital in postcolonial studies and memory studies. These issues—such as the question of migration and the legacy of the empire among others—have spurred the "emerging proximity"[38] between postcolonial studies and memory studies as well as the development of the subfield now popularly referred to as "postcolonial memory studies."[39]

It is worth reiterating that despite the relatively recent openness to postcolonial issues, memory studies is still steeped in a colonial framework. The dominant postcolonial memory discourses still focus largely on the colonial metropoles and less on the colony—which, broadly speaking, reveals the power asymmetries in the curation of history and the production of knowledge in our so-called postcolonial epoch. In addition, the prominent scholarly works in and on postcolonial memory are the ones that show how Europe is (or is not) dealing with its colonial hangovers.[40] Most research grants and sponsored academic projects in the postcolonial memory field are channeled into how Europe needs to deal with looted artifacts and how it needs to decolonize its museums.[41] While these conversations are very important and should continue to be had, they still position the colonial powers as the center of analysis and, as a result, play into the intransient violence of erasing colonial subjects. Dipesh Chakraborty's insights are particularly instructive here. In his seminal essay "Postcoloniality and the Artifice of History," he challenges the logic behind Europe's dominance as the subject of all histories and reveals the ways in which all other histories tend to become variations of the history of Europe.[42] This logic also applies (and is often unchallenged) in postcolonial memory studies where Europe remains the sovereign subject of all discourses.

By the same token, mainstream memory politics is still stuck within the narrow framing of the history of the postcolony as one that begins and ends with colonialism or slavery. That is, with a few exceptions, critical imaginings on postcolonial memory tend to pigeonhole or reduce African history to slavery/colonialism—nothing before, nothing after. This, of course, does not necessarily negate the idea that the history of the postcolony is fragmented and that the experience of slavery/colonialism produced a temporality that is tragically out of joint.[43] However, as a work in postcolonial memory studies, *Continuous Pasts* investigates intervening postcolonial[44] histories that have distinct "memory narratives and political challenges"[45] but are still recalcitrantly shaped by—but not necessarily the same as—the colonial encounter. It also explores the traces of colonial post-memories as well as the subtle and not-so-subtle afterlives of colonialism.

Filip de Boeck eloquently avows that "once the space of colonialism has been defined as a 'space of death,' . . . the question then becomes how to speak about the postcolonial afterlife, that which lies beyond the grave. What remains to be told in the *post*, in the postcolonial as *post mortem*."[46] In the same vein, I investigate, in this book, the continuing and overlaying shades of political violence in post-independence African countries. To echo Mahmood Mamdani, I explore how political violence explodes rather than diminishes after the independence of many African countries.[47] In essence, *Continuous Pasts* examines the memory of post-independence civil conflicts in

Africa. It formulates post-independence Africa as a distinct memory regime, albeit with the awareness that some of its political skirmishes are—to use Frantz Fanon's words—an "arsenal of complexes that has been developed by the colonial environment."[48] This "arsenal of complexes" remains salient in the procedures of political modernity among African countries.

If coloniality is defined as a space of death and postcoloniality as postmortem, a postcolonial memory work could then be conceptualized as being with the dead.[49] That is, the question of memory in the postcolony is a question of the continual presence of the dead. Postcolonial memory is a marker of the oscillating tension between summoning the dead and laying them to rest.[50] After all, Berber Bevernage, in his study of historical memory in Sierra Leone and South Africa, instructs that one can learn a lot by approaching history as a practice of mourning and discourse of death.[51] Similarly, Mamadou Diawara, Bernard Lategan, and Jorn Rusen, in their work on historical memory in Africa, assert that "issues like trauma, mourning, confession, forgiveness and reconciliation have to be considered as part of such an extended understanding of the memory process."[52] Therefore, despite the calls to move away from trauma paradigms in memory studies,[53] postcolonial memory is still very much marinated in the discourse of memory as a discourse of trauma and mourning.[54] There is a continuous interconnectedness of working through (mourning) and acting out (melancholia) of traumatic pasts in the postcolony.[55] To put it another way, the postcolonial narrative is a narrative of mourning.[56] Post-conflict fictions of memory in Africa are engaged in wake work—wake being the process in which we think about the dead, the rituals through which we enact memory, and the avenue through which those among the living mourn the passing of the dead.[57] In post-conflict fictions of memory in Africa, we are bound to encounter various instances of anamnestic solidarity with the dead as well as various forms of ancestral veneration. These fictions also present us with the inextricable link between cultures of mourning, complexities of witnessing, and modes of writing. Therefore, in reading post-conflict fictions of memory in Africa as wake work in this book, attention is given to contextualized portraitures of commemorative culture, funerary rites, and other ways of mourning depicted in the selected literary texts. In a similar vein, questions of ghostly presences and tropes of spectrality are still very topical in postcolonial memory discourses. Most postcolonial fictions of memory present haunting as an intensely literal and visceral experience. Haunting is, in fact, a constituent element of postcolonial life. It is one way "in which abusive systems of power make themselves known and their impacts felt in everyday life, especially when they are supposedly over and done with (slavery, for instance) or when their oppressive nature is denied."[58] Essentially, memory in the postcolony still very much serves as a conceptual space through which experiences of trauma, mourning, and haunting are anatomized. This is not to say that trauma is all there is to postcoloniality but that there is so much insight to be gleaned from reading postcolonial history as posttraumatic.[59]

Speaking of the interconnectedness of memory and mourning in the postcolony, David Scott reminds us that the work of mourning is basically an intertwined work of time and memory.[60] That is, memory is a temporal site of mourning—the kind of mourning that seeps into the present and makes time fall outside the plane of teleological progression. Scott, skeptical of the teleological time of progress which plots the past, present, and future "as a kind of romance," notes that the temporality of the postcolony is a "temporality of the aftermaths of political catastrophe, the temporal disjuncture involved in living in the wake of past political time, amid ruins, specifically, of postsocialist and postcolonial future pasts."[61] Put simply, the unfinished businesses of the past in the postcolony lead to disjunctive[62] and entangled[63] temporalities as opposed to Western modernity's linear times. Therefore, *Continuous Pasts* demonstrates how post-conflict fictions of memory in Africa often present a calibration of time that is based on a structure of mourning—a time of/in the wake. It shows how the selected fictional texts present a situation where a grievous past is embedded within a grieving present.

Ever since the critique of homogeneous empty time by Walter Benjamin[64] and the embrace of the spectral, non-contemporaneous time by Jacques Derrida[65] as well as the espousal of the coevality of the past with the present by Theodore Adorno,[66] memory scholars have increasingly moved away from progressive historicism and have embraced the logic of "present pasts"[67] and the possibility that "all things pass except the past."[68] While all of these temporal configurations are obtainable in postcolonial contexts, it is crucial to take seriously not only the present-ness of the past but also the past's continuity into the future. In view of this, Scott, arguing about Black and postcolonial futurity, posits that "we no longer have any confidence that the present will give rise to a future significantly different from the past. A future without the present's burdened inheritance of the past violation, subjugation and dispossession."[69] Therefore, taking Wole Soyinka's concern (in this chapter's epigraph) about the diabolical continuity of the past into consideration, one wonders if the cumulative and palimpsestic memories of slavery, colonialism, apartheid, and the manifold unresolved conflicts in the present could be formulated as a kind of concatenation. After all, Ian Baucom has pointed out that time does not pass; it accumulates.[70] And if that is the case, the logic of a concatenated memory in the postcolony is useful in explaining how the past is not only persistent but also continuous precisely because of the way it cycles—predictably so—into the future. It is important to clarify that this continuity of the past in the postcolony is not in any way suggestive of a progressive temporality; rather, it is a non-progressive temporality that gestures toward the interminability of mourning, reversal of history, and cyclicality of time.

Additionally, if we read the work of Pierre Nora on national sites of memory[71] along with Benedict Anderson's on nation-states[72] very closely, we would realize that the idea of the nation-state is founded upon a logic of temporal homogeneity and simultaneity. However, to fully grasp the non-teleological and non-progressive dialectics of time in postcolonial climes, we need to move beyond all modes of methodological nationalism and give attention to decolonial reconstructions of nationhood. In light of this, Mahmood Mamdani, writing about post-genocide Rwanda, faults the approach of methodological nationalism which tends to "see state boundaries as boundaries of knowledge, thereby turning political into epistemological boundaries."[73] Therefore, while colonialism, by its very nature, is transnational and has resulted in intercontinental migrations of people, the nature of genocide and civil conflict in the postcolony is also very transnational. Postcolonial African memory works need to be more attuned to the transnationality of memory in all of its modes. Analyzing post-conflict fictions of memory in this book proves insightful for thinking about these modes of African transnationality that, on the one hand, correct the impression that Africa is a country and, on the other, inspire reflections on the concept of African transnational memory (ATM), which I have earlier alluded to. An ATM work is useful in understanding the transnational nature of anticolonial struggles on the continent. It enhances our understanding of the connected histories, shared presents, and common futures of African nation-states. It creates a conceptual space for thinking about collective memory and a potential commons in Africa.

ATM decenters the nation as the container of memory and, by so doing, weakens the hold of atavistic nationalisms and promotes relations of solidarity across the continent. ATM is important because of the way postcolonial memories have been reduced to marginal memories within the global memory framework that still hegemonizes Euro-American memories. It is also important because of the biased salience that First World memories have over the Third World within the global memory politics.[74] As Astrid Erll argues, memory scholars, in their attempt to move from national to global frameworks of memory, have a tendency to overlook the significance of regional memories.[75] Hence, a regional perspective is important precisely because of its potential to "even out some of the failures of national and global approaches to collective remembering."[76] In *Continuous Pasts*, African transnational memory is formulated as a regional memory work that speaks to the ways collective memory in post-conflict African societies is produced and circulated. ATM also accounts for the ways in which the post-conflict fictions of memory analyzed in this book provide a contextual logic that sometimes contests and other times aligns itself to globalized forms of memory (particularly the Holocaust) while at the same level providing alternative ways of reading memory narratives coming out of the African continent. In all, postcolonialism has various memory dimensions. The act of "writing back"[77] is invariably an act of "re-membering" a past that is marked with ruptures and dismembered by colonial violence. A postcolonial memory work is, among many other things, a work that attunes itself to deconstructing orthodox structures of witnessing and configurations of temporality. It is a work that challenges the espousal of the Holocaust memory as hegemonic memory, questions the construction of the nation-state as a natural container of memory, and seeks instances of lateral mnemonic connections among postcolonial nation-states.

FRICTIONS OF MEMORY

Literature has a special relationship with memory; it functions as one of the paths through which the past is *acted out* and *worked through*. It helps us to understand the nature and function of memory. It is capable of portraying "individual and collective memory—its contents, its workings, its fragility, and its distortions—by coding it into aesthetic forms such as narrative structures, symbols and metaphors."[78] There are several approaches to studying literature's resonances with memory, and one such approach involves looking at literature as an art—as well as an act—of memory. Put differently, literature is a mnemonic art that often embodies and archives the memory of a culture.[79] Certain literary texts, more than others, take a prominent place in the cultural memory of certain nations—and this is usually brought about and consolidated by the process of canonization. In addition, just as museums and monuments are understood as media of memory, literature functions as a medium of cultural memory. It is an agent of, and an indispensable force in, memory culture.

As Renate Lachmann rightly argues, the memory of a text is in its intertextuality.[80] Although literature cannot literally "remember" the way individuals do, a way of approaching its dalliance with memory is through the lens of intertextuality or what Erll calls the "memory of literature."[81] Through intertextuality, earlier stories are retold and earlier texts are "re-membered." The memory of literature, therefore, points to the "idea of an inner-literary memory, a memory of literature as a symbol system which is manifested in individual texts."[82] For example, as I will show in chapter 1, Adichie's *Half of a Yellow Sun* as a work of postmemory retells earlier stories about Biafra and brings the memory of earlier literary texts to bear through different forms of intertextual and metatextual references.

Literature's relationship with memory is most commonly approached as *memory in literature*, which, to put it simply, means the portrayal of individual and collective remembering in literary texts. While the past can be represented in all the genres of literature, prose literature is the most common literary genre within memory culture. Ansgar Nünning coined the phrase "fiction of memory"[83] to describe how prose fiction provides an imaginative reconstruction of the past—both structurally and thematically—in a way that is useful for understanding and navigating the present. This is also why Ulrich Rauff asserts that novelists were ahead of historians in their ability to use fiction to problematize the relationship between the past and the present.[84] Through fiction, readers can access and assess conflicting interpretations of the past. More so, fiction has the capacity to unsettle memory by opening up cracks in doctored histories. Therefore, because the past is always a contested territory, good fiction is able to come to grips with the complexities of memory. Meanwhile, because of its fabricative and inventive quality, fiction itself can become a source of conflict about the past. One could even think of the friction that emerges when the process of remembering itself is considered (especially by cognitive psychologists and neuroscientists[85]) to be intrinsically constitutive of fictitious elements. That is, just as fiction as a narrative genre is highly imaginative, the act of memory is also inextricably bound up with figments of the imagination. From this stance emerges the idea that there are fault lines inherent in human acts of remembering; therefore, memory is characteristically (re)constructive and malleable. As I will show in chapter 2, fiction can expose the frictions of memory by mirroring the inherent falsificatory propensities in individual remembering or individual retelling of remembered events. This is all the more reason why fictive representations of the past, according to Toni Morrison, are—and should be—more attuned to the question of truth rather than fact.[86]

Again, a fiction of memory, especially the one that zooms in on the interiority of its characters, is capable of giving clarity to knots of memory as well as giving voice to erstwhile silenced voices. In the context of *Continuous Pasts*, fictions of memory function as counter-memory to hegemonic memory structures; they serve as an alternative site of memory in the face of militant memorialism and institutionalized amnesia. One may even argue that all fictions are fictions of memory because, from a narratological point of view, "the distinction between an 'experiencing I' and a 'narrating I' already rests on a (largely implicit) concept of memory, namely on the idea that there is a difference between pre-narrative experience on the one hand, and, on the other, narrative memory which creates meaning retrospectively."[87] Realist fictions often capture the general atmosphere of the time they are set in and, in turn, become repositories of memory themselves. However, post-conflict fictions of memory, which often do not follow a chronological plot structure, are usually set during and after civil conflicts. They portray—and invite—reflections on the aftermaths and afterlives of a conflict. They use a lot of traumatic flashbacks and are particularly notorious for inspiring memory debates (and frictions) in the wake of their publication. While some of the novels analyzed in this book—especially *Half of a Yellow Sun* and *The Memory of Love*—could be categorized as war fiction,[88] I read them as post-conflict fictions of memory because they provoke conversations about justice, healing, reconciliation, and responsibility in the aftermath of civil conflicts, something that is not necessarily a feature of war fictions. Therefore, while all war fiction may be read as post-conflict fiction, not all post-conflict fiction is war fiction.

In this book I argue that fictions of memory in Africa often employ complex chronotopes and multiperspectivity as a way of potentially inciting agonistic memory reactions in their readers (although, in practice, they tend to attract more antagonistic memory reactions[89]) and how that shapes politics and identities on individual and collective levels. I also explore, especially in chapter 4, how fictions of memory in Africa sometimes question their own fictionality, reject genre pigeonholing, and employ multiple genres in telling their stories despite being under the umbrella category of fiction. In essence, *Continuous Pasts* illustrates how form and content interact in enhancing our understanding of the intergenerationality, transnationality, temporality, and corporeality of traumatic memories in the accounts of survivors, children of survivors, and distant/secondary witnesses in post-conflict Africa. It also explores how fiction takes on a critical function in memory culture by highlighting several theoretical questions as well as new models of memory that the selected texts bring to fore.

FICTION OF MEMORY IN POST-CONFLICT AFRICA

Leela Gandhi reminds us that the postcolony is often inclined to a "will to forget" the past even though its narratives attempt to un/consciously "counter this amnesiac tendency by revisiting, remembering and crucially interrogating the past."[90] In that sense, post-conflict fictions of memory in Africa—as I have already argued—are works of mourning precisely because they participate (and invite others to participate) in coming to terms with, and thinking through, the atrocities of the past in order to better understand the present and imagine the future. Werbner, in *Memory and the Postcolony*, acknowledges the role that literature—more than any social science and humanities discipline—plays in shaping memory in postcolonial Africa. He recognizes the relentless efforts that African writers make in bringing the past to our doorsteps as he writes, "While memory has been movingly envisioned by African artists, poets and novelists, such as Yvonne Vera in the transgressive disclosures of her *Under the Tongue* (1996) and Jack Mapanje in his reflections on justice and memory (1995), the political and moral problematics of postcolonial memory in Africa has hardly been recognized—not to say analyzed or theorized in any depths by social scientists."[91] In view of this, fiction has always been a strong and steady vector of memory in Africa. It was and is still at the forefront of investigating Africa's colonial histories. Some of the African fictions that have come to shape the collective memory of colonialism on the continent include Chinua Achebe's (1958) *Things Fall Apart*, Ferdinand Oyono's (1956) *The Old Man and the Medal*, Ousmane Sembene's (1960) *God's Bit of Woods*, Tayeb Salih's (1966) *Season of Migration to the North*, and Ngugi wa Thiong'o's (1964) *Weep Not, Child*, among numerous others. Susan Z. Andrade notes that the authors of these novels are part of the first generation of postcolonial African novelists and that "the most obvious manifestation of political commitment in their works took the form of anti-colonial resistance and agitation of national sovereignty."[92] While Andrade's point is accurate, we need to take more seriously the problematics of using generational markers and the crisis of periodizing African literature (and perhaps all literatures). In the light of this, Harry Garuba notes that there are always semantic ambiguity, thematic fluidity, and temporal overlaps whenever we "generationalize" African literature.[93] While the problem of periodization seems like something the African Literature discipline will continue to grapple with, I want to suggest that it might be more productive to think in terms of the phases in African writing rather than the generations of African writers. Hence, while a new generation of writers sprang up during the second phase of modern African writing, some of the first-generation writers that Andrade is describing also explored new thematic concerns that characterized this second phase. The second phase of African writing was characterized by multiple layers of postcolonial disillusionment. It was during this phase that "anticolonial utopias gradually withered into postcolonial nightmares."[94] Therefore, writers who wrote during this period painted what it meant to inhabit a collective disenchantment in post-independence Africa. Examples of such writings include Festus Iyayi's (1979) *Violence*, Ayi Kwei Armah's (1968) *The Beautyful Ones Are Not Yet Born*, Ngugi wa Thiong'o's (1977) *Petals of Blood*, Meja Mwangi's (1976) *Going Down Road*, and Abdourahman Waberi's (1994) *The Land without Shadows*, among many others.

The third phase of African writings involves a company of writers who were born or grew up during the years of civil wars, military dictatorships, and economic collapse in post-independence Africa. As a consequence, these writers task themselves with representing the traumatic memories of war "through the logic of distance, mediated by inheritance."[95] Because of the major thematic preoccupations in their writings, Abdourahman Waberi refers to these writers as the "children of the postcolony."[96] It is important to note that this was a phase that also marked the beginning of the mass exodus of Africans to the West that is still ongoing. Hence, Dominic Thomas—commenting on the third phase of African writing—explains that themes such as colonialism, anticolonialism, and the questioning of occidental superiority have now been displaced by concern for immigration, democratization, civil conflicts, genocide, globalization, and the disintegration of the nation.[97] F. Abiola Irele also notes that many of these third-generation African writers are based outside of the continent because of the push factor of political instability and that they are part of a "global Africa" or the "new African diaspora."[98] By the virtue of their mobility, these African writers do not only attract a cosmopolitan readership, but their works are also transnational in nature—that is, the content, characters, and settings of their writings are often intra- and intercontinental. Their works mirror what Anna Tsing describes as "aspirations of global connections and how that comes to life in *friction*."[99] In the same vein, contemporary African fiction is said to be both introverted and extroverted because it addresses multiple kinds of publics.[100] It is introverted because it is oriented toward a particular national public. It is extroverted because it has a strong presence in the global literary market and, in turn, attracts a global audience. All the writers whose works I have chosen to analyze in this book fall into this category of global African writers. They are very cosmopolitan and their works mostly fall within the third phase of African writing, except for Véronique Tadjo, whose first novel dates back to 1984, making her works fit into the second and third phases of African writing. Therefore, in the succeeding chapters, I investigate the frictions (of memory) enabled and produced by the transnational exchanges and impetuses in the selected writers' works. I provide various modes of reading post-conflict African fiction through and against the lens of critical and cultural memory studies. In what follows, I provide the outline of this book and lay out the specific ways I have read the selected novels.

OUTLINE OF THE BOOK

In chapter 1, I read Chimamanda Adichie's *Half of a Yellow Sun*, a novel centered on the Nigeria-Biafra War (1967–1970), as a work of postmemory because the author was born seven years after the war. With this novel, I investigate what it means to write about a past that one does not have lived experiences of. I begin by establishing the fact that Adichie's parents were survivors of the war and that Adichie inherited the trauma of the war within the embodied space of the family. I argue that it is this traumatic inheritance that bestows the imperative to bear witness vicariously on Adichie. Hence, the novel becomes not only her way of working through her traumatic inheritance but also her way of memorializing—and bearing posthumous witness and fidelity to—some of her ancestors who died in the war. It is also her way of humanizing history and provoking the public to remembering after half a century of state repression. Also in this chapter, I investigate—through a reading of Adichie's interviews and other autobiographical writings—how family stories became the "raw material" for writing *Half of a Yellow Sun*. I look for instances where Adichie may or may not have sacrificed historical accuracy for sentimentalism or a romanticization of the past in the novel. I elucidate on how postmemory is bound up with the imagination and how, in that process, Adichie reconstructs a past that beckons to the future. I explain that the novel's frequent recourse to metatextuality qualifies it as a historiographical metafiction. I also argue that the novel, as a postmemory work, is a rewriting of earlier stories on Biafra. This is evident not only in the obvious intertextual references but also in the bibliography provided at the end of the novel. The photographs (taken by a journalist during the war) provided at the end of the novel underscore the importance and centrality of photos to postmemory work. They also partly explain how and why photos of malnourished Biafran children came to shape global perceptions about war in Africa. In addition, I examine the intersections of postmemory and postcolonialism and argue that postcoloniality shares certain overlaps with postmemory and that while Adichie is a "child of the postcolony," she is at the same time a "child of memory." However, despite the potential interconnectedness, postmemory has its limits in postcolonial contexts. Hence, drawing again from Adichie's interviews, I propose the concept of ancestral memory as a reworking of postmemory in a postcolonial African context. I argue that Adichie's copious references to her ancestors in her interviews gesture toward the possibility of harboring—uncannily and even unsuspectingly—the memories of her ancestors' experiences. I conclude the chapter by arguing that *Half of a Yellow Sun*, as a work of postmemory, provokes uneasy conversations about justice and contributes to the (re)production of the various frictions of memory (of Biafra) observable in Nigeria today.

In the second chapter of this book, I read Aminatta Forna's *The Memory of Love*, a novel based on the Sierra Leonean Civil War (1991–2002). I examine the novel's portrayal of post-conflict technologies of survival and the everyday. With insights from the works of Jay Winter, Paul Ricoeur, Friedrich Nietzsche, and Elizabeth Loftus, I explore the novel's portraitures of memory's (im)morality, unreliability, and plasticity. More importantly, I show how Forna brings to fore the various textures of silence that the Sierra Leonean Civil War is shrouded in. I zero in on the novel's portrayal of the kinds of frictions that occur when memory is interposed by silence. I begin my analysis by investigating the novel itself as a form of textual silence. I examine how it thematically and narratologically represents the polysemy of silence observable in post-conflict Sierra Leone. In addition, I investigate the mnemonic consequences of these silences that Forna brings to bear in the novel—that is, I show instances where silence enhances memory or induces forgetting in the post-conflict Sierra Leone. I argue that in *The Memory of Love*, silence becomes the third leg of memory and forgetting. Also in my engagement with the novel, I highlight the distinction between silent memory and silenced memory. I argue that while some of the characters are silent in the wake of the war, they do covertly remember (silent memory); however, some other characters, especially Elias Cole, try to cover up their atrocity in the war by remembering so many details but disremembering the details about their complicity in the atrocities (silenced memory). I look for traces of silent complicity—or complicity of silence—and extend the discussion to the various forms of complicity that fueled the embers of the war. I conclude the chapter by examining how the novel portrays the place of time in the complex processes of remembering, forgetting, and healing in post-conflict Sierra Leone. Drawing from other violent histories in the postcolony, I argue that many post-conflict African countries may still be going through a silent time characterized by public silence about violent pasts. Drawing also from the example of the pact of silence in Spain and the one or two decades of silence in post-Holocaust Germany, I argue that perhaps a time will come in Sierra Leone (and other post-conflict African countries) when this culture of silence will be overturned and people will be able to revisit hegemonic memory narratives. However, without the risk of sounding pessimistic, I conclude that silence might just be pivotal in the construction and sustenance of certain postcolonial nation-states.

In the third chapter, I analyze Dinaw Mengestu's *Children of the Revolution*, a novel based on the memories and experiences of Ethiopians who fled their country to America during the communist revolution of the 1970s and '80s. I examine how the novel depicts the traversal of traumatic memories across continental borders (from Africa to America). I show how the characters come to terms with their traumatic pasts, which led to their emigration to America, as well as their interactions—as Black African immigrants—with America's racialized past and present. In essence, in chapter 3 I examine the frictions that occur when immigratory and emigratory memories come into contact. Focusing on the main character, Sepha, I argue that the experience of migration, in and of itself, is based on a structure of mourning. I argue that Sepha suffers from a condition called "immigrant melancholia" that results from his inability to integrate after seventeen years of living in America. He is continuously haunted by the traumatic witnessing of his father's brutal death at the hands of communist soldiers; hence, the past for him is another country.[101] I argue that the novel indeed can be read as a melancholic text because of the narrative melancholy, forlorn tone, and pensive mood with which it is written. Drawing on his other novels, I argue that Dinaw Mengestu himself might be regarded as a melancholic author because of the repetitive compulsion with which he writes about his family's involuntary migration from Ethiopia to the United States during the Derg revolution. I also examine how the novel portrays the Ethiopian community living in Washington, DC. I explore how this community is able to emplace the memory of Addis Ababa in Washington, DC, creating a translocal connection between the two cities. In light of that, I argue that memory, for immigrant groups, creates continuity between their experience of displacement and a connection to their original place of dislocation.[102] The chapter ends with an exploration of how Sepha and his two African immigrant friends, Kenneth the Kenyan and Joseph from Zaire, form the habit of "remembering together" in America. While America excludes them from its national memory discourse, these immigrant friends insurgently suture themselves into America's memory through symbolic acts such as learning America's history and obsessing over America's national memorials and monuments. But beyond that, these immigrant friends also keep their pasts in Africa alive by always talking about the post-independence civil wars and revolutions that led to their emigration to America. This performance of remembering, which I discuss in detail in this chapter, is what I describe as an African transnational memory in a migratory setting. The third chapter, in essence, is about the entanglement of memory, migration, melancholies, and practices of belonging.

In the fourth chapter, I continue to explore the idea of an African transnational memory, albeit in a different context. I begin the chapter by establishing the transnationality of the Rwandan genocide, after which I analyze the 1998 "Rwanda: Writing as a Duty to Remember" project as an ATM project. Four years after the genocide, a group of ten African writers from Kenya, Chad, Ivory Coast, Guinea, Senegal, Burkina Faso, Djibouti, and Rwanda came together to Kigali to write about the genocide and its aftermath. This is what became known as the "Rwanda: Writing as a Duty to Remember" project. I read the project as an ATM project because of the way it assembled African writers of different nationalities with the aim of commemorating the genocide from a Pan-African viewpoint. After laying this background, I zero in on one of the texts that came out of the project: *The Shadow of Imana* by Véronique Tadjo. Drawing on the works of Avishai Margalit, I examine how the text provides insights on the ethical dimensions to the production of narratives about other people's traumatic memories. I read the text along the line of what Saidiya Hartman eloquently describes as "the precariousness of empathy and the uncertain line between witness and spectator."[103] I also examine the text as a work of secondary and intellectual witnessing before moving on to the im/possibility of considering Tadjo's memory (presented in the text) as prosthetic memory. In view of this, I give attention to Tadjo's embodied interactions and affective encounters with the Rwandan memorial sites. I end the chapter with an investigation of the stylistic techniques that Tadjo uses in writing from a position of a secondary witness. In all, I explore in this chapter the kinds of frictions that occur—ethically and aesthetically—when one witnesses the past from the position of exteriority. The main insight gleaned from this exploration is that the past is not simply present; it is present-ed through subject positions, either of the victim, perpetrator, or, in Tadjo's case, the "outsider within."

In the fifth chapter, the concluding chapter, I highlight the connecting strands between all the texts. I establish what the texts altogether reveal—theoretically and politically—about (traumatic) memory in the postcolony. I explain how each of the texts has dealt with the question of memory and positionality and argue that the relation between memory and distance might, in fact, be necessary for the performance of solidarity and comradeship. I return to my idea of concatenated memory in the postcolony and argue that while the selected texts focus on particular histories, they also hint at how cumulative pasts continue in the present. This corroborates Achille Mbembe's position that the postcolony consists of "multiple durées made up of discontinuities, reversals, inertias and swings that overlay one another, interpenetrate one another and envelope one another."[104] I also note in the concluding chapter that what the selected post-conflict fictions of memory bring to bear is the fact that memory is implicitly about futurity. Therefore, while some characters in the novels want to bury memory, the authors of the novels perform the ethico-political duty of remembering which, as Paul Ricoeur[105] also suggests, is important for the construction of a just future. I conclude that the selected texts constitute a form of textual mourning and that they offer an idea of a postcolonial temporality that is of—and in—the wake. In all, this book investigates the representation of violent histories and traumatic memories in post-conflict African fiction. It frames memory as a conceptual domain in which the experiences of trauma and the intricacies of mourning are interlocked.

CHAPTER 1

The Past Is a Contested Territory

Half of a Yellow Sun as a Postmemory Fiction

All wars are fought twice, the first time on the battlefield, the second time in memory.
—Viet Than Nguyen, *Nothing Ever Dies*

People may indeed experience the persistent residues of the distant past and unsuspectingly harbor memories of the most significant experiences of their ancestor.
—Laura Murphy, "The Curse of Constant Remembrance"

Of all cults, that of the ancestors is the most legitimate: our ancestors have made us what we are.
—Ernest Renan, "What Is a Nation?"

It is all on the shoulder of the living that the burden of justice continues to rest . . . and few will deny that justice is an essential ingredient of social cohesion.
—Wole Soyinka, *The Burden of Memory, The Muse of Forgiveness*

THE SHADOW OF BIAFRA

Seven years after independence from the British, Nigeria went into a civil war that lasted for three years—from 1967 to 1970. The war claimed the lives of over a million[1] Igbo people who had decided to form an independent nation, called Biafra, following the repeated killings aimed at them in the Hausa-dominated Northern Nigeria. In January 1970, after a brutal defeat, Biafra surrendered and reunited with Nigeria. The Nigerian president at that time, Yakubu Gowon, made a rather specious declaration that the war had no victor and no vanquished. This declaration marked the beginning of the strategic and political silence placed on the subject of Biafra by the Nigerian government. To this day in Nigeria, there are no reputable national memorials or acts of commemoration of the war. The government has achieved a repressive erasure[2] by ensuring that this history is not taught in schools or engaged publicly. However, while the state repression remains unswerving, Nigerian artists and intellectuals challenge and interrogate this "will to forget" through their continuous engagements with this violent history. To put it another way, over the years in Nigeria, literature has served as a tool for countering the official amnesia about Biafra—and one such literary intervention is Chimamanda Adichie's *Half of a Yellow Sun* (2006). What is remarkable about this novel is that it was not written by a direct, firsthand witness of the war. Adichie had not been born when the civil war broke out. She belongs to the "born-after" or "postwar" generation. She was born in 1977 (seven years after the war) into an Igbo family that was deeply affected by the war. While her parents survived the war with scars and numerous losses, her grandfathers died in refugee camps and were buried in mass graves.[3]

Adichie's generational distance did not prevent her from being haunted by the war. She grew up in the "shadow of Biafra"—a phrase she uses in many of her interviews to describe how, despite not being a direct witness, she saw the specters of the war everywhere and was affected by its phantomlike sensations. From Adichie's statements, which I will get to later, one gets a sense that not only is the state silent but that some of the victims and survivors of the war—including Adichie's parents—are also given to silence as a result of trauma. Therefore, despite belonging to the postwar generation, Adichie inherited the traumatic memories of Biafra. The silence of her parents troubled her to the point that she started to do her own research on Biafra and, as a way of working through her own traumatic inheritance, wrote *Half of a Yellow Sun*. More importantly, Adichie wrote *Half of a Yellow Sun* as a way of engaging in a dialogue with history and urging the masses to remember what happened in Nigeria between 1967 and 1970.

The novel is a narration and an amplification of the experiences of Igbo people during the war. It begins in the early 1960s and chronicles the ordinary lives of Nigerians along with the various events that precipitated the war. It ends in the early 1970s by showing the immediate aftermaths and ruins of the war. It is told through the eyes of three major characters: Olanna, Ugwu, and Richard. Olanna is an upper-middle-class Nigerian woman who went to school in the United Kingdom but chose to work as an instructor in the Department of Sociology at the newly established University of Nigeria in Nsukka. In Nsukka she lives with her revolutionary and idealistic lover,

Odenigbo, who is also a professor at the same university. Ugwu, who is more or less the soul of the novel, is the houseboy in Olanna and Odenigbo's house. He is at first presented as a naive and illiterate thirteen-year-old boy whose master (Odenigbo) teaches how to read and write. But during the war, he is forcefully conscripted into the army and becomes indifferently violent and even rapes a girl. By the end of the war, he decides to write a book about his experiences as a conscripted Biafran soldier. Richard, on the other hand, is an English writer who goes to Nigeria to research Igbo-Ukwu art. When the war breaks out, he chooses not to be repatriated to England, moves to Biafra, falls in love with Olanna's twin sister (Kainene), and shows his support for the Biafran cause by writing articles (with a Biafran viewpoint) for a Western audience. Through these characters, the novel explores how the experience of war tests the human spirit and drives people to the end of their tethers. It details how trauma, starvation, and betrayal during a war can put a strain on the ties that bind us as humans, but it also illustrates the possibility of redemption, love, and forgiveness even amid social and political extremities. In addition, the novel explores the politics of ethnicity and nascent democracy in postcolonial nation-statehood; it complicates political and civil conflicts in the postcolony by showing how colonial powers are, more often than not, the enabler or even the cause of such conflicts.

Because Adichie is writing from a transgenerational position, her novel becomes a work of postmemory. She writes as part of a growing community of writers who inherited the memories of Biafra. By virtue of their works, these writers—Uzodinma Iweala, Helon Habila, Uwem Akpan, and Chika Unigwe, to mention a few—are part of the "generation of postmemory." Their works, among many others, constitute what Pius Adesanmi and Chris Dutton categorize as the third generation of Nigerian writing.[4] Adesanmi and Dutton particularly describe *Half of a Yellow Sun* as one of the leading texts to emerge within this third generation and "as one of the richest creative works yet to appear on the subject of the Nigerian Civil War."[5] It is therefore not surprising that the novel has attracted the attention of many literary scholars.[6] In fact, there is a consensus among critics that the novel is a literary masterpiece and an instant African classic. In 2006 it was listed as one of the *New York Times'* "100 Most Notable Books of the Year."[7] It won the 2007 Women's Prize for Fiction and in 2020 was voted the best novel to have won the Women's Prize for Fiction in its twenty-five-year history. In 2019 *The Guardian*[8] voted it the tenth-best book written in the twenty-first century, and the British Broadcasting Corporation (BBC)[9] listed it as one of the "100 novels that shaped our world." In 2013 *Half of a Yellow Sun* was adapted into a movie that starred Chiwetel Ejiofor and Thandie Newton in the lead roles.[10]

While earlier studies have established the novel as a work of postmemory,[11] I want to show how theory and text illuminate each other by exploring the various postmemory tropes and underpinnings in the writing of *Half of a Yellow Sun* (hereafter, *Yellow Sun*). In view of this, I read the "inside and outside" of the text—that is, in order to unravel the postmemorial workings of the novel, I employ an extratextual and a transtextual reading of the novel. This kind of reading allows me to assess Adichie's narrative corpus, her autobiographical writings, authorial discussions, interviews, and other epitextual data that are central to the making (and the reception) of the novel. This kind of reading also grants me access to the unconscious of the novel and sheds light on how form constitutes an integral part of meaning-making for the postmemorial novel. I argue that while Adichie's postmemorial endeavor gestures toward the necessity of repair[12] on national and familial levels, it also represents, complicates, and even anticipates the ongoing frictions over the memory of Biafra in Nigeria today. Overall, I read *Yellow Sun* as a way to understand postmemory's founding on a structure of mourning, its reliance on re/mediation and its dis/connections with postcoloniality. In the next section, I provide a brief overview of the concept of postmemory as a means of setting the stage for my discussion of *Yellow Sun* as a work of postmemory.

POSTMEMORY

A lot of scholars have established and theorized trauma's inheritability.[13] Sigmund Freud used the term "archaic inheritance" to refer to the transgenerational transmission of trauma that may not necessarily be overt but traces back to very distant pasts.[14] W. G. Sebald also used the phrase "secondhand memories" to capture how those who experience a traumatic event pass on their memories of the event to the younger generation.[15] Martha Minow notes that children and grandchildren (of survivors) often receive bitter legacies in their own experiences "with unexplained sadness and anxiety."[16] However, it is Marianne Hirsch who has written most extensively about the transgenerational effects of trauma. She coined the term "postmemory" to describe what it means to own the memory of a violent history that one did not experience firsthand but is continuously haunted by. The term, according to Hirsch, illustrates the "relationship of the second generation to powerful, often traumatic, experiences that preceded their births but that were nonetheless transmitted to them so deeply as to seem to constitute memories in their own right."[17] Another reason why postmemory is constructed as memory is because of the obsessive grip it has on its carriers. However, it cannot be overemphasized that postmemory is different from (survivor) memory—"it is 'post' but, at the same time, approximates memory in its affective force and psychic effect."[18] It is distinguished from memory by a "generational distance" and from history by "deep personal connection." It is belated, indirect, and secondary in comparison to memory, which is supposed to be more directly connected to the past.[19] Essentially, members of the second generation "remember" through the lens of the stories, images, and behaviors among which they grew up.

Of all the scholars[20] who have interrogated the legitimacy of Hirsch's claims, Guy Beiner's[21] and Liz Stanley's[22] critiques stand out. Beiner expresses skepticism over the extension of the term from the transmission of trauma by familial relationship to adoptive and distant witnessing.[23] He points out that when postmemory is not restricted to autobiographical recollections passed on from parent to child, the boundaries between memory and postmemory become blurred. He also expresses concern over the propensity to sweep historical experience into oblivion in this ever-expanding transgenerational memory discourse. In response to this, Hirsch notes that "the expansion of the postmemorial community beyond family boundaries is enabled by the conventionality of the familial tropes prevalent in postmemorial writing, which provides a space for identification that can, in theory at least, be occupied by any reader or viewer."[24] Meanwhile, Stanley's critique stems from the fact that all memories are "post" memories because of their belatedness, mediation, and separation from the actual event. Despite these debates, postmemory continues to gain traction among memory scholars and students as a theoretical and analytical framework for discussing the transgenerational transmission of memory. As I will show later in this chapter, the various arguments for and against postmemory are relevant for conversations about the Nigeria-Biafra War.

It is worthy of mention that postmemory overlaps conceptually with Toni Morrison's notion of rememory that similarly explores how later generations remember via imaginative investments.[25] Rememory accounts for how, based on the traces of someone else's memory, someone can reconstruct an event they did not experience. It is perhaps not surprising that before Hirsch became known for postmemory, she had worked with Morrison's concept of rememory. Hirsch defines rememory as "neither memory nor forgetting, but memory combined with (the threat of) repetition; it is neither noun nor verb, but both combined."[26] While Morrison's rememory is often applied to the African American slavery context, it can fit into any history of trauma. In the same vein, postmemory, initially solely applied to the Holocaust context, is applicable to any context of trauma. While the concept of rememory may be undoubtedly useful for reading *Yellow Sun*, I embrace postmemory as a deliberate analytical choice because of my vested interest in how Adichie's writing process and style are blended with her familial attachments to Biafra. Therefore, in the following section, my discussion is grounded in Adichie's experience: What was transmitted to her at personal and intimate levels? What structures of experience ensured the continuity of the past within the family space? How does the war generation serve as the bridge to the past for the postwar generation?

CHIMAMANDA ADICHIE AS A VICARIOUS WITNESS

To understand *Half of a Yellow Sun* as a work of postmemory, it is pertinent to know why the novel was written in the first place. In "Stories of Africa," an addendum to the novel, Adichie states:

> I wrote the novel because . . . I grew up in the shadow of Biafra, because I lost both grandfathers in the Nigeria-Biafra war, because I wanted to engage with my history in order to make sense of my present, because many issues that led to the war remain unresolved today, because my father has tears in his eyes when he speaks of losing his father, because my mother still cannot speak at length about losing her father in a refugee camp, because the brutal bequests of colonialism make me angry, because the thoughts of the egos and indifference of men leading to unnecessary deaths of men and women and children enrages me, because I don't ever want to forget.[27]

Growing up "in the shadow of Biafra" suggests Adichie's experience of the spectral presence of an incomprehensible past. It means she saw her parents entangled in a loss they could not articulate and became a vicarious witness to that inarticulable loss. It also connotes the arduous experience of relating with—or being closely related to—scarred people whose silence she found very deafening. Later she says:

My parents did not talk about their experience until I started asking questions and I really cannot explain in an intellectual way why I was haunted by that experience but I have been since I was 13. And I would ask questions endlessly.... The stories my father told me formed the basis of the novel.[28]

It is apparent, from the foregoing, that the family is a privileged site for the transmission of heritable memories. That is, Adichie's fragmented memory of the war, which formed the raw material for *Yellow Sun*, came primarily from the family space—she draws from a communicative memory to build the cultural memory of the war.[29] In addition to family stories, the landscape also bears the traces of the past and tells its own story for postgenerational witnesses. In view of this, Adichie writes:

There are buildings in my hometown with bullet holes; as a child, playing outside, I would sometimes come across bits of rusty ammunition left behind from the war. My generation was born after 1970, but we know of property lost, of relatives who never "returned" from the North, of shadows that hung heavily over family stories. We inherited memory.[30]

Therefore, apart from the memories and silences within the embodied space of the family, Adichie's postmemory of Biafra also emanates from her interactions with topographical incarnations of the past. This stirred her inquisitiveness so much that she decided to embark on the journey to recover the unclaimed. She says that writing *Yellow Sun* felt "like an obligation . . . an obsession."[31] The obligatory impulse, on the one hand, serves to reclaim the dignity of her ancestors who died in the war and, on the other, challenges the taboo label that the state had placed on discussions relating to the war. However, this (moral) obligation that Adichie felt came with a lot of baggage. At first she was unnerved by the thought of writing about the dead. She asked herself repeatedly, "If dead people can see, what would they think about the book?"[32] She was also anxious about what the war survivors would think when they read the book. This ethical quandary certainly has nothing to do with the quality of Adichie's writing but with the fact that she was (re)writing a historical experience she did not live through. She defended her (post) memorial obligation to write about Biafra when she said:

I have often been asked why I chose to write about Biafra, and I like to say that I did not choose Biafra, it chose me.... It is a subject I have known for a very long time that I would write about.[33]

That Biafra "chose her" and not the other way around suggests some kind of fate or an indeclinable duty to belatedly witness. That is to say, Adichie felt historically—and ancestrally—appointed to bear posthumous witness to the past. In fact, she went on to write, "Most families have that one child who wants to know the story of who they are, and I think in my family I am that child."[34] Being that "one inquisitive child" in the family illustrates how traumatic memories are not always inherited with the same intensity in lineal (and even public) spaces. Adichie's commitment to remembering and writing about Biafra is therefore an ethico-political duty and a historical responsibility that, by consequence, makes her novel not only a familial but also an affiliative postmemory project.[35]

Apart from the anxieties that Adichie felt about the reception of the novel, the writing itself was revelatory as well as traumatizing for her. It was in the writing and shaping of characters that she really began to acquire an affective knowledge of, and an imaginative clarity about, the war. Her writing journey, as overwhelming as it might have been, became a witnessing journey; it authenticated her position as a postgenerational witness. In view of this, she said:

> Writing *Half of a Yellow Sun* took a lot from me emotionally. . . . *Half of a Yellow Sun* is deeply personal. . . . I cried writing it.[36]

She also said elsewhere:

> The writing was a bruising experience. I struggled to maintain many fragile balances. I cried often, was frequently crippled with doubt and anxiety, often wondered whether to stop or to scale back.[37]

The writing was emotional for Adichie because she had to come face-to-face with horrifying stories of massacre, starvation, and disease. In addition to confronting these horrors of the past, writing *Yellow Sun* was Adichie's way of displaying ancestral piety; it was her way of bearing an unbearable fidelity to the dead as well as suturing herself into her ancestors' memories. After all, she mentioned that she wrote the book for—and even dedicated it to—her grandparents who died during the war (*Yellow Sun*, ix). The novel is therefore a kind of textual commemoration or literary memorial for the dead. In the absence of a reputable national commemoration of the war, the novel serves as an archival memory. More technically, it serves as what Ann Rigney, in another context, refers to as a "portable monument."[38]

Jacques Derrida argues that the dead no longer lives in himself or herself, and that the only being of the dead is "in us" and in our "bereaved memory." We, the living, bear the grave of the dead within us, and it is in this process of "interiorizing the deceased other" that the past is kept alive.[39] In spite of that, there is usually a pressing urge to bury the dead and rid ourselves of their ghosts. It is this oscillating tension between interiorizing the dead and exorcising their ghosts that produces the inconsolable mourning that impelled Adichie to keep returning to the subject of Biafra. At the age of sixteen, she wrote a play[40] about Biafra, which would be followed by a couple of short stories[41] (and poems[42]) about Biafra and, eventually, *Yellow Sun*. On the one hand, the continuous writing about Biafra is a form of repetition compulsion and a melancholic attachment to the source of trauma that is Biafra. On the other hand, this attachment to Biafra reaffirms the fact of transgenerational transmissions which, in Adichie's case, realizes itself in the form of what I have so far been describing as postmemory. Put differently, Biafra, in and of itself, is a site of an interminable mourning and a narrative of an inconsolable loss for the victims and survivors of the war. It is precisely this interminable quality of (Biafran) mourning that produces melancholic attachments in both the survivors and the generation that succeeds them.

As a work of postmemory, *Yellow Sun* allows us to see Biafra in a renewed light. One of the distinctive qualities of the novel is that it provides readers with a repository of details on a scale and intensity that have not been seen in earlier fictional works on Biafra. And to be clear, Adichie's melancholic attachment to Biafra cannot be interpreted as pathological in the traditional psychoanalytic sense. Rather, it boosts her artistic prolificacy (she has written a play, short stories, a collection of poems, and a novel on Biafra) and is precursory to a viable work of mourning. In what follows, I examine the stylistic devices and aesthetic choices that make this postgenerational witnessing possible.

AESTHETICS OF POSTMEMORY IN *HALF OF A YELLOW SUN*

In one of her interviews, Adichie said, "I knew that the book would be read as history by my generation. That's why I had to *stay true to fact*."[43] Of course, Adichie's novel can certainly be read as a historical text, but there are risks embedded in doing so. First, her statement that *Yellow Sun* would be read as history by members of her generation, although veracious to an extent, sounds dangerously prescriptive. It risks downplaying the significance of Biafra's historiography, but maybe that is the point: to write history differently. Adichie's statement also obliterates the fact that, being a child of survivors, she writes from a victim's perspective; in fact, she once admitted that the novel is filled with "unapologetic Biafran sympathies."[44] Therefore, her fictive representation of the past is only one—but necessary—version of the war. Readers need to be aware of this so as not to base their assessment of Biafra on Adichie's perspective only. Even Adichie herself will agree that there are still stories to be told about Biafra, especially from the Nigerian side of the war, and that telling such stories will allow for a democratic and pluralistic interpretation of the past.

Still on history, Adichie does not only attempt to humanize history, but she also fictionalizes it. *Yellow Sun* serves as that space where history and fiction are entwined in a way that allows for a more sublime and affective representation of the past. In the novel, history dissolves within fiction for the purpose of producing emotional and narrative truths about the past.[45] This privileging of a fictive narrative of history as a form of truth-telling bestows some new historicist predilections on the novel. In fact, there are many instances in the novel where historical facts are intercalated within the conversations of the characters. For example, there is a scene where Olanna, having been bedridden as a result of the trauma of witnessing the Igbo pogroms in the north, listens in on the conversations between Odenigbo and his friends from her room. The narrator describes the conversation in the following:

> Then she [Olanna] heard Okeoma say "Aburi." It sounded lovely, the name of that Ghanaian town, and she imagined a sleepy cluster of homes on stretches of sweet-scented grasslands. Aburi came up often in their conversations: Okeoma would say that Gowon should have followed the agreement he and Ojukwu signed in Aburi, or Professor Ezeka would say that Gowon's reneging after Aburi meant that he did not wish the Igbo well or Odenigbo would proclaim, "on Aburi we stand."

The Aburi Accord is a historical fact that took place in January 1967 when the tension of war was suddenly mounting.[46] By sliding Aburi into her characters' conversations instead of centering it within the novel, Adichie avoids the monotonous expectations of historiography in her attempt to animate the everyday life in Biafra. This injection of historical facts into the characters' dialogues also enhances Adichie's effort at incorporating "history into her novel as a spectral presence rather than attempting to recover it as a fully narratable subject."[47] In essence, *Yellow Sun* is, no doubt, a historical fiction, but it is even more of a memory-making fiction because it is less burdened by historical facts—although it prioritizes historicity—and is more attuned to producing emotional and narrative truths.

As a postmemorial technique, *Yellow Sun* also offers a postmodern approach to history through its use of metatext.[48] Some of the chapters in the novel end with a short (meta)text under the title "The World Was Silent When We Died." Readers get the impression that this metatext is a book (within a book) with its own prologue and epilogue. But it is not exactly a finished book because it is still being self-consciously and self-referentially written by an extradiegetic narrator. It offers historical details about Nigeria's past while, at the same time, commenting on the fictional world of the novel. The metatext is laden with a subtle authorial impulse to legitimize the events described in the fictional world of the novel which, in the long run, cements *Yellow Sun* as a historical fiction that also bears the burden of postmemory.

Additionally, the metatext is written with an awareness of the political and compromised nature of history. It is presented as a kind of a decolonial historiography that accommodates creative language and experiments with style. In other words, the metatext in the novel incorporates poetry, prose, and journalese as a way of critiquing conventional (and colonial) historiography and narrative forms. In light of this, Dori Laub asserts that it is inconceivable to attempt to construct the past through the use of a single methodology or approach.[49] Therefore, by way of representing a "people's history,"[50] the metatext, as we later find out, is written by Ugwu, a houseboy-turned-vernacular-intellectual[51] rather than the earlier suspected British professional writer, Richard. The twist in the authorship of the metatext represents the repudiation of elitist memorialism of Biafra. Overall, *Yellow Sun*'s metatextuality is what enhances Adichie's use of fiction to fill archival silences and historical gaps. More importantly, it is what allows for the smooth re-presentation of history within the world of fiction. Hence, the novel qualifies as what Linda Hutcheon calls "historiographic metafiction" because it is at "once metafictional *and* historical in its echoes of the texts and contexts of the past."[52]

Despite having read and heard a lot of stories about Biafra, Adichie, as a postgenerational witness, still needed to reactivate and reanimate the past through a painstaking work of the imagination. One could argue that all works of fiction require the work of the imagination, but for Adichie the imagination is not simply an apparatus for fictional inventions but a political tool and a memory tactic. After all, Toni Morrison writes that the act of imagination is bound up with memory and that for memory narratives, the imaginative act yields a kind of truth.[53] Therefore, while Adichie's imaginative investments as a postgenerational witness come from an absent memory, it is precisely these same imaginative investments that enable her to narrate the past in a believable way. For example, in the novel, we see an imaginative recollection of the popular cultural signature of the early post-independence Nigeria defined by High Life music (*Yellow Sun*, 26) and cultural icons like Rex Lawson (26) and Bobby Benson (37). Also in the novel, we find fictitious inventions at play in the depictions of characters and settings. Adichie said the following about her inventions in *Yellow Sun*:

> While writing *Half of a Yellow Sun*, I enjoyed inventing a train station in a town that has none, placing towns closer to each other than they are, changing the chronology of conquered towns. ("Stories of Africa")[54]

In addition, there is a fusion of history, memory, and imagination in the way most of the characters in the novel are modeled after real-life actors or figures in the war. For instance, Adichie reveals in "Stories of Africa" that the character Richard was inspired when she read Frederick Forsyth's *The Biafra Story*. Forsyth, like Richard, was a British journalist with strong sympathies for Biafra. Likewise, the character Okeoma bears striking resemblances to the renowned Nigerian poet Christopher Okigbo. Okeoma, just as Okigbo, believed in the Biafran cause so much that he dropped the pen to carry the sword but unfortunately died in the war. Adichie does not only bring these real-life personalities back to life in her fiction, she also reinvents some of them to the extent that they are almost unrecognizable. For instance, the character Ugwu, who was inspired by Mellitus (Adichie's parents' houseboy during the war), was fictionalized quite differently from his real-life parallel. In view of this, Adichie explains:

> When my mum spoke about Mellitus, what a blessing he was, how much he helped her, how she did not know what she would have done without him, I remember being moved and also thinking that he could not possibly have been the saint my mother painted, that he must have been flawed and human. ("Stories of Africa")

One of the concerns that immediately come to mind with Adichie's inventive and imaginative investments is the possibility of imagination inflation or the danger of romanticizing Biafra. But it appears that in a bid to avoid romanticizing memory, Adichie largely detaches herself from the story and allows her characters to be driven solely by their impulses without losing sight of the overall narrative arc. We see an instance where one of the main characters, Kainene, raises allegations against Chukwuemeka Odumegwu Ojukwu, the heroic Biafran leader, who is still regarded as a leader without blemish among many Igbo survivors today. Kainene critiques Ojukwu by pointing out how he had led Biafrans to go to war with poor weaponry compared to the British-armed Nigerian army. Likewise, when Biafrans started pointing accusing fingers at the minority group within Biafra as saboteurs, Kainene came to their defense by indicating that:

> The only saboteurs we have are the ones Ojukwu invented so he can lock up his opponents and the men whose wives he wants. Did I tell you about the Onitsha man who bought up all of the cement we had in the factory shortly after the refugees started coming back? Ojukwu is having an affair with the man's wife and had just had the man arrested. . . . Really, when Biafra is established, we will have to remove Ojukwu. (*Yellow Sun*, 313)

Therefore, *Yellow Sun* is told through a multiplicity of perspectives, a plurality of voices/opinions and through what Chris Ouma describes as a "composite consciousness" in order to avoid the trap of romanticizing the memory of Biafra.[55] Drawing from Kainene's statement above, the novel exposes the ethnic divisions and tensions within Biafra itself. It reveals how minority (non-Igbo) groups within Biafra were sidelined and, sometimes, victimized. Thus, *Yellow Sun*, as a postmemory fiction, disrupts the mystery woven around— and exposes the frictions in—the memory of Biafra among the survivor generation. This becomes possible partly because of the "privilege of distance"[56] that enables Adichie as a member of the postwar generation to investigate the truth about Biafra. In other words, the historical imperative to bear witness could essentially not be met during the actual occurrence of a traumatic event; hence, the "innocent children" removed from the actual experience find themselves in a position to ask questions.[57] It is precisely the paradoxical (generational) distance from, and (personal) attachment to, Biafra in Adichie's postgenerational positioning that makes *Yellow Sun* an extraordinary work of postmemory.

REMEMBERING BACK AND WRITING BACK: THE NEXUS BETWEEN POSTMEMORY AND POSTCOLONIALISM IN *HALF OF A YELLOW SUN*

If postcolonialism is conceived as a memorializing project that is concerned with the afterlives and aftereffects of colonialism, then it is arguably—and inherently—postmemorial. In the introduction, I showed how postcoloniality operates within the logic of mourning, and in this chapter, I am arguing that the same could be said about postmemory. That is, while postcoloniality is partly concerned with working through colonial losses, postmemory is an attempt at working through familial losses. They are both concerned—albeit in different ways—with memory ruptures and temporal disruptions. In addition, while postmemory deals with intergenerational (trauma) transmissions, the postcolony is fraught with persistent haunting and the presence of melancholia which is born of a transgenerationally transmitted colonial trauma.[58] Put differently, postcolonialism is postmemorial precisely because colonialism involves a break in the "intergenerational communicative memory of a colonized group."[59]

In writing *Yellow Sun*, Adichie simultaneously reaches for familial and national pasts which, in consequence, make the novel both a postcolonial and postmemorial work. On the one hand, the novel "remembers back" in the way it reflects Adichie's inherited memories of Biafra and in the way it guides the readers through the colonial history that gave rise to the war. On the other hand, it "writes back" in the way it sharply critiques Western (mis)conceptions of post-independence African wars and subverts colonial ideological edifices and power structures. Additionally, *Yellow Sun* presents a palimpsestic vision of memory in the way it details the diabolical layering of colonial violence on the continuing violence of Western exploitative and unequal relationship with Africa. In light of this, we find in the novel how the memory of the Nigeria-Biafra War cannot be completely divorced from the memory of British colonial violence in Nigeria which, in a sense, is also an aftermath of the transatlantic slave trade.[60]

As a postcolonial novel, *Yellow Sun* provides a counter-narrative to the stereotypical renderings of Africa within colonial discourses. In the early part of the novel, Odenigbo hints at the need to decolonize the world's map when he says to Ugwu (while showing him Africa on the map):

> This is our world, although the people who drew the map decided to put their own land on top of ours. There is no top or bottom. (*Yellow Sun*, 10)

This seemingly simple statement reflects the cartographic manipulation of the world as well as the hierarchization of space which fuels the embers of colonial domination. Beyond illustrating geography, the map becomes a manifestation of the colonialist's desire to control and mold the world in his own essentialist image. In another instance in the novel, the revolutionary Odenigbo says to Ugwu:

> They will teach you that a white man called Mungo Park discovered River Niger. That is rubbish. Our people fished in the Niger long before Mungo Park's grandfather was born. (*Yellow Sun*, 11)

Here, we see Odenigbo's rejection of the foisting of colonial knowledge on the colonized as well as his stern repudiation of the colonial gaze. Odenigbo's words, therefore, provide a decolonial counterclaim to the coloniality of memory. On the whole, *Yellow Sun* is a critique of the colonial practice that constructs Africa as "an object of consumption," especially through the character of Richard, who represents the colonial voice and its privileges.[61] Kainene gives expression to this anticolonial sentiment when she calls Richard "a modern-day explorer of the dark continent" (*Yellow Sun*, 62). Likewise, on a local (Nigerian) flight full of white Europeans, Richard imagines how Kainene would have mockingly described them as "the marauding Europeans" (150). The problematic (Western and colonial) gaze of Africa is also illustrated when Olanna speaks about Kainene's racist boyfriends in England who looked at Africans condescendingly and had a "familiar superiority of English people who thought they understood Africans better than Africans understood themselves" (36).

The West's knowledge of Africa is inundated with what Adichie calls a "single story"[62] that often becomes the definitive story of Africa in the global imaginary. In the same vein, Achille Mbembe writes that more than any other continent, Africa has been the "supreme receptacle of the West's obsession with, and circular discourse about, the facts of 'absence,' 'lack,' and 'non-being,' of identity and difference, of negativeness—in short, of nothingness."[63] In light of that, *Yellow Sun* exposes Western biases in the media coverage of the Nigeria-Biafra War and, by extension, other post-independence wars in Africa. In the novel, an editor for an international press asks Richard to write about the human angle of the war, and by that he means if the people ate "body parts like they did in the Congo" (*Yellow Sun*, 167). Similarly, Martin, who lives in Britain, is so curious about the war that he writes a letter to Richard. In the letter, he asks, "Were hands chopped off in Africa as well? I'd imagined it was only in India. I'm intrigued!" (137). At the end of the novel, after having lived through the war, Richard realizes the problematics of the colonial gaze and gives up writing about Biafra because the "war isn't [his] story to write" (345). This radical shift in authorship is Adichie's way of creating "a voice that is not reliant upon a Western subject for testimony."[64]

Yellow Sun does not only critique the colonial gaze; it also challenges phallocentric narratives that have long dominated the accounts of the Biafran war by centering women's experiences. The novel is replete with stories of independent and educated Nigerian women who showed unequaled resilience and optimism in the face of war—Olanna is the most focalized of these women. The decentering of colonial and patriarchal gazes launches *Yellow Sun* into a postcolonial feminist discourse, and in view of that, Adichie has stated the reason why she had to carefully craft the character Olanna:

> Olanna's trajectory, I think, was inspired by reading about women, but I was struck when researching by how little the stories of women were told, how rarely women's stories were the centre of narratives about that period. And I would read something and there would sort of be a "by the way" mention of what a woman had done.[65]

Yellow Sun essentially becomes Adichie's way of writing Biafra's *herstory*, a way of feminizing the Biafran war narratives that had hitherto marginalized female voices. Thus, one could say that Adichie's postmemorial and postcolonial impulse is unapologetically gendered.

Another postcolonial memory dimension to the novel is how it strategically "remembers" and represents the involvement of Western superpowers in the war as well as how it subtly presses for transnational forms of solidarity and justice. In other words, the Nigeria-Biafra War is a transnational site of memory because of the involvement of other—mostly imperialist—nations. The novel recounts the memory of British complicity in the 1966 anti-Igbo pogrom that culminated in the war. It reminds us of several instances where British academics and other white expatriates encouraged "anti-Igbo sentiments" in prewar Nigeria (*Yellow Sun*, 165). It also elucidates how the prewar ethnic distrust in Nigeria is predicated on the divide-and-rule policy of British colonialism that manipulated the differences between the ethnic groups and ensured that unity did not exist (298). We are also informed about the reactions of Western countries to the news of Biafra as the narrator notes:

> He [*Ugwu*] writes about the world that remained silent while Biafrans died. He argues that Britain had inspired that silence. The arms and advice that Britain gave Nigeria shaped other countries. In the United States, Biafra was "under Britain's sphere of interest." In Canada, the prime minister quipped, "Where is Biafra?" The Soviet Union sent technicians and planes to Nigeria, thrilled at the chance to influence Africa without offending America or Britain. (257)

Here, *Yellow Sun* addresses a transnational audience, especially the British and American governments. It recalls the betrayal of the countries that failed to recognize or share solidarity with Biafra's pain although they were in the position to do so. It is in the same vein that another character in the novel says lamentably that "the world simply cannot remain silent while we die" (305). This statement, which would later become the title of the poem in the novel's metatext, strikingly resonates with the Yiddish title of Elie Wiesel's (1956) Holocaust memoir, *Un di Velt Hot Geshvign* (*And the World Remained Silent*). Therefore, *Yellow Sun* contributes to a multidirectional memory discourse by pointing to the link between the Holocaust and colonial violence which, in a sense, is not unconnected to the independence and post-independence wars in Africa.

In view of this, Odenigbo says, "If Europe had cared more about Africa, the Jewish Holocaust would not have happened. . . . In short the World War would not have happened" (*Yellow Sun*, 50). While there might be a bit of exaggeration in Odenigbo's statement, it is not necessarily untrue. His statement is significant because it, on the one hand, invokes a global ethics of care and, on the other, alludes to the transnational memory of modern wars. Put differently, by stating that the Holocaust would not have happened if Europe had cared about Africa, Odenigbo is making a historical allusion to the first genocide of the twentieth century: the genocide of the Herero people of today's Namibia by German imperialists. This particular genocide—as scholars such as Aimé Césaire, Frantz Fanon, Michael Rothberg, and Elizabeth Baer have established—set a precedent in imperial Germany and would later be followed by the genocide of European Jews by Nazi Germany.[66] In essence, colonial violence, the violence of the world wars, and the violence of the Nigeria-Biafra War are arguably interconnected because they function as either a pre-life (prememory)[67] or an afterlife of one another.[68] More importantly, *Yellow Sun* can be read as a site of an African transnational memory and Black internationalism because it constantly reminisces on, and gives recognition to, Black suffering and struggles across the world at that point in history. For instance, through Odenigbo and his intellectual friends, the novel invites the readers to remember "the Rhodesian and Algerian wars of independence, the Sharpeville killing in South Africa, the Gambian independence, the unjust killing of Lumumba among others" (305). Having established the nexus between postmemory and postcolonialism in *Yellow Sun*, the next section of this chapter explores how the novel (as a postmemory work) relies on, and draws from, the literary works on Biafra that came before it.

REMEDIATION OF MEMORY

Memories are always mediated. What is remembered about a war or any other event in the past is not the "actual event" but a representational form or a mediated re/construction of that event. As many scholars have argued, Adichie's postmemory or derivative recollection of Biafra is a product of accumulated exposure to oral stories, photographs, and books, among other sources.[69] These memories that are contained in *Yellow Sun* have also been remediated into other media forms, such as film,[70] music videos,[71] and even new social media platforms such as Facebook[72] and YouTube.[73] Therefore, *Yellow Sun* itself is arguably becoming a *lieux de memoire* of the Biafran war because of the way it remediates earlier stories as well as how it is being remediated into other media forms. Adichie gives insights on how she remediated the memory of Biafra into a novel form when she mentions:

> The inspiration for *Yellow Sun* came from a faded beautiful photograph of my grandfather David Adichie, it came from seeing tears in my mother's eyes as she told the story of her father's death in a refugee camp. It came from the novels of Flora Nwapa and Chukwuemeka Ike.[74]

From this statement we see exactly how Adichie taps into the oral, visual, and literary archive in order to create her own story. She stresses, in particular, the importance of oral accounts in the creation of *Yellow Sun* when she says:

> In the four years that it took to finish the book, I would often ask older people I met, "Where were you in 1967?" and take it from there. It was from stories of that sort that I found out tiny details that are important for fiction. My parents' stories formed the backbone of my research. ("Stories of Africa")

Thus, *Yellow Sun*, as a postmemory work, is not a single-handed achievement but a narrative built on other narratives of Biafra—that is, the "story" in *Yellow Sun* is a literary afterlife of the preceding stories of Biafra. The novel is a spectral narrative not only because it imaginatively resurrects the dead but precisely because it bears traces of earlier writings on the war. Interestingly, some of the authors of these earlier writings on Biafra are already dead (Chinua Achebe, Christopher Okigbo, Buchi Emecheta, and Flora Nwapa are examples of these Biafran ancestors). *Yellow Sun*, therefore, is Adichie's way of paying tribute to preceding artists—dead or alive—who, despite the state repression, have managed to keep the memory of Biafra alive in their works. One could even conclude with Chris Ouma that Biafra's story and its cultural memory constitute a "network of collective ownership."[75] *Yellow Sun* is a part of the narratives that cement "Biafra as a heritage";[76] it is an addition to the literary archaeology of loss and trauma from the Nigeria-Biafra War.

One way to explain Adichie's recourse to earlier writings on Biafra is through the lens of intertextuality. That is, *Yellow Sun* derives a memory of its own through an intertextual relation with other texts on Biafra. This intertextual relation borders on the existing literary tradition in which "every creative artist is inescapably influenced by precursors."[77] With this understanding, the allegations of plagiarism leveled against Adichie based on the fact that she did not live through the war—and therefore could not have been able to masterfully write about the interior lives of those who did—become groundless.[78] Adichie herself reveals, in many of her interviews, how Chinua Achebe gave her "the permission to write."[79] She writes about how she felt immensely validated by Achebe's reaction to reading *Yellow Sun*.[80] Moreover, the epigraph of *Yellow Sun* is taken from "Mango Seedling," a poem in Achebe's collection of poetry titled *Biafra and Other Poems*. There are also many scenes and events in the novel that we have come across in earlier narratives of Biafra. For example, the Affia attack in which characters such as Mrs. Mekeoku and Kainene were involved has been depicted in earlier Biafra narratives, most notably by Flora Nwapa and Buchi Emecheta. The depictions of Biafran refugee camp experiences in the novel are reminiscent of the refugee camp experiences in Chinua Achebe's *Girls at War*. The suspicion about acts of sabotage by the minority tribes within Biafra, which is an important trope in the novel, has also been earlier depicted in Nwapa's *Never Again* and Emecheta's *Destination Biafra*.

In a sense, the intertextual references in *Yellow Sun* suggest Adichie's mapping of her literary genealogy. At the end of the novel, Adichie provides a bibliography of thirty-one books (memoirs, novels, short stories, nonfiction, biographies, autobiographies, and poems) on the war written by firsthand and secondary witnesses whom she consulted while writing her own novel. She even goes on to highlight the specific ways in which some of the books helped her to structure her own story:

> In particular, Chukwuemeka Ike's *Sunset at Dawn* and Flora Nwapa's *Never Again* were indispensable in creating the mood of middle-class Biafra; Christopher Okigbo's own life and *Labyrinths* inspired the character of Okeoma; while Alexander Madiebo's *The Nigerian Revolution and the Biafran War* was central to the character of Colonel Madu. (*Yellow Sun*, author's note)

The bibliography provided at the end of *Yellow Sun* establishes it as a work of postmemory because it symbolizes the fact that Adichie picks from the memories of the artists who came before her and also corroborates the idea that we often remember through other people's memories. Also as a postmemorial tactic, Adichie goes beyond the written medium and provides photographs at the end of the novel, rendering it not only an intertextual but also an intermedial work of memory. As has already been established, Adichie draws inspiration from family photographs to tell her story, but, more importantly, at the end of the novel, she provides photos of emaciated Biafran children who suffered from Kwashiorkor—commonly referred to as "Harold Wilson Syndrome" (*Yellow Sun*, 338)[81]—during the war in order to make a point about the historical role that photographs played in the international perceptions of the war. With the photos, we are reminded of how today's Western vision of war in Africa was cemented by the photos of malnourished Biafran children (Biafra being the first post-independence African war). In the same vein, Adichie (and, perhaps, her editor and publisher) strategically positioned the photos at the back of the novel[82] as a reminder to the readers that they have not simply read a work of fiction. The photographs draw the viewers into the sacred horror of looking at the dead and being looked at by the dead. The spectrum (the object that is photographed) therefore represents "the life that was no longer to be and that, against all odds nevertheless continues to be."[83] It undoes the finality of a camera snap and narrates, visually, the story of the dead in the present tense. The photos bring the dead back to life in the form of a "ghostly revenant" or "living dead."[84] Of course, without the photos, readers can visualize the events that the novel depicts, but the postmemorial impulse behind the writing of the novel necessitated the need for a piece of material and documentary evidence of the sufferings of the victims of the war. It is almost as if there is an underlying move to solidify the reader's experience and, in turn, implicate them in this hauntological frame of memory. Therefore, as part of the (anti)aesthetics of postmemory, the photos serve as a visual testimony to the horrors of the Nigeria-Biafra War. Ultimately, *Yellow Sun* as a postmemory work moves slightly beyond the conventional purview of fiction to provide a fusion of visual and written stories.

POSTMEMORY AND THE POSSIBILITY OF JUSTICE FOR BIAFRA

Earlier in this chapter, I showed how Adichie feels the historical imperative to bear witness to the past and give voice to the muted victims and survivors of Biafra. But it is also worthwhile to explore how this postgenerational witnessing stimulates conversations about justice and repair. In many cases of historical violence, it takes a temporal, spatial, generational, and reflective distance before the question of justice surfaces. In the case of Biafra, *Yellow Sun*, as Eleni Coundouriotis argues, becomes "an imaginative historical project that engages with the people's suffering in war, hoping that its vision will yield a more just society."[85] The novel is a much-needed intervention in contemporary Nigeria precisely because the "ultimate witness"[86] of the war is dead and is thus unable to seek justice. Therefore, Adichie's postmemorial endeavor becomes resonant with Walter Benjamin's position that the living possess a "messianic power" to remedy the injustices of the past.[87] Adichie maintains an anamnestic solidarity with her ancestors and hopes that their pains will be recognized, especially since there has been no public acknowledgment of the injustice done to Biafra by the Nigerian government. She expresses a strong feeling of historical injustice when she writes:

> I feel very strongly that there was so much more that could have been done about Biafra that wasn't done. I feel the number of deaths would have been drastically reduced if the United Kingdom was not arming Nigeria. If the US had done more. If Russia had not become involved with the aim of spreading its influence in Africa.[88]

One can almost feel the tone of righteous indignation in the above statement, but beneath that indignation is a postgenerational cry for justice and accountability. This cry comes with a burden of responsibility—the kind of burden that Adichie shoulders as a chronicler of the past. The invitation to bear the burden of responsibility for the past is then extended to us,[89] the readers and members of the postwar generation. Memory, after all, is—and should be—a "rectitude of responsibility" for all.[90] By and large, *Yellow Sun*, for Adichie, is "something larger than art";[91] it is her attempt at atoning for history.

Furthermore, Martijn van Gils rightly points out that *Yellow Sun* gestures to the need for reconciliation through various allegorical representations. He also notes that the novel stresses the role of dialogue in ensuring a reconciliatory future that Adichie firmly believes in. The failure of dialogue between Nigeria and Biafra, which is one of the main causes of the war, is allegorically depicted in the strained relationship between Olanna and her twin sister, Kainene.[92] This argument for dialogue is not an attempt to oversimplify the complex tensions and frictions surrounding the memory of Biafra in contemporary Nigeria. Rather, dialogue becomes a first step in acknowledging the fact that Nigeria is, in a sense, still at war.[93] It is also a first step in acknowledging that the condition for justice in the Nigeria-Biafra context remains largely equivocal. Is justice in Biafra's ability to eventually secede from Nigeria, or would it require material reparations for survivors and their offspring? Should justice require a public apology from the Nigerian government, or would it involve the prosecution of the key players in the war (some of whom are no longer alive)? Is it a Truth and Reconciliation Commission that is needed? Or maybe more attention should be given to changing political structures rather than seeking prosecutorial justice? After all, Mahmood Mamdani argues that the postcolonial crisis is first and foremost a political crisis, not a criminal one. Therefore, political reform, not criminal prosecution, is what might enable a breakage from the cycle of violence in post-conflict/postcolonial nation-building.[94] While these are seemingly knotty questions, what is certain is that Nigeria and Biafra can benefit from instituting a dialogue.

Toward the end of the novel, we find in the attitudes of Olanna and Odenigbo two potential ways in which survivors bequeath memories to the succeeding generation. By religiously keeping the Biafran flag, Odenigbo demonstrates how linking objects[95] to the past are preserved for the coming generation, while, on the other hand, Olanna burns every forensic evidence of the war. Odenigbo, who strongly disapproves of Olanna's attitude, accuses her of "burning memory," but she responds that she does not want to "place her memory on things strangers could barge in and take away" (*Yellow Sun*, 433). She says, "My memory is inside me" (433), which means that her memory is sensorially inscribed within her and that, even when everything else fails, her body keeps the score of history. Many survivors, just like Olanna, dissociate themselves from any linking object to the past by burning material evidence of memory but (un)consciously embody its spectrality, which then becomes a prologue to, and a portal for, the next generation's rememory.

Adichie, in her author's note, emphasizes the importance of keeping memory alive as she ends with the supplication "may we always remember" (*Yellow Sun*, 437). However, there is a need for caution with regard to this blanket ethico-political quest for memory as well as the assumption that the impetus of postmemory's transgenerational quality lies in its warning against repeating the violence and errors of the past. While Adichie's novel has inspired conversations and interrogations, especially among the postwar generation, it has also sparked some controversies. There appears to be a surge in Igbo nationalism since the period after the publication of the novel. The film adaptation of the novel was initially banned by the Nigerian Film and Censorship Board because of the concern that it would incite ethnic violence. We have seen Biafra secessionist movements spring up in the years following the release of *Yellow Sun* (ethnic tensions became remarkably fiercer after the publication of Chinua Achebe's *There Was a Country* in 2012). The Indigenous People of Biafra Movement (IPOB) kicked off in 2012, the same year that the Biafra Zionist Movement (BZM) was born. The Movement of the Actualization of the Sovereign State of Biafra (MASSOB) launched the Biafran passport in 2009 and has been encouraging the hoisting of the Biafran flag in recent years. Attacks and counterattacks between the Nigerian army and Biafran secessionist groups continue even today. Of course, Adichie does not necessarily have personal ties with these groups and may not even buy into their politics, but *Yellow Sun*, among other recent stories on Biafra, has directly or indirectly sustained and aggravated conversations—and agitations—about the secession of Biafra despite the ongoing state repression. These are difficult issues with no easy solutions but, nonetheless, play a pivotal role in determining the future of Nigeria and in shaping the question of justice for the victims of the war and their offspring.

CONCATENATED MEMORIES, ANCESTRAL MEMORIES

As much as the concept of postmemory provides a productive lens for engaging with Adichie's novel, my engagement raises two provocations that I want to briefly end with. As revealed in the novel (especially in the metatext), the memory of Biafra is not unconnected with the memory of colonialism, and as I have shown, Adichie's postmemorial endeavor certainly has a postcolonial side to it. Still, the concept of postmemory does not seem entirely adequate in articulating the concatenated and cumulative memories of slavery, colonialism, and the relatively recent civil wars in the postcolony. This, in all fairness, was not Marianne Hirsch's intention when she first coined the term. She developed the concept in order to process her personal experiences as a child of Holocaust survivors. Hence, as the concept continues to gain currency among memory scholars, caution must be taken over its universal applicability and contextual specificity.

The second provocation comes from my engagement with Adichie's interviews. In these interviews, I noticed her frequent use of the word "ancestors," and that got me thinking about ancestral memories. In one particular interview, she notes that "writing the book felt like being held by something.... It really did feel as though my ancestors wanted me to do this."[96] Therefore, in provincializing postmemory and in refashioning it for postcolonial contexts, maybe we could think critically about the idea of ancestral memories. Drawing on Laura Murphy's quote in this chapter's epigraph, "People may indeed experience the persistent residues of the distant past and unsuspectingly harbor memories of the most significant experiences of their ancestors."[97] Ancestral memory, I imagine, transcends the psychoanalytic framings of archaic inheritances. It includes but also transcends the domains of genetic memory; it is in the bequeathing of feelings, phantom sensations, and tacit knowledge to a succeeding generation. It is in the mystical and covert incorporeal bestowals that precede an individual's birth. It invokes a transcendental—if not esoteric—language of ancestors and is in the return of ancestral voices crying out in the wilderness of justice. It is in the weight of our ancestors' traumas that we bear and in the amorphous yet definitive "memory contracts" that bind us to our progenitors. It is in the things we know but never learned and in the things we learned that opened us to the vast morphology of the unknown. It is our ancestors' losses visited upon us and their experiences relived in the central nervous systems of our memories. It is the push-and-pull factor of cultural epigenetics. It is also the return of strangely familiar ghosts of deep history as well as the in-body and out-of-body reappearance of long-repressed and latent progenitorial experiences. Our ancestral memories are in the things that know us; they are our embodiment of our ancestors' footprints. They are the memories (broadly defined) that are transferred, sometimes unfathomably, from distant and dead progenitors to the living.

In this chapter, I showed how text and theory productively illuminate each other by analyzing *Half of a Yellow Sun* as a work of postmemory. I described how Adichie uses the novel to process her inheritance of loss and to revive suppressed memories of Biafra in Nigeria. I analyzed the role that the novel has played, either directly or indirectly, in the frictions of memory (of Biafra) in Nigeria today. I argued that it was precisely in the writing of the novel that Adichie was able to vicariously witness the past and that this vicarious witnessing was made possible through various forms of imaginative investments. I also argued that the use of metatext in the novel serves to blur the line between fact and fiction by engaging with history while not losing sight of the fictional world of the novel. I explained that the photographs provided at the end of the novel point to the importance of intermediality and intertextuality in postmemory works. I showed how the bibliography provided at the end of the novel confirms it as a postmemory fiction that bears traces of earlier writings on Biafra. Ultimately, because of her generational distance from—and familial obsession with—Biafra, Adichie is able to weave a complex narrative of loss that does not advocate closure but gestures toward the possibility of repair.

CHAPTER 2

The Past Continues in Silence

Memory, Complicity, and the Post-Conflict Timescapes in *The Memory of Love*

For you, healing looks like talking and transparency / For them, it is silence and burying / And both are probably valid.
—Koleka Putuma, *Collective Amnesia*

Confronted with a taboo, people can fall silent out of terror or panic or because they can find no appropriate words. We cannot, of course, infer the fact of forgetting from the fact of silence. Nevertheless, some acts of silence may be an attempt to bury things beyond expression and the reach of memory; yet such silencings, while they are a type of repression, can at the same time be a form of survival, and the desire to forget may be an essential ingredient in the process of survival.
—Paul Connerton, "Seven Types of Forgetting"

Surviving is the other name of mourning.
—Jacques Derrida, *The Politics of Friendship*

READING SILENCE

The civil war in Sierra Leone lasted for eleven years (1991–2002). By the end of the war, over fifty thousand people had died with about two million displaced and thousands of bodies dismembered.[1] Following independence in 1961, the country was dragged into about twenty-five years of authoritarianism that culminated in the war. Aminatta Forna is committed to putting this war on the literary map[2] and, in turn, attracting much-needed conversations about its aftermaths. On her motivation for writing *The Memory of Love*, she said, "My country had a civil war. It would be extraordinary not to write about that."[3] Forna's family was enormously affected by both the dictatorship and the eventual civil war that caused the implosion of the country. Her father died as a political prisoner in 1975 when she was just eleven years old. The death of her father was a watershed moment in her life, and it compelled her, later in life, to delve into her family histories as a way of understanding the genesis of her country's collapse. This partly explains why most of her creative works are centered on the themes of war, family, memory, trauma, and human rights. Unlike Adichie, Forna, arguably, does not fit into the category that has come to be known as the generation of postmemory because she was a *child witness* of the brutal authoritarian regime (not the war) in Sierra Leone. Susan Suleiman refers to child witnesses like Forna as the "1.5 generation."[4] They are different from the second generation because they were alive during the atrocity even though they were too young to have an adult understanding of what happened. In other words, Forna experienced the traumatic years of dictatorship in Sierra Leone but was too young to fully grasp its intricacies. It was only when she became much older that she began to research the political climate of 1970s Sierra Leone.

In 2003 Forna published a memoir, *The Devil That Danced on Water*, which details her attempt to sift through the past in order to unearth the secrets and silences around her father's death. In 2006 she wrote *Ancestor Stone*, a novel told in the voices of four women whose lives accentuate the interconnectedness of lineal and national histories. *The Memory of Love* (2010) is a fictional exploration of memory in post-conflict Sierra Leone; it chronicles the prelude and the aftermath of the civil war in the country. It presents characters anguished by the spell of the past and a post-conflict society engulfed in silence as victims and perpetrators continue to live side by side. It narrates the imbrication of the past in the present and, at the same time, demonstrates how the Sierra Leonean Civil War is nothing but a continuation of the violent years of dictatorship that preceded it. The story is told through the eyes of three major characters: Adrian Lockheart, Kai Mansaray, and Elias Cole. Adrian, a British psychologist, has come to Sierra Leone to treat war survivors, 99 percent of whom are allegedly suffering from posttraumatic stress disorder. He experiences a strange configuration of time and is taken aback by the overwhelming presence of silence among the people. It is only when he stops expecting the country to explain itself to him that he makes faintly modest headway as a psychotherapist in the war-torn country. Elias Cole, on his deathbed, struggles with his conscience over his complicity in the violence unleashed on those who opposed the authoritarian regime in prewar Sierra Leone. He chooses to tell his version of the past to Adrian, the "outsider" and the only therapist in the hospital. Kai Mansaray, on the other hand, is a Sierra Leonean surgeon who spends all of his time treating victims of amputation during the war; it is the only way he can deal with the nightmares and incessant flashbacks of his own traumatic experience of being brutally beaten by rebel soldiers. Kai and Adrian coincidentally—and all too neatly—find themselves in a love triangle with Elias Cole's daughter, Mamakay, who is also weighed down by the yoke of her past. It is with this backstory that Forna explores several issues affecting post-conflict Sierra Leone.

The novel has attracted much scholarly attention, and numerous essays have been written on the profound insights it offers on the subjects of empathy[5] and post-conflict nationalism.[6] Dave Gunning[7] and Stef Craps[8] have also written about the novel's generative exploration of postcolonial trauma. Craps particularly shows how the novel provides a balanced view of trauma treatment and recovery in a non-Western culture. He notes that although the novel does not entirely disavow Western trauma treatment methods, it is skeptical of an exclusive focus on these methods in a non-Western context such as Sierra Leone. On many occasions, Adrian, the British psychologist, feels like a failure because his patients (postwar Sierra Leoneans) do not initially respond to his Western-style treatments. He later owns up to his own Eurocentric biases and begins to notice—and acknowledge—how the people resort to "local healers and religious leaders" (*The Memory of Love*, 87) in a bid to find healing to their trauma. He also becomes aware of the people's embrace of fatalism as a coping mechanism and a survival tactic. Perhaps Zoe Norridge is currently the only scholar who has written on almost all the literary works of Aminatta Forna. In her book *Perceiving Pain in African Literature*, she explores the bodily inscription of pain and trauma in *The Memory of Love*; she shows how the novel contributes immensely to understanding pain as a psychosomatic phenomenon. Elsewhere, Norridge explores Forna's use of sex as a synecdoche of violence in the same novel.[9] While these scholarly interventions have helped anatomize Forna's complex novel and have illuminated our perceptions of post-conflict Sierra Leone, I am rather interested in the novel's portraiture of the different kinds of silence ingrained within the Sierra Leonean post-conflict landscape.

The novel begins with the depiction of a nation-space going through some sort of national melancholia. Elias Cole, the character encountered on the first page, talks about a "premonition of loss" which many characters struggle to articulate and, as a consequence, turns them into melancholic subjects in the Kristevan sense.[10] The narrator describes these melancholic subjects in the following:

> All over town, you see them. Slumped on the balconies of their homes, amid the traffic fumes, staring into space, gradually being covered in a layer of dust from the street. The living dead. (*The Memory of Love*, 4; hereafter, *TML*)

These melancholic subjects are not only beset by their present pains; they are also haunted by the memories of the torture they were subjected to during the war. They visit the doctor with complaints about pains that began only after the "trouble." They talk about their war experiences in hushed tones and "huddled whispers."[11] They choose less menacing words like "trouble" and "a few things" when referring to the war. Adrian notices this silence concealed in metaphors and euphemisms and insists that the people recount their experiences in plain logocentrism, but they continue to talk "in dampened voices about what they had endured, as though the events described belonged to somebody else" (*TML*, 21). To Adrian's chagrin, the people's lives unfold "like a reel of silent film" (254). Their sparse speeches are punctuated with long silences that are "more eloquent than anything their barbed tongue could produce" (294). Adrian finds conversations in postwar Sierra Leone very challenging because "the notion that a conversation is a continuous act is bred into his bones and silences like nudity should be covered up lest they offend" (48). As previously mentioned, the novel explores, on both individual and collective levels, the different kinds of silence that obtain in post-conflict Sierra Leone. It presents the manipulative, deadly, spectral, complicit, companionable, and deafening silence observable in the country in the wake of the war. The novel equally maps out silences that are nuanced, ambivalent, sometimes indeterminate, and, overall, just as complex as spoken language. What is not said is as important as what is said, and, just as every word has consequences, every silence in the novel has consequences too. In a nutshell, one could say that *The Memory of Love* is filled with, and haunted by, silences.

Silence in the novel possesses a polysemous quality too. It is manifested in the semiotic inability to speak, realized in the absences of conventional verbal exchanges, but also concealed beneath a calculated loquacity. It takes on the status of a character because of its heavy performative presence. The postwar subjects in the novel nestle in silences that are sometimes driven by the urge to protect, exhale, or survive. Their silences sometimes develop as a result of fear and other times as a mark of bravery. They also often resort to silence as a way of either recounting or repressing the past.

This chapter is an attempt at reading the silences in *The Memory of Love*; it is an inquiry into the multiple connotations and denotations of silence in the novel. To put it another way, this chapter contains a dissection of the hidden and open spaces of silence and their implications for memory or forgetting in post-conflict Sierra Leone. Overall, this chapter investigates the ways in which *The Memory of Love* animates reflections on the nexus between political silence and the construction of a postcolonial, post-conflict nation-state. Thus, I begin my analysis by showing how silence is embedded within the unconscious of the novel and how the novel, in consequence, becomes a form of textual silence. I identify the multilayered shades and multiple shapes of silence that the novel brings to bear and how they play out in post-conflict Sierra Leone. More importantly, I look for instances where the novel presents silence as an act of remembering or where silence is employed in the service of forgetting. I also zero in on the character of Elias Cole as a launchpad for discussing the role and consequence of silent complicity in the war. I end the chapter with reflections on the idea of "silent time" as a *chrono-trope* in the novel and how this particular configuration of time might not only be a postwar Sierra Leonean reality but also a reality of many post-conflict (African) countries.[12]

A SENSE OF SOMETHING UNSPOKEN:
THE MEMORY OF LOVE AS TEXTUAL SILENCE

Just as the characters in *The Memory of Love* often communicate in silence, the novel itself is a tapestry of silence at both thematic and narratological levels. It showcases silence as an essential part of the strategies that underlie and permeate discourses. Hence, though silent—not in the sense of a silent film, nor can it be called a silent novel—*The Memory of Love* is not quiet; it speaks in a grammar of silence. It is a form of textual silence precisely because of the interpretability of its many silences that are steeped in what the Prague school linguists describe as "communicative dynamism."[13] The silences in the novel bear an illocutionary function, and it is only when one immerses oneself into this intricate syntax of silence that post-conflict Sierra Leone starts to become legible.

Silence has always been a crucial part of narrative making, and narratives, by their very nature, require the use of silence for the plotting of a cohesive story.[14] *The Memory of Love* embodies this complex interplay of silence and narration in the way it tells of the prelude and aftermath of the war in great detail but remains strategically silent about the war itself. That is to say, the war maintains a spectral presence—and is told in ellipses— throughout the novel. However, despite this narrative silence, the novel is still able to implicitly convey the horrors of the war to its readers in such a way that they can appreciably grasp its emotional weights and affective truths. The melancholic mood, pensive language, and the silent, often imperceptible, switch of narrative voice from the first to the third person all contribute to the simmering textures of silence in the novel. Further, silence is not only inscribed into the entrails of the story; it is also visible at the typographical level. For example, apart from the silence clothed in verbosity and excessive attention to detail, the thirty-eighth chapter of the novel consists of only five sentences, which are immediately followed by a large, blank space. This advertent structural arrangement in the novel further illustrates the inexhaustibility and equivocality of the silences that the novel brings to bear.

In addition, we come across several instances where silence functions as an illocutionary act in the novel. An example of this illocutionary silence is in a conversation between Kai and Adrian in the second chapter. In this conversation, Kai is silent about the death of the baby he had just helped to deliver when Adrian asked him about it. The conversation goes thus:

> "What happened?" . . .
> "The baby was stuck. The woman was in labour for two days."
> "And now?"
> He shrugs. "Well, now it's out." (*TML*, 26)

In this excerpt, even though Kai replies to Adrian, he is covertly silent about the death of the baby, but Adrian is able to decipher the illocutionary force beneath his reply. Beyond the proliferative speech-act silences in the novel, there is also a pervading discreet silence noticeable among the war survivors. For several reasons, which I will get to in a bit, the war takes on the status of a taboo topic among the survivors to such an extent that they completely refrain from talking about it. In view of this, Mamakay tells Adrian:

"Have you never noticed? How nobody ever talks about anything? What happened here. The war. Before the war. It's like a secret." (321)

Silence, therefore, is presented as an integral part of everyday life in postwar Sierra Leone in the novel. It is also a way of mourning, of surviving the almost unbearable aftermaths of war. For example, a character named Agnes resorts to silence as a way of mourning her husband and children who died during the war. However, as subsequently revealed in the novel, this is in fact how many of the women cope with their losses. The narrator recalls that "for days Agnes neither spoke, nor moved, nor ate, Isatta was not disturbed by Agnes, for many were the women who mourned in such a way" (231). These women's silent mourning, on the one hand, is emblematic of a nation that mourns in silence and, on the other, indicative of how women are left to bear the weight of mourning in many post-conflict African nations. Also in the novel, we find instances where silence serves as a code among the war survivors as well as where they (the survivors) become bound together in the fellowship of silence (225). In general, Aminatta Forna uses *The Memory of Love* to look at the dynamics of loss and mourning in post-conflict Sierra Leone through the intimate and public zones of silence. Drawing from her interviews, Forna seems to subscribe to three kinds of silence in postwar Sierra Leone: the silence of trauma, the silence of oppression, and the silence of culture. These silences are not mutually exclusive but interconnected at both individual and collective levels. While they may not necessarily provide the most accurate picture of postwar Sierra Leone, they serve as a useful anchor point for reflective engagements with the country and for a better appreciation of Forna's novel. In the next section, I take a cursory look at these three kinds of silence.

SILENCE OF TRAUMA

Following the civil war, many Sierra Leoneans embraced silence as a way of keeping their traumas at bay.[15] From the characters in *The Memory of Love*, we learn that traumatic silence is a form—not a loss—of language. Trauma victims in most places often articulate their pain and grief through the register of silence.[16] For example, Pumla Gobodo-Madikizela observes how some trauma victims, during the Truth and Reconciliation Commission (TRC) hearings in South Africa, "chose" silence, body language, and other nonverbal cues to communicate their experiences because they found verbal communication inadequate.[17] Therefore, silence, albeit traumatic, can be said to be an "inexpressible expressiveness" that has an effect on political meaning and is capable of challenging social discourse.[18] More so, this kind of traumatic silence challenges the Western psychoanalytic framing of the psychic experience of trauma as non-communicable because, in the non-Western context in *The Memory of Love*, silence is not a lack of communication but instead a different kind of expressiveness.

In the novel, Kai and Mamakay are two focal characters who embrace silence as a result of trauma. Kai "occupies the present" and reveals "little about his traumatic past" (*TML*, 105). He sublimates his trauma into working rigorously at the hospital while Mamakay invests her energy into her music career, says nothing about what happened to her during the war, and avoids her father, the source of her trauma. These two characters may seem very active on the surface, but their activity is an act of repression and a kind of deflective silence. Put differently, Kai's sublimation and Mamakay's avoidance are silence mechanisms—and acts of silencing memory's ghosts.

Furthermore, *The Memory of Love* constructs silence in postwar Sierra Leone as a consequence of what Cathy Caruth describes as a "crying wound" that is too deep for a simple resolution.[19] It suggests some sort of "silence cure" as complementary but not necessarily oppositional to the Freudian "talking cure." It demonstrates the fact that the talking cure is a Western construct rooted in the "Western belief that every problem must have a solution" (*TML*, 176). The survivors in the novel resort to silence so as to protect themselves from the fear of being listened to—and of listening to themselves.[20] Therefore, importing Western forms of therapy into the Sierra Leonean situation proved initially unsuccessful because, as opposed to talking, the people found a safe haven in silence. It also proved unsuccessful because the idea of the talking cure was produced in a distinct cultural context with infrastructures that support its viability, unlike in Sierra Leone, where such infrastructures may not exist. In view of this, Ileana, another European psychiatrist in the novel, says to Adrian, "After all, it was us Europeans who invented the talking cure. And most of the maladies it's designed to treat" (169). In essence, the survivors in *The Memory of Love* are committed to silence as a way of processing their grief because they know full well that talking, in their situation, is unavailing. This argument provokes many questions about traumatic silence which I shall return to later in this chapter. How long can one remain silent as a result of trauma? Does traumatic silence fuel forgetting? And what exactly is the price of silence in a post-conflict context like Sierra Leone?

SILENCE OF OPPRESSION

Reading *The Memory of Love*, one gets a sense that when people are confronted with a long history of violence and violence of history, talking is not always the first resort. In the novel, we encounter characters who embrace silence for many reasons that do not include the inability to remember. One of the reasons the survivors choose silence is associated with the fear of the resurgence of violence. They are afraid that their violent past could, in the Nietzschean sense, become a gravedigger of the present. And as Caruth reminds us, violence is not only the encounter with death but also the ongoing experience of surviving it.[21] The embrace of silence among the survivors in the novel is, therefore, constitutive of the crucial victuals needed on the journey of survival in the Sierra Leonean post-conflict climate. Put differently, *The Memory of Love* as a non-redemptive narrative[22] constructs silence as a space where "the poetics of trauma shifts to a poetics of survival."[23]

In the novel, postwar Sierra Leone is presented as a place of "terrifying dreams" (*TML*, 4) where people are more fearful than they were before the war because they now have to live side by side with their assailants. As a matter of fact, the Special Court instituted after the war indicted only thirteen men and granted blanket amnesty to the majority of the offenders. The underlying effect of this on the survivors is the reignition of the feeling and memory of oppression that prevailed during the war. Therefore, silence may appear to be a risk in a situation such as this, but talking bears even more risk. For example, in the novel, Agnes is forced to live under the same roof with her husband's murderer who is now her son-in-law. She is silent because she is afraid of what might happen to her and her daughter if she speaks up. It is in light of this that Berber Bevernage argues that after the war a large part of Sierra Leoneans chose to keep quiet rather than testify before the Sierra Leonean Truth and Reconciliation Commission (SLTRC) because of the fear of awakening the past.[24] Hence, silence in the novel is also a strategy for containment in a melancholic nation-space; it is a price or a condition for peace.[25] But the question is, How does one measure peace at both individual and collective levels? In view of this, Mamakay partly addresses the fragility of peace in Sierra Leone when she says, "People think war is the worst this country has ever seen: they have no idea what peace is like" (*TML*, 282). Therefore, while the survivors' silence is a traumatic one, it is at the same time induced by the fear that speaking up may awaken suppressed memories and continue the cycle of violence.

A CULTURE OF SILENCE[26]

Adrian discovers that, unlike Britain, where he hails from, silence in postwar Sierra Leone has a "different quality, [and is] entirely devoid of expectation" (*TML*, 29). He realizes that silence—apart from being a result of trauma or fear—is an intricate part of the people's sensibility. He therefore "came to understand it [silence] as also part of a way of being that existed [t]here" (321). To put it another way, the silence in postwar Sierra Leone is not only a product of oppression or trauma but also something that people are culturally comfortable in. *The Memory of Love* invites us to imagine silence as being an ontological component of the Sierra Leonean populace. This culture of silence might even be said to trace back to more distant pasts, the period before colonialism and transatlantic slavery in Sierra Leone. This deep time of extreme violence—or what Paul Basu, in his study on Sierra Leone, describes as a "palimpsest of violence"[27]—may have contributed to the formation of this culture of silence.[28] In view of this, the novel's narrator asks rhetorically: "If we are to rewind the past, how far back would we go?" (374). That is, if history—as Caruth argues—is inherently traumatic,[29] the endemic and existential silence deducible in the novel is not simply an immediate response to the eleven years of civil war but a result of a trauma deeply rooted in history. Therefore, the silences in the characters' conversations serve as bearers of—distant and recent—history as well as a repository of memory. If humans truly exist in a penumbra of their ancestors' time and space,[30] the moments of silence in the novel become, subliminally, moments of connection with ancestors far removed in time and space. In other words, the space of silence in *The Memory of Love* serves as the confluence where the past and the present collide; it is a space for the incarnation of ancestral memories.

The question, again, is: What are the mnemonic implications of these silences in *The Memory of Love*? Do they induce forgetting, enhance remembering, or exist in between? Where does the postwar Sierra Leonean silence fit on the forgetting curve? In light of these questions, Paul Connerton details how silence as a result of humiliation or oppression leads to forgetting with the passage of time.[31] On the other hand, Rosalind Shaw argues that the silence of Sierra Leoneans after the war and their resistance to reparative remembering in the form of the SLTRC involves some sort of "social forgetting."[32] This kind of forgetting does not equal total erasure or even amnesia; it is rather a conscious, selective, and collective suppression of memory. It is close to a state of oblivion,[33] or what Paul Ricoeur calls *oubli de reserve*.[34]

Hence, with time, there is a possibility of resuscitating or reactivating memories archived in silence. After all, it took several years of silence before people started engaging with their violent pasts in countries like Spain, Chile, Indonesia, Argentina, and Germany. Spain's history is particularly interesting because of the "pact of silence" (*el pacto del olvido*) that served as the foundation for the country's transition from dictatorship to democracy. This "pact of silence" (or "pact of forgetting") was an unwritten agreement among major political parties that wanted the country to "move on" from its brutal past. Implied within the pact is the silencing of the horrific episodes of the Spanish Civil War (1936–39), which was immediately succeeded by four decades of Francisco Franco's violent dictatorial rule. However, with the Law of Historical Memory passed in 2007, there is now an allowance for the un-silencing of modern Spain's repressed and painful pasts. The point, therefore, is that silence enters history at different times. Between memory and silence is the contingency of time; there is time for everything, a time to speak and a time to be silent.[35] After all, Luisa Passerlini reminds us that something may be unsaid because its memory has been repressed (by trauma) or because the conditions for its expression no longer (or do not yet) exist.[36]

Despite these arguments in favor of silence and remembering, it is important to reiterate that silence, over time, is equally capable of contributing to the effacement of memory. Thus, given the silence over recent atrocities in Sierra Leone,[37] can we really conclude that silence has become a cultural life of the nation or that there comes a time when memories will boom? Or is the silence a consequence of a plummeted postwar economy that impelled survivors to put their traumas aside and scramble for a sustainable livelihood? When does silence become morbid? When is it a conspiracy against the self? In *The Memory of Love*, Aminatta Forna presents us with silences that oscillate between memory, forgetting, and the complicity of time. In the following section, I explore more closely the idea of silence as a mnemonic device in individual and collective contexts in the novel.

SILENT AND SILENCED MEMORIES

In their essay "Unpacking the Unspoken: Silence in Collective Memory and Forgetting," Teeger Chana and Vered Vinitzsky-Seroussi (2010) note that words hide much more than they reveal in certain situations while silences, on the other hand, reveal more than they hide. Similarly, my reading of

The Memory of Love reveals how overt silence facilitates memory while covert silence, clothed in wordiness, enhances forgetting. While Chana and Vinitzsky-Seroussi use the terms "overtness" and "covertness" to illustrate two dimensions of silence, Charles B. Stone and his colleagues use the same terms to illustrate two dimensions of remembering—overt and covert remembering.[38] They contend that when a memory is expressed in a conversation, it is remembered overtly, but when it is not expressed but recollected, it is remembered covertly. Therefore, in my reading of silence as a mnemonic process in *The Memory of Love*, I propose the term "silent memory" to denote a kind of covert remembering (remembering in silence) and the term "silenced memory" to refer to a form of covert silence veiled in utterances but aimed at denying, concealing, and forgetting the past.

Forna's novel is replete with instances where silence functions as covert remembering. One particular instance is when Adrian interrogates Agnes, whom he suspects to be suffering from fugue because of her habit of absconding from home without the ability to trace her way back. In the conversation that ensues between Adrian and Agnes after she is found and taken to the hospital, she tries to remember the first time she left home. She remembers almost all the details. She remembers that her daughter was not at home the day she absconded but remains silent about her son-in-law who was at home on that day. After several interrogations, Adrian asks:

> "What about your son-in-law?"
>
> Silence. Perhaps she has not heard him. Adrian repeats the question. And then, thinking too that maybe the phrase has not translated well, he adds, "Your daughter's husband, I mean."
>
> Agnes looks distracted. She puts her hand up to her throat, feeling with her fingers around the base of her neck. She seems upset about something. (*TML*, 140)

In this excerpt, Agnes divulges all she remembers but is cautiously silent about the details involving her son-in-law. The son-in-law, we later realize, is the rebel soldier who killed Agnes's husband during the war, but her daughter, Naasu, is oblivious of it. This is the reason behind Agnes's habitual abscondence, as she is unable to bear living under the same roof with her husband's murderer turned son-in-law. Her silence in this particular conversation (and in the overall situation) does not equal forgetting or forgetfulness. She does remember that her son-in-law was at home on the day she absconded, but she is too traumatized to express it verbally. The non-verbal cues such as putting her "hands up to her throat" and "feeling her fingers around her neck" signal the fact that she remembers, corporeally, something she has repressed in the recesses of her mind.

Adrian, in the same conversation, notices her disquiet and tries to save the moment by asking her if something is wrong, but she replies immediately:

> "Where is my gold chain? I cannot find my gold chain. Somebody's taken it. Has this matter been reported? Why has nobody returned the chain to me?" (*TML*, 140)

Here, Agnes quickly changes the subject by remembering something else so as to "blank out her mind"[39] on what is currently being discussed. From a cognitive perspective, what obtains here is that Agnes is remembering something else as a way of disremembering the traumatic. Of course, Agnes is not psychotic, as Adrian himself confirms, but her "sudden switches of subject were sometimes a marker of [her] *wanting to avoid something*: [her] subconscious steered them away" (*TML*; emphasis mine). In addition, Agnes's dislocated memory of the gold chain is a reminder of her melancholic condition. She knows she lost something but cannot place the memory of that loss (she actually pawned the chain herself but had forgotten). Her silence is a silence of knowing and not knowing at the same time. The fact that she has forgotten that she pawned the gold chain may be indicative of a psychogenic fugue, but what is certain is that she remembers—in silence—her son-in-law and his (mis)deeds.

Another instance of silent remembering and "switching of subject" is found in a conversation between Adrian and Mamakay. Adrian questions Mamakay on why she left college:

> "Did you ever think about getting a position at the university?"
>
> She replies, "I never finished my studies."
>
> "Because of the war?" . . . She stands up, changing the subject. "Are you hungry? I'm hungry. I need to eat. Let's go out." Suddenly she is no longer relaxed but restless. (*TML*, 299)

Mamakay's "standing up" and "changing of the subject" are silent expressions of memory. She remembers why she quit studying but refuses to recount the memory because it is a source of agony for her. Apparently curious and unsatisfied with Mamakay's response, Adrian raises the issue in another conversation but is again met with silence:

> "But you never finished your degree."
> "No."
> Adrian waits for Mamakay to continue, but she does not. For the second time Adrian has a sense of something unspoken. (322)

The "sense of something unspoken" shows that Mamakay undoubtedly remembers (did she ever forget?) in silence. Her silence is a silence of knowing what it means to be culpably ignorant; it comes from the shame and guilt of discovering one's implication in wrongdoing. Her father's collaboration with the authoritarian government ensured her survival and safety while many of her schoolmates and friends died or were expelled because they dared to stand up against authoritarianism. Worse still, she was used by her own father, without her knowledge, to betray her schoolmates (350).

Both Agnes's and Mamakay's silent memories are not publicly shared but privately held. Their cases demonstrate the process of covert remembering (in silence) on the individual level. They demonstrate very clearly how silence is often a language of memory. However, while Agnes's silent memory is more or less a kind of repression, Mamakay's is a case of suppression because, in traditional psychoanalysis, repression happens in the unconscious while suppression is a conscious act. Agnes's silence is a failure of overt remembering while Mamakay's is a refusal to remember overtly. This implies that there is a difference between the inability and the refusal to remember overtly. Nonetheless, I believe these two women are capable of sharing their privately held memories under an auspicious condition—which leaves us with memory's open secret: there is just a thin line between remembering and forgetting.

Having examined silent memory on an individual level, what might it look like on a collective scale? Perhaps the answer lies in Adrian's observation of the silence that encapsulates postwar Sierra Leone (*TML*, 25, 429). He notes, "It's as though the entire nation is sworn to some terrible secret. So they elect muteness, the only way of *complying* and *resisting* at the same time" (322; emphases mine). A mnemonic rendition of the latter part of this statement would be that the people collectively choose silence as a way of *forgetting* and *remembering* at the same time. Therefore, while Adrian's observation provides a clue on the mnemonic consequence of silence on a collective scale, it also complicates it. It suggests that the collective Sierra Leonean silence is not synonymous with forgetting, nor is their non-silence an act of remembering. Of course, societies do not remember literally, because remembering exists only in the faculty of the individual, which in many cases serves as an index of collective memory. However, I like to argue that the novel portrays a kind of collective silence that is characterized by an un/conscious act of "remembering to forget" and "forgetting to remember"—or what Homi Bhabha in another context refers to as the "fibrillation of remembering-forgetting."[40] The novel also offers a portrait of silence as a kind of acting out that does not know itself as remembering or forgetting yet is somehow both at once.[41]

Furthermore, an instance of silence and remembrance on a collective scale in the novel occurs when, forty days after the death of Julius Kamara, the students observe a forty-minute of silence in the form of a march from the university campus to Julius's house. Elias Cole describes the event as follows:

> There was singing, as I recall, but not much. In the main we walked in silence. Forty minutes. A minute for each day that had passed. (*TML*, 249)

For the marchers, the moments of silence serve as moments of remembering and reflecting on the life of Julius. The silence is performative yet commemorative; it establishes the importance of silence in a collective ritual of mourning. Of course, the "minute of silence" culture is a widespread way of mourning or honoring the memory of the dead, but what is remarkable about the one described above is the way it collapses time; each minute is spent on remembering each day in the life and death of Julius.

To reiterate the position of Stone and his colleagues that I earlier referred to, much talk can enhance forgetting (and denial) just as silence can foster memory. The character of Elias Cole in *The Memory of Love* epitomizes this position. Adrian wonders why "in the land of the mute, only Elias Cole has elected to talk about the past" (*TML*, 327). But he eventually realizes that Cole, who is struggling with his own conscience over his role in the authoritarian regime, is only attempting to sanitize memory and "create a version of truth for himself" (154). We, the readers, are not privy to this until much later in the story because of the way Forna strategically allows Cole's voice to be heard in the first-person point of view, unlike all the other characters, whose stories are told in the third person. Forna presumably employs this technique because she does not want readers to be too quick at judging Cole. Nevertheless, what remains certain is that the novel, through the character of Cole, enables us to see through the eye and memory of the complicit and, more importantly, to see how every act of remembering carries a dimension of selective forgetting. We are also made to witness the inherently malleable nature of memory in the way Elias Cole remembers the past with such impressive details but does not quite remember—almost convincingly so—the details pertaining to his contribution to the perpetuation of evil in 1970s Sierra Leone.

While it is no longer a debate that personal memories are often quite subjective and fallible, Elias Cole forces us to grapple with another important (moral) question: When does subjective memory become manipulative? Cole's prolific memory reeks of suppressive silence as the details of his complicity are omitted. Adrian, Cole's listener, eventually becomes aware of this intentional forgetting, just as it also becomes clear to the readers that Cole "elected to talk about the past" only in order to silence memory. He "concealed uncomfortable truths in order to confess to something lesser" (*TML*, 374). The silences in his memory talks are covert; they are in the very "undetectable lies" (346) he repeatedly tells himself and others who listen to him. By silencing memory, he downplays the truth, obfuscates reality, absolves himself from guilt, and untethers himself from the past. In his calculations, the memories he silenced, by lying or by omission, will not only be forgotten but also erased from history. In other words, by silencing memory, he aims to reconstruct the way history will remember him, which is why he chooses to tell his story to Adrian, a Westerner in the privileged position needed to propagate Cole's version of history. But after becoming aware of Cole's intention, Adrian gives an interesting analysis of his conduct:

> A liar should have a good memory, said Quatilian. The trouble with fantasists is that, in their eagerness to impress, they become careless about details. The purists are of distinctly cooler temperament. Intellectually-minded, they understand the fallibility of memory, prefer to lie by omission. The silent lie that can neither be proved nor disproved. The fantasists and the purists have one thing in common, and this they share with all liars—the pathological, the compulsive, the delusional, the ones who suppress and repress unbearable memories. They all lie to protect themselves, to shield their egos from the raw pain of truth. (346)

While Agnes's and Mamakay's cases are examples of silent memories arising from a traumatic experience, Cole's is an example of a silenced memory arising from the inveterate need to manipulate the truth and "re-member" the past by erasing memories that incriminate while magnifying the ones that exonerate. These instances of silent and silenced memories in the novel force us to think more critically about the gendered dimensions of memory. That is, the stories of Agnes, Mamakay, and Elias reveal how silence (en)genders certain modes of remembering and forgetting. Overall, *The Memory of Love* reveals how remembering and forgetting are not polar opposites but two sides of the same process—and how silence is not a mere consequence of this process but an intrinsic part of it. In the next section of this chapter, I explore another layer of silence that the novel brings to bear: the silence of complicity. I focus on the character of Elias Cole in order to investigate the nexus between silence and complicity and to further reflect on the broader effect of complicity in the prelude and aftermath of the Sierra Leonean Civil War.

SILENCE OF COMPLICITY

The factors that led to the Sierra Leonean Civil War, like most postcolonial wars, are complex, but what mostly stands out is the multiple layers of complicities that fanned the embers of the war. There is the corporate complicity of international companies in the diamond mining business that left the majority of ordinary Sierra Leoneans frustrated and impoverished. This frustration would become the justification for some who joined the rebel forces. There is also the role of Muammar Gaddafi of Libya and Charles Taylor of Liberia as accomplices in the gross violation of human rights that took place during the war—which, by the way, provides interesting details for the discussion of the (African) transnational dimensions of the war. But in the rest of this chapter, I am more interested in Forna's remarkable ability to tease out "the small but far-reaching complicities of communities and the cowardice of inaction experienced by people in positions of privilege."[42] I want to explore how *The Memory of Love* sheds light on silence as the hallmark of complicity and how it provides insights into the moral and political consequences of complicity in post-conflict situations.

The truth of the matter is that it was not in the 1990s that things began to fall apart in Sierra Leone. The country started experiencing a rapid decline with the institution of a one-party state under the leadership of Siaka Stevens (1968–1985). Forna notes that during this period, "there were those who stood up above the rest to condemn the authoritarian regime but, over time, those people were killed or fled, or simply fell silent. . . . And for those who were complicit in their silence it is taking a huge amount—it is a war—to get them to recognize that."[43] Forna's disappointment is mainly with the prewar Sierra Leonean intelligentsia who were supposed to be the voice of reason but kept mute and allowed evil to prevail. Their inaction and dereliction of the duty to speak make them accomplices in wrongdoing because the desire not to be complicit in injustice is usually realized in the ability to speak up against it. In the novel, Elias Cole represents this body of intellectuals who chose silence over justice.

As a university lecturer, Cole makes friends with other university lecturers such as Julius, Yansaneh, and Kekura, and they all form the informal habit of discussing the sociopolitical situation of their country. While Julius, Yansaneh, and Kekura are open about their dissatisfaction with the authoritarian government, Cole is rather indifferent. Julius—the most vocal critic of the government—often uses Cole's office to write some of his revolutionary articles. The government soon begins to clamp down on freedom of speech and arrest the so-called activists across the country. Julius, apparently, is the biggest target here, but Cole also gets arrested because of his association with him. Cole gives his journal, which contains information about Julius and his activism, to Johnson (the police officer and government informant who is instrumental in the arrests of all those who opposed the government). While Cole and Julius are both in Johnson's detention, Cole—from his cell—hears Julius's struggle to breathe and witnesses his eventual death but chooses to keep the information to himself even after he is released from detention. He is afterward promoted to the rank of dean at the university while Yansaneh is sacked and Kekura flees the country. Cole eventually becomes Johnson's "friend" and informant.

As I earlier mentioned, *The Memory of Love* is written to make us see through the eye of the complicit, which is why Cole's account occupies a substantial part of the story. His first-person narrative voice gives us direct access to his complicitous memory. Cole uses his power as a narrator to justify his actions and rationalize his decisions; he makes statements such as "I made my peace with power. I had no other choice" (*TML*, 405), and "I was scarcely in a position to do otherwise" (213). He also tries to absolve himself of guilt by saying, "I did nothing wrong except to give Johnson what he asked for, which was a small amount of information" (376). He confesses that speaking up against tyranny would have cost him his career and marked him as a "troublemaker" (213). Hence, his complicity lies in his supine collaboration with an evil regime out of his lust for survival. It also stems from a place of fear—the fear of the punishment that comes with resisting tyranny. In reference to

Cole, Mamakay says, "Courage is not what it took to survive. Quite the opposite. You had to be a coward to survive. To make sure you never raised your head above the parapet, never questioned, never said anything that might get you into trouble" (350). This fear or cowardice inspires silence—the kind of silence that is tantamount to acquiescence. And this acquiescent or complicit silence is the ransom for survival, *a morally questionable survival*.

Meanwhile, Adrian offers another possible way to think about Cole's complicity. He notes that beyond fear and cowardice, Cole's complicity is a question of "self-interest and betrayal" (*TML*, 375). That is, large-scale complicities are usually traced down to small acts of betrayal by one's neighbor or friend. In Cole's case, what has become a historic complicity began as small acts of envy and rivalry with Julius. He is envious of Julius's fame and effortless ability to command the attention of people while he, himself, "has the kind of face that people forgot" (13). He also lusts after Julius's wife, Saffia, whom he later marries after Julius's death. Despite this, Forna is careful not to cast moral aspersions on Cole; rather, she uses his character to show the inherent moral ambiguities and contradictions in human nature. For example, Cole mentions in the novel that he acted in self-defense by giving information about Julius to Johnson. But the question is, Where do we draw the line between self-defense and self-interest? Although Adrian is not a scholar of complicity, he provides an accurate answer to this question by noting that "good moral thinking and self-interest are one and the same" (377). This statement resonates with what many scholars of complicity have also said. Mark Sanders, for example, suggests that resistance and collaboration may be interrelated,[44] while Debarati Sanyal notes that complicity and solidarity may actually be two sides of the same coin.[45] However, what is crystal clear is that Elias Cole is complicit not only in the death of Julius but also in the death of a nation. It is also clear that he uses his power as (an unreliable) narrator to solicit sympathy from his audience and to make himself the victim of the situation. He notes, for example, that everything he did was not for himself but for the safety and survival of his only child—Mamakay. However, the conscientious daughter does not buy her father's excuse; she feels like an implicated subject,[46] bears the weight of her father's complicity, and assumes "vicarious responsibility"[47] for an offense she has not committed. Consequently, she breaks ties with her father and willfully terminates her studentship at the university after she finds out that her activist friends have all been rusticated. Toward the end of the novel, she laments:

"Everyone talks about they. Them. But who is *they*? Who are *they*? People like Johnson? Paid to do the things they do? Or people who help them along, who keep their mouths shut and look the other way? My father survived. No, he didn't just survive, he thrived! And there came a point . . . I had to ask myself, how could that be?" (351)

The latter part of the statement above illustrates how it took another generation to ask why people like Elias Cole could have survived a political climate that brutally clamped down on the voice of reason. Also in this statement, Mamakay brings more nuance to the problem of complicity in the Sierra Leonean context by indicating how there are different degrees of complicity. In view of this, Mark Sanders differentiates between "acting-in-complicity" and "responsibility-in-complicity." He notes that acting-in-complicity involves acts subject to a system of accountability while responsibility-in-complicity is assuming responsibility for an "other" in the name of generalized "foldedness" in human beings.[48] Of course, Johnson's complicity is easy to point out; in fact, some people would regard him as an accessory perpetrator who deserves to be criminally charged. However, Elias Cole's case demands a closer examination. His complicity stems from the act of "contributing to wrongful action knowingly though not as a co-participant."[49] His silence counts as complicity because he fails "to act on the knowledge that crimes are being or likely to be committed or failing to try at least to prevent them happening, despite having the means to do so."[50] In other words, while Johnson's complicity is a participatory action, Cole's is more of a contributory action.

What is more dismaying is that the postwar Sierra Leonean society venerated people like Elias Cole. The SLTRC focused mostly on "exceptional" victims and perpetrators, and as a result, people like Cole absolved themselves of any responsibility toward rehabilitation and reparation. In light of this, the narrator explains:

Adecali [one of the perpetrators], tortured by those acts he had committed. Elias Cole unperturbed by the many he had not. Adecali was made to feel shame, was held culpable. Cole was venerated. Yet where does the greater evil lie, if evil is what you call it? Somewhere in the place he calls a soul, Elias Cole knows. Adrian has been his last attempt at absolution, his last attempt to convince himself of his own cleanliness. (*TML*, 410)

The exclusive focus on core perpetrators in the reconciliation process is in itself a kind of silence. Hence, the postwar Sierra Leonean society is, in a way, complicit in overlooking the sins of people like Cole. Perhaps that is the paradox of complicity: everyone is complicit, so no one is complicit. More so, the fact that the postwar veneration of Cole makes him "convince himself of his own cleanliness" (410) is not entirely surprising because it is often in the psychology of complicity to shift the blame to others. For example, Cole shifts the blame to Johnson and claims to be a victim of "coerced collaboration" (410). He even goes as far as blaming Julius for being the architect of his own death. He says to Adrian, "The truth, if you want to know—and I have thought about this for many years. The truth is Julius brought it upon himself. He never knew what was good for him. He presumed too much" (410). What sounds more like the truth, of course, is that although Elias Cole absolved himself of any responsibility for the eleven years of civil war in Sierra Leone, the war would not have happened and would not have been so prolonged without his quiet cooperation with power. Adrian provides a summary of Cole's action in the following:

> A life, a history, whole patterns of existence altered, simply by doing nothing. The silent lie. The act of omission.... Elias Cole would never take responsibility for his hand in Julius fate. The fragmentation of conscience. Cole absolved himself the moment he handed responsibility for Julius to Johnson, in the same way he handed the list of students to Johnson knowing yet refusing to acknowledge the likely outcome. He absolved himself of responsibility for the greater crime and yet it could not have occurred without him. There are millions of Elias Coles the world over. (410)

As the popular saying goes, evil prevails when good people do or say nothing. With the character of Elias Cole, we see the power of complicity in the perpetuation of evil. Therefore, there is the need to think more critically about questions of accountability and responsibility—on the part of the complicit—in the aftermath of historical violence. Finally, having established how the postwar Sierra Leonean society itself is complicit in venerating people like Cole, I like to argue that time is equally complicit in silencing the offenses of the likes of Cole. Time is complicit in the sense that it renders certain conversations impossible in the wake of the war. In the next section, I explore this tension between silence and the complicity of time in *The Memory of Love*.

POST-CONFLICT TIMESCAPES IN *THE MEMORY OF LOVE*

The Memory of Love, like many postcolonial novels, offers an alternative chronosophy to Western modernity's historical time. It provides an outstanding critique of absolute, homogeneous, empty time and projects another calibration of time that is based on a politics of mourning. In the novel, we hear Kai Mansaray saying aggrievedly, "Now they say it's over, but it is not over" (*TML*, 304). He is referring here to the war which many other characters, like himself, consider unfinished because the circumstances that precipitated it remain unchanged. Likewise, for many in postwar Sierra Leone, time collapses and contracts as the present becomes interlocked with the past and the future in a kind of Venn diagram logic. This experience of disjunctive temporality is mostly a result of trauma, which has been said to be capable of breaking the mind's experience of time.[51] Hence, the timescape of *The Memory of Love* is reflective of a traumascape.

Adrian notes that for people in postwar Sierra Leone, "time had taken on a kind of shapelessness" (*TML*, 20), and all that they are left with is a pervading sense of "ambivalent temporalities in the nation-space."[52] He finds the postwar Sierra Leonean timescape enigmatic and observes that in this melancholic nation-space, "There was before. And there is now. And in between a dreamless void" (114). The "void" between "then" and "now" points to the hazy line between the past and the present. Likewise, oftentimes in the novel, the past and the future become compressed into the spontaneity of a timeless present[53] such that the "pain of the past, the unbearable present and the possible future all ran together" (269). Therefore, while the survivors live in a chronological time of ordinary life experiences, they also inhabit a durational time of a past that resists closure and is continuously present.[54]

Time in *The Memory of Love* is subjective—that is, within the text's disjunctive temporal substructure are subjective times dictated by individual experiences. And as Achille Mbembe rightly points out, "There is a close relationship between subjectivity and temporality—and, in some way, one can envisage subjectivity itself as temporality."[55] Therefore, the multiple subjectivities splattering through the novel account for its multiple temporal underpinnings and polyontologies of time.

It makes sense at this juncture to zoom in on some of the characters' experiences of time before examining the novel's overall narrative time. Kai Mansaray is said to occupy only the present and reveals little of his past

(*TML*, 105); as far as he is concerned, "There was no before" (48). His attempt at expunging the past, it turns out, is a defense mechanism, but, that notwithstanding, the past reveals itself through him. His corporeality mediates between the past and the present as the past is acted out in his nightmares and daydreams. We get more insights into his experience of time when the narrator says, "Another time. Before or after, he cannot be sure" (118), which simply means he is unable to distinguish the present (after the war) from the past (before the war). He exists in a disjunctive phenomenological time.[56] He is also unable to imagine a future for himself because he experiences an omni*presence* of a traumatic time that leaves him incapacitated. The war not only affects his experience of time; it also "frustrated his hope, shut out the light. And everything ceased" (342). He immerses himself in his work at the hospital as a way of "unforgetting,"[57] but like flies unto wanton boys, he is in the hands of time.

Agnes is another character who has "no idea where the time went" (*TML*, 139). Her affective resource of *being-in-time* makes the present almost ahistorical and fleeting. She has lost her "sense of time and count of seasons" (113) and can hardly differentiate the past from the present. It is only in her silence that she is able to navigate between her "experienced past" and "experiencing past." Adrian suspects that she is suffering from fugue because she seems to "inhabit a state of obscured consciousness from which [they] eventually emerged with no memory of the weeks, months or even years they had spent away" (128). Even though throughout the novel it is not established whether she truly suffers from psychogenic fugue, there is no doubt that she as well as the other war survivors experience a sociotemporal fugue. They un/consciously wear a psychology of silence as an *alternative state* in their minds. This fugue-like experience of time is also given expression in Kai's statement that his dreams and experiences, in some ways, connect with Agnes's (325) and, by extension, those of all the survivors. Similarly, the experience of an unbounded time translates to a disjuncture in the characters' experience of reality and illusion. Hence, a breach of their mind's experience of time co-occurs with a rupture in their selves and identities.[58] For example, Agnes cannot tell if "those things occurred or were part of her dreams" (*TML*, 163). Mamakay's neighbor is also unable to "work out what was real and what was not" (278).

From these two instances, we see how an intimate scene of violence oftentimes blurs the boundaries between one's sense of reality and general external reality. It is for this reason that Juliet Rogers avers that for many trauma survivors, fantasy becomes reality and reality becomes fantasy.[59] In light of this, Elias articulates what it is like for many in postwar Sierra Leone in the following:

> A day passed. Then another. The clouds hung thick over the city, only their patterns altered with wind. It was as if we were trapped on the dark side of a mirror. (*TML*, 186)

Adecali is another character whose disjunctive experience of time is reminiscent of Marcel Proust's idea of an "involuntary memory" which accounts for how the past can be triggered through the senses of sight, smell, and taste. For Adecali, the past floods back any time he comes across a burning fire or smells roasted meat because it reminds him of a woman he had burned alive during the war. This traumatic return of the repressed, as well as a puncture in optic and olfactory nerves, produces a puncture in his experience of time. In some ways, his story corroborates the idea that perpetrators also suffer from trauma because, as the narrator notes, the screams of the woman whom he set ablaze "follow him in dream and in real life" (373). Adrian explains Adecali's situation as a flashback of memory "so strong that it feels as though the thing [past] is happening all over again, as though you are back in the same place. Sometimes you forget who you really are" (373).

Time in *The Memory of Love* is slippery. The characters struggle to map time; their traumatic grief takes place in time but equally evades time. The constantly shifting time signatures in the novel complicate its time setting. The convolution of/in time is backed up by an *episodic plot* structure, long interior monologues, and copious flashbacks. For instance, Elias Cole, for the most part, narrates his past to Adrian in the form of uninterrupted monologues. In addition, Kai's and Mamakay's stories are told through nonlinear flashbacks. The narrative point of view, as I have indicated earlier, shifts constantly but almost imperceptibly. The novel's kaleidoscopic pattern of temporality synchronizes well with this constantly shifting point of view which eventually produces a silent narrative tempo that submerges the readers into the story. In a sense, the narrative itself becomes a kind of fugue because of its structural, philosophical, thematic, and aesthetic complexity[60] which, arguably, is symptomatic of the Sierra Leonean postwar heterogeneous timescapes.

In the novel, there is also an abounding reference to the fact that the characters are oblivious of time's passage which, as I have already explained, is mostly traceable to trauma. Adrian, a Westerner, is taken aback by the strange configuration of time in this alien landscape, and in comparing his experience of time in Britain to postwar Sierra Leone, the narrator notes that "without the order of his previous life, time had taken on a kind of shapelessness" (*TML*, 20). After spending some time in postwar Sierra Leone, Adrian feels trapped in this frigid silence of time; "he tries to imagine himself into a future, somewhere past this point, but he cannot" (417), and all he sees is disorder, "a tangle of days, weeks and months" (422). He is unable to do anything but "to keep on existing, in this exact time and place" (417). Because he is not particularly used to this non-chronological sequence of time in Sierra Leone, he grows into becoming "acutely aware of the slow and silent passage of time" (22).

Adrian's dalliance with the postwar Sierra Leonean temporality raises a couple of provocations. First, it suggests that the experience of time of the traumatized—victim time[61]—is different from that of the non-traumatized. Also, it confirms the idea that time and space are not really separate entities but a blended continuum. Hence, in the novel, we see a silent time that is co-constitutive of a silent space. Through the eyes of Adrian, we see a postwar Freetown where "the clouds are unmoving. Everything is quiet. No traffic on the roads. Even the birds are silent" (*TML*, 320). In this "silencescape," both flora and fauna are affected to the extent that even the goat bleats a repetitive melancholy sound (304). Adrian is puzzled by the "silence that overlays the entire place" (84) as well as the "terrible stillness" of Freetown (25, 429). He wanders around and wonders about the "silent streets" (157) and worries about the families that have become "silent islands" (163). On that note, *The Memory of Love* can be said to be embedded with a chronotope of silence. With expressions such as "hours dragged by," "the day wore on" (5), and "every action slowed down" (246), the novel points to a peculiar mechanism of time that moves in slow motion, a time without duration—a silent time. The characters' quotidian lives unfold in silent temporal rhythms, and in this silence of time, they struggle to locate their existence (in time). The narrator emphasizes the presence of silent time in post-conflict Sierra Leone by stating, "In this country there is no dawn. No spring or autumn. Nature is an abrupt timekeeper" (27). Silent time in the novel suggests a time wherein clock time is erased, suspended, and transformed. It is both a temporal atemporality and an atemporal temporality. It is entangled between cosmological, phenomenological, ecological, and psychological times. It is a "human time"[62] in all of its complexities. It conveys an intricate interconnectedness of moments.

More than being a literary time, silent time is multi-scalar—it operates on the individual, familial, social, national, and even transnational scales. Therefore, while it constitutes a "chrono-trope" in the novel, it also reveals a lot about the post-conflict Sierra Leonean society. The fact that the survivors are silent suggests that words—in post-conflict Sierra Leone—lose their meaning. Or, to put it another way, because people are still processing their traumatic experiences, they are unable to find the words to capture what has happened. A silent time is what usually follows a period or experience of immense violence. During this period of silence, discussions about the past often sound vulgar while coming to terms with what happened seems obscene. Silent time corroborates the fact that some memories silence time just as some times silence memories. However, drawing from other histories of atrocity from around the world, silent time is not a permanent time. It is transitory. It is a phase of disillusionment with(in) the present. After all, it took over a decade before people began to break the silence of the Holocaust in Germany[63] and over twenty-seven years before people started talking about the Hiroshima crisis in Japan.[64] Maybe there will come a time of talking about the past in Sierra Leone. Maybe that time has even arrived with local initiatives such as Fambul Tok.[65] Whatever the case may be, *The Memory of Love* helps us think through this temporality of silence, which is not only peculiar to Sierra Leone but is obtainable in many post-conflict African countries.

As I hope I have shown in this chapter, *The Memory of Love* is about the plurality of silence. It explores the silences of place, time, and action as well as their mnemonic consequences; it depicts how time is complicit in the silence of memory as well as how memory is complicit in the time of silence (and silence of time). While silence may not be regarded as an auspicious resolution in some post-conflict situations, the novel sketches a more complex and ambivalent silence that serves as a condition for stability on the one hand and an indication of traumatic suppression (of the past) on the other. The novel, as a non-redemptive narrative, portrays a nation that is struggling to cope with festering wounds from the past but is not in a hurry to heal—at least not with the Western psychoanalytic approach to healing and therapy. The novel tells of a kind of past that continues in silence and a kind of silence that bears the burden of memory. It tells of a kind of silence that is not simply an absence of sound but is hidden in loquacity, a kind of silence that is imbued with aesthetic and performative qualities. On the whole, the novel gives insights into the frictions of memory in postwar Sierra Leone by showing how different people, at different points, struggle to remember, misremember, forget, and, most of all, silence the past.

CHAPTER 3

The Past Continues in Another Country
African Transnational Memory in a Migratory Setting

When one leaves one's place of origin—voluntarily or involuntarily—there are a host of losses both concrete and abstract that must be mourned.
—David Eng, "Melancholy/Postcoloniality"

Migrant communities often become memory-makers themselves because of their absence from national memories.
—Irial Glynn and Olaf Kleist, *History, Memory, and Migration*

Modern colonialism and the modern state were born together with the creation of the nation-state. Nationalism did not precede colonialism. Nor was colonialism the highest or the final stage in the making of a nation. The two were co-constituted.
—Mahmood Mamdani, *Neither Settler nor Native*

IMMIGRANT MELANCHOLIA

A postcolonial African memory discourse is incomplete without the discourse of migration. Postcolonial migration is, to a certain extent, a sequel to colonialism and an afterlife of imperial subjugation. As I already laid out in the introduction, Africa, between the 1970s and 1990s, experienced various forms of political and economic violence that resulted in the mass migration of its peoples to the Global North. This history of emigration directly or indirectly precipitated the emergence of a new wave of African writings with diasporic leanings. There is also a transgenerational dynamic to this history, as some of the émigrés fled with their children, who later came of age in the West but still maintained various forms of affiliations and attachments to Africa. Dinaw Mengestu is one of these "children." He has been described by critics as an Africa-born American writer whose stories are laced with Pan-

African sensibilities coupled with intricate attention to the politics of race, identity, and class relations in America.[1] He was born during the Derg revolution of the 1970s which saw the overthrow of Emperor Haile Selassie and the establishment of a vicious communist state in Ethiopia. His parents fled Ethiopia (along with him) to America in 1980 when he was only two years old. Mengestu's experience as an Ethiopian child (of a) migrant in America has been a crucial influence in his writings. All of his novels so far have been preoccupied with the memory and legacies of the Ethiopian communist revolution of the 1970s and the Ethiopian migrant experience in America.

His trilogy—*Children of the Revolution* (2007),[2] *How to Read the Air* (2010), and *All Our Names* (2014)—has a leitmotif of involuntary migration of people from Ethiopia to America. *Children of the Revolution*, for example, is about a man named Sepha Stephanos, who is forced to leave Ethiopia for America during the revolution but is unable to work through his traumatic memories after many years of residing in America. He struggles to maintain his fragile balance and finds a bit of solace only when he is in the company of his two friends—Kenneth the Kenyan and Joseph from Zaire—who share a similar story of violent displacement from Africa. *How to Read the Air* is about Jonas Woldermarian, a man born in the United States to refugee parents from Ethiopia. To make sense of his distressed adult life, Jonas needs to rummage through the generational and familial stories that preceded him. *All Our Names* is also premised on an unwilling migration to America from a "revolutionizing" African country. The anonymous narrator leaves Ethiopia, his home country, for Uganda and then goes to a racist Midwestern American town where his affair with a white woman exposes him to the continuous past of racial bigotry in America.

These three novels are arguably semiautobiographical. Mengestu, just like his main characters, left Ethiopia for the United States; he also at one point or another lived in many of the American cities described in his novels. He said in an interview that in *Children of the Revolution*, he created the character of Shibrew Stephanos (Sepha's father, who died as a victim of the revolution) in memory of his uncle of the same name who faced a similar fate. He also mentioned in the same interview that his grandfather named him Stephanos at birth.[3] Thus, *Children of the Revolution* falls within the category of transgenerational memory narratives not only because of the author's generational connection to the memory of the revolution but also because—as the title of the novel suggests[4]—it broadly illustrates the legacies of the revolution among a succeeding generation now established in the diaspora. To put it another way, Mengestu represents a generation of children born during or after the Derg revolution in Ethiopia; he is a child of the revolution and is affected by its aftermath even though he is now an American citizen.[5]

On children and immigration in America, Alison Landsberg notes that the child of an immigrant "must necessarily engage in a creative form of amnesia, constantly editing and negotiating the past, creating and taking on prosthetic memories in order to imagine himself or herself as one of "America's children."[6] On the contrary, Mengestu, as a child of immigrants in America, is more invested in writing novels that negotiate familial and generational losses in Ethiopia than taking on prosthetic memories of America. It is in light of this that James Arnett posits that Mengestu's novels amplify the trauma of origin in the experience of immigration and "invoke specifically the coincidence of parentage and history."[7] Mengestu himself makes a similar statement following the publication of *How to Read the Air*:

> I knew that I wanted to write from the perspective of somebody imagining this family history that they have no real access to. So the book was very much about this process of imagination, the distance between one generation and the next, and the attempts to recreate the past and to write fiction out of that. Jonas, the character who's controlling the story, is so internally isolated, he's so walled off from his own past and sense of identity, that the only way he has of achieving any peace is through the process of, *"Let me go back and recreate what I don't know."*[8]

In essence, children of immigrants do get encumbered with the question of home and, in Mengestu's case, often bear the burden of the memories of their parents' (forced) migration. As a way of making sense of this burden of memories in *Children of the Revolution*, Mengestu creates characters who struggle to hold on to the memories of Africa despite America's relentless push for the suppression of those memories. Consequently, these characters find themselves in an existential dilemma where they have to juggle between the painful memory of their natal home (Africa) and the harrowing experience of disenfranchisement in their new home (America).

My argument in this chapter is that *Children of the Revolution* is not your typical, hackneyed immigration story, nor is it a facile narrative about an immigrant's fixation on the past. Rather, the novel explores the complexities and paradoxes of the experience of involuntary migration. This chapter also examines how the novel portrays the traversal of memory across continental borders as well as the frictions that occur when immigratory and emigratory memories come into contact. Put differently, I am investigating how the characters in the novel negotiate their traumatic pasts that impelled their emigration to America and their interaction—as Black African immigrants—with America's racialized past and present. I explore how they negotiate the ghosts of home and how they navigate diasporic intimacies—the kinds of intimacies constituted by displacement and dispossession.[9] I also examine the structures of melancholy that emerge from the collision of traumatic memory and migration. I demonstrate how the novel as a postcolonial fiction of memory challenges the idea of the nation-state as an automated container of memory as well as how it imagines alternative forms of belonging and memory-making beyond nation-statehood.

The novel opens with an informal Pan-African meeting (in America) among Kenneth the Kenyan, Joseph from Zaire, and Sepha Stephanos from Ethiopia, three African friends who form a habit of debating Africa's coups and wars. Kenneth, an economic migrant, is dangerously optimistic and "irrationally hopeful" (*Children of the Revolution;* hereafter *Children*, 145). Joseph and Sepha sarcastically call him the "perfect immigrant" who goes to work on Christmas Day like the "perfect house nigger of the 1800s" (182). Joseph, on the other hand, is an ambivalently nostalgic immigrant who sees "flashes of the continent everywhere he went" (100). Sepha, the narrator, whose experiences and thoughts are most focalized, is irredeemably melancholic and persistently fails to integrate into the American neoliberal capitalist culture after seventeen years of living there. He constantly remembers the cruel torture that his father suffered at the hand of communist soldiers in Ethiopia. And as a result, the past, for him, continues even in his new country. The communist past and its legacies invade his present in America such that "the real world in which he lives fades into a past he tried to put to rest" (89). He is also described as living his daily life in America with an "overwhelming sense of loss" (149). In other words, hanging between his traumatic memory of emigration and his precarious experience of immigration is a mixture of an inarticulable loss and an implacable grief—all of which form the basis of his migrant subjectivity.

Sepha's experiences illustrate how migration itself is based on a structure of mourning.[10] His immigratory and emigratory griefs constitute what in similar contexts have been described as "immigrant melancholia"[11] or "migratory grief."[12] Involuntary migrants usually carry with them a baggage of material and symbolic losses that they must mourn upon their arrival in a new country. Sepha provides insights on his own migratory grief when he laments:

> I was hit with the sudden terrible and frightening realization that everything I had cared for and loved was either lost or living on without me seven thousand miles away and that what I had here was not a life but a poorly constructed substitution made up of one uncle, two friends, a grim store and a cheap apartment. (*Children*, 40)

Beside the concrete loss of family and displacement from home, Sepha, in the statement above, refers to the life he lives in America as a "poorly constructed substitution," a life saturated with the monotony of grief and loneliness. But why is Sepha unable to find closure to his traumatic losses after almost two decades of living in America? Perhaps one could find the answer to this question in the Freudian theory of mourning, which accounts for how one works through traumatic losses through the "withdrawal of cathexes" and an investment in new objects or fixations.[13] For many immigrants in America, investing in the enticing American dream is where they sublimate the feelings of loss and trauma that they might have brought from their home country. For instance, in the novel, Kenneth the Kenyan enthusiastically embraces the American dream and its leftover capitalist schemes. He says proudly, "God bless America. . . . Only here can someone become the Buddha" (3). On the contrary, Sepha's immigrant melancholia is anchored in his inability to invest in the American dream. The bleeding memories of home weaken his prospects of embracing America's capitalist ethos which is notorious for fostering amnesia.[14] Likewise, his failure to ignite a romantic relationship with Judith, his white American neighbor to whom he is attracted, is symbolic of his inability to be devoted to America which Judith represents. He says:

> I did not come to America to find a better life. I came here running and screaming with the ghosts of an old one firmly attached to my back. My goal since then has always been a simple one: to persist unnoticed through the days. (41)

As much as he would want to, Sepha could not "find the guiding principle that relegated the past to its proper place" (*Children*, 127). His inability to let go of the past is rather compulsive than intentional and cannot be interpreted as nostalgic because only memories that are not defined by trauma are likely to slide into nostalgia.[15] He also finds himself frequently conversing with his dead father and "passes his mother, brother, father and friends in the aisles of grocery stores, in parks and restaurants, [so] that at times it hardly felt as if

[he] had really left [Ethiopia]" (175). This, in a way, provides a clear picture of how haunting is often a mark of melancholia and how Mengestu's novel is, in and of itself, a spectral narrative.

Freud describes melancholia as a situation in which an object loss is withdrawn from consciousness. He also explains that the melancholic "knows whom he has lost but not what he has lost in him."[16] The implication of this is that the melancholic is unable to fully comprehend his loss and, as a result, experiences "a profoundly painful dejection, cessation of interest in the outside world, loss of the capacity to love, . . . a lowering of the self-regarding feelings to a degree that finds utterance in self-reproaches and self-revilings, and culminates in a delusional expectation of punishment."[17] Therefore, all the times Sepha attempts to reroute cathected energies and rise above his migrant precarity, he ends up saying to himself:

> I told myself that I had no right to expect more. . . . I cursed myself for silly expectations. I thought I saw the situation for what it was—a case of mistaken identity. I had forgotten who I was. . . . I had to recast myself. (80)

From the statement above, it seems quite evident that Sepha's melancholia is given expression in his self-indictment; however, as much as his confession conveys a deep feeling of sadness mixed with self-reproach, one must be careful not to pathologize or interpret it as debilitating helplessness. The immigrant melancholia is not necessarily clinically morbid; it is, instead, a depathologized structure of the everyday life of immigrant groups.[18] Sepha's melancholia, which is behind his inability to genuflect to America's neoliberal capitalism, is an inadvertent weapon of the weak,[19] an (un)intended act of resistance to America's blindness to his migrant subjectivity.

As I have mentioned earlier, Sepha's relationship with Judith is symbolic of his relationship with America as a whole. Although he managed to gain Judith's trust and friendship, he constantly feels undesirable and inadequate. Slavoj Žižek's insight on melancholia is useful for making sense of this fraught relationship between Sepha and Judith. In "Melancholy and the Act," Žižek, drawing from the work of Giorgio Agamben, explains that the melancholic thinks what he possesses is lost; he even mourns the object before it is lost.[20] In other words, although Sepha and Judith enjoyed a platonic friendship that had the potential to become more intimate, he mourned the loss of that friendship even before it was shattered by the inhibitions of race and class. Sepha's melancholia manifests in his attachment to the cufflinks given to him by his father during his "days in the Ethiopian government" (*Children*, 50). The cufflinks—on which the Ethiopian flag is imprinted—are the only objects he has brought with him to America, and they symbolize the entangled links between familial and national histories. They also serve as the linking object that takes him back in space and time to Ethiopia every now and then.[21] Therefore, while physically located in America, Sepha psychically transits between two spaces and temporalities just as the temporal and geographical settings of the novel constantly alternate between past and present and between Addis Ababa and Washington, DC, respectively.

Furthermore, *Children of the Revolution* aesthetically mourns the symbolic losses of its immigrant characters through different narrative techniques.[22] The novel's elegiac narrative voice and overall dirge-like tone render it as a kind of textual mourning. In addition to the elegiac narrative voice, the main character, Sepha, makes a lot of meditative and aphoristic statements that, in a sense, corroborate the notion that grief often generates insights in and for its subjects. Many a time in the novel, we find Sepha asking rhetorical questions that could have been generated only from an itinerary of loss. For example, after seventeen years in America, he asks, "How did I end up here? . . . . Where is the grand narrative of my life?" (*Children*, 147). Readers can almost visualize Sepha's teary eyes as he asks these rhetorical questions. He also expresses his sense of despondency when he talks about his "idle dreams" (169), "unrealized ambitions" (148), and incessant feeling of "loneliness and occasional despair" (96). Therefore, the novel qualifies as a melancholic text not only because of its depressed narrator or plaintive narrative progression but also because it is, quite literally, a pessimistic read. However, it is worth reiterating that the novel's narrative melancholy has a political function in that it forces us to see involuntary migrant subjects (refugees, economic migrants, exiles, asylum seekers) not only as a silent population with no political voice[23] but also as people who are culturally constituted and historically situated.

One may even regard Mengestu as a melancholic author because of the ambience of melancholy that spreads through all of his novels. Just as in *Children of the Revolution*, Jonas, the main character of *How to Read the Air*, is also melancholic. He wants to be "just obscure enough to always blend into the background and be quickly forgotten" (*How to Read the Air*, 207). He chooses a reclusive life in which he only enjoys reading "pastoral poetry." He feels like a failure because of his inability to pursue a PhD and, just like Sepha and Judith's relationship, his relationship with Angela (an American) is fraught with anxieties and instabilities. Also in *All Our Names*, we find a depressive depiction of an African immigrant in a Midwestern American city. He is severely haunted by a past marked by horrific violence (of 1960s Uganda) and also agonized by a racist America that had just come out of the civil rights movement. His romantic relationship with Helen, a white American, is fraught with tensions not simply because of Helen's whiteness but because of his own inability to find closure to his traumatic (emigratory) memories. The similar storyline in the three novels suggests a repetitive compulsion on Mengestu's part, a compulsion to return again and again to the primal scene of violence which, in this case, is in Africa.

Mengestu explains that Sepha's situation is "less about trying to figure out how to occupy these two cultural and racial boundaries and more about what it's like when you are not particularly attached to either of these two communities."[24] Hence, this fragmented existence and the melancholic in-betweenness that characterize many involuntary immigrants' lives propel Sepha to ask, "How was I supposed to live in America when I had never really left Ethiopia?" (*Children*, 79). His suspended memories make him neither here (America) nor there (Ethiopia). He describes himself as a man "stuck between two worlds" and resigns, melancholically, to the possibility of "dying alone" (450). One would expect that the company of other Ethiopian migrants in America will at least be a source of comfort to him, but he avoids such company like a plague. He moves out of his uncle's apartment precisely because it is full of Ethiopians. He says, "I count the number of Ethiopian friends still in my life with two fingers. I go out of my way to avoid the restaurants and bars frequented by other Ethiopians of my generation. My phone calls home are infrequent. I eat injera [a type of bread] only on social occasions. I consider the old emperor to be a tyrant, not a god" (118). The migrant paradox in this confession is in the way Sepha tenaciously holds on to his memory of Ethiopia while, at the same time, avoiding anything that associates him with it. His internal and external isolation is compounded by the "melancholy of no return."[25] That is, while trying to grapple with the disappointments of America's market democracy, he is confronted with the irreconcilable possibility of never returning to Ethiopia. In view of this, the thought of going home becomes a contradiction that evokes a sense of moving forward and backward at the same time. He says:

There is a simple and startling power to that phrase: going back home. There is an implied contradiction, a sense of moving forward and backward at the same time.... How long did it take for me to understand that I was never going to return to Ethiopia again? It seems as if there should have been a particular moment when the knowledge settled in. (350)

Essentially, Sepha is a migrant at point zero,[26] whose trauma of origin, migratory grief, and melancholy of no return have rendered him estranged from the world and from his own ego. His multilayered subjectivity—poor, Black, migrant—contributes to his anonymity in America, and this anonymity is what he eventually embraces as the "shield against all of the early ambitions of the immigrant which had long since abandoned [him]" (41).

Despite the politics of exclusion and invisibility, Sepha is forced to navigate his way through the stormy waters of America's racial past and present. For instance, while the city's graffiti confers a "crazy nigga" (*Children*, 46) appellation on him, Mrs. Davis, his African American neighbor, ceaselessly reminds him of his immigrant status. In an attempt to rationalize the ongoing gentrification in Logan Circle and find a justification for America's liberal democratic utopia, Sepha says to Mrs. Davis, "It's a free country, people can live where they like" (23), but Mrs. Davis's withering response is not without a tinge of xenophobic nationalism:

> What do you know about free countries? You didn't even know what it was till you came here last week and now you are telling me people can live anywhere they like. (23)

It is interesting, in the above conversation, that it is one of those rare moments when Sepha tries to embrace America that he is reminded of his immigrant status. It is also striking that Mrs. Davis, who is playing a nationalistic game here, is a poor Black subject who is also at the risk of being displaced by the ongoing racialized gentrification in Logan Circle. Therefore, while Sepha may be an exile from Ethiopia, Mrs. Davis herself is an exile within America.[27] After making peace with this reality, she begins to fault America's racial neoliberalism. She initiates some kind of racial solidarity with Sepha by asking him not to be "one of those people" (the middle-class white Americans behind the gentrification). The migrant double bind here is that Sepha, a longtime resident of Logan Circle, is expected to protest against the ongoing racialized gentrification but, at the same time, is strategically excluded from the struggle because of his immigrant status. Sepha eventually embraces his precarity as he says, "I have never really been a part of Logan Circle[,] at least not in the way Mrs. Davis and most of my customers were. . . . I knew my place, not in the dispute in which I had no part to play" (*Children*, 90). The exchange between Sepha and Mrs. Davis also reveals how memory is central to the processes of inclusion or exclusion of migrants from national narratives. Mrs. Davis indirectly invokes the memory of Black people's struggle for emancipation in America—when she asks Sepha what he knows about "free countries." It is this same memory (especially the memory of the 1968 riot in Washington, DC, after the assassination of Martin Luther King Jr.) that many African Americans invoked in order to reject the official proposal to rename some neighborhoods in Washington "Little Ethiopia" in 2005.[28] This brings me to the next part of this chapter where I examine how the Ethiopian—and, by extension, African—migrant groups in *Children of the Revolution* negotiate their exclusion from America's national memory discourses.

MEMORY, TRANSLOCALITIES, AND ALTERNATIVE PRACTICES OF BELONGING IN *CHILDREN OF THE REVOLUTION*

Children of the Revolution gives a close-up portrait of Sepha's life as an exile in America and situates it in a broader context of the lives of Ethiopians who fled to America during the revolution. Washington, DC, where the novel is set, was the common destination for many of these immigrants. Statistics show that outside of Africa, Washington, DC, has the highest concentration of Ethiopian migrants and that Ethiopians constitute the second-largest Black population after African Americans in this area.[29] Some parts of the neighborhoods in DC (such as Shaw and Alexandria) are commonly and unofficially known as "Little Ethiopia." In addition to the Ethiopian restaurants, boutiques, and coffee shops that flood these areas, there is also a bilingual (English and Amharic) Ethiopian newspaper (*Zethiopia*) company based in Washington, DC. "Little Ethiopia" (which can also be found in Los Angeles and some other parts of the United States) is apparently not the only micronational enclave within America. There are other enclaves, such as Chinatown, Little Japan, Little Egypt, Koreatown, Yoruba town (South Carolina), and other older, multicultural cities that share a similar history of migration, such as Little Italy, New Britain (Connecticut), Dutch Town, German Town, New Madrid (Missouri), and New Amsterdam (now known as New York City). These micronational enclaves turn the United States into a "postnational network of diasporas."[30] Hence, the United States—popularly and controversially labeled "a nation of immigrants"[31]—is the migratory setting in *Children of the Revolution*.

By conceiving America in this way, *Children of the Revolution* shifts our perspective from the idea of "migration as a movement from place to place" to the idea of "migration as installing movement within places."[32] The novel portrays America as having the potential to become a fertile site of entangled histories, transnational identities, and multidirectional memories. Also in the novel, Washington, DC, becomes the site of transnational urbanism and a translocal space where migrants settle and transform into a place "intricately shot-through with other places, memories and imaginations."[33] In one of Sepha's flaneur-like strolls through the city, he spots America's promise of multiracial and multicultural conviviality in a school ad campaign that showcases four students from different racial backgrounds. He then comments that "the liberal idea of America is at its best in advertising" (*Children*, 98). This comment subtly yet perceptibly critiques America's haste to amplify her cultural pluralism when, in practice, many immigrants struggle to maintain a balance between their cultural memory of home and their displacement from America's cartography of belonging. As a consequence, the Ethiopian migrants in the novel become "in-betweeners" who make America their home but also bring Ethiopia into its streets.[34]

Further into the novel, we see how Ethiopian immigrants retain their cultural memory in weddings, funerals, dressings, and foods that contribute to the formation of a vibrant Ethiopian diasporic community in America. This community, in fact, rises above the pejorative label of "immigrant" and its regular image of permanent rupture and abandonment of old patterns of life.[35] It becomes a community of *transmigrants* who live in a world shaped by interconnections between their society of origin and their host nation. These transmigrants in the novel develop subjectivities embedded in networks of relationships that connect them to both Ethiopia and America.[36] Sepha's uncle—one of the first few Ethiopians to arrive in America during the communist revolution—performs this transmigrant identity in the letters he writes to presidents Carter, Reagan, and other U.S. government officials, requesting their intervention in the political violence going on in Ethiopia. The letters reveal how Sepha's uncle negotiates his political and civil transnationalism; they reverberate with a tone of patriotic sentiments of a "concerned and active US citizen" (*Children*, 121) relaying a heartfelt message to his government. At the same time, they constitute the way Sepha's uncle performs a long nationalism as an Ethiopian in the diaspora.

Sepha's uncle refers to Ethiopia as his "home country" although he admits that nothing is left for him there (*Children*, 124). His position invites a question: What do involuntary migrants really mean when they talk about their "home country"? The reference to "home" in that phrase implies more than national descent; it also points to a seemingly inexplicable attachment to an ancestral home or a place of origin. This attachment, on the one hand, is puzzling because—in Sepha's uncle's case—this "home country" is also a source of disillusionment. On the other hand, it is this same attachment that the Ethiopian immigrants as a collective in the novel seek to enact and install in their new abode in America. Consider, for example, how the transporting of home and locality is given expression in the following lines where Sepha describes the Ethiopian neighborhood where his uncle lives:

> There are twenty-eight floors to the building, and of those twenty-eight floors, at least twenty-six are occupied by other Ethiopians who, like my uncle, moved here sometime after the revolution and found to their surprise that they would never leave. Within this building, there is an entire world made up of *old lives and relationships transported perfectly intact from Ethiopia*. To call the building insular is to miss the point entirely. Living here is as close to living back home as one can get, which is precisely why I moved out after two years and precisely why my uncle never left. . . . The older women still travel from apartment to apartment dressed in slippers and white blankets that they keep wrapped around their heads, just as if they were still walking through the crowded streets of Addis. (*Children*, 115; emphasis mine)

This neighborhood illustrates the idea that place, in and of itself, is mobile and that in a migratory setting, movement is installed within place. The Ethiopian migrants whom Sepha describes in the excerpt transform their inability to return to their natal home into building a familial and communal life that connects them to it. The neighborhood, therefore, forges a translocal connection between Addis Ababa and Washington, DC. In other words, the Ethiopian immigrants, even when they are in DC, can also be said to be in Addis Ababa because of the way they have managed to create connections between the two settings. This corroborates the idea that locality is relational rather than scalar or spatial. The translocal paralleling of Addis Ababa and

Washington, DC, proves that geography is not only a matter of a map but also a lived reality, one that is always shrinking and expanding.[37] Sepha's warning against reading the Ethiopian neighborhood described in the excerpt as "insular" speaks to the broader practice of immigrant profiling that usually fosters willful blindness to the numerous ways in which involuntary immigrants add to the cultural currencies of their host nations.

The installation of Addis Ababa into Washington, DC's socio-sphere is made possible by the work of memory. The Ethiopian migrants engraft the Ethiopia of their memory to their memory of Ethiopia in America. Therefore, memory is central to the production of translocalities. It provides continuity and connection to the original place of dislocation for displaced individuals and social identities.[38] In other words, as people and places move, memories also follow suit. That the memory of Africa is entangled with the memory—and experience—in America in the novel suggests a kind of relational remembering "that connects diverse cultural memories" and advances the claim that "the other is co-constitutive when it comes to the making of our own memory and identity."[39] The translocal negotiations between Addis Ababa and Washington, DC, also point to the "intertextuality of settings"[40] that Mengestu uses to showcase the interconnectedness of the human world.

Therefore, for Joseph, the violence that erupts in Logan Circle because of the displacement caused by gentrification is not very distant from the violence that caused his displacement from Zaire. As someone who has had a firsthand experience of violence and displacement, he remarks, "Everything is connected.... They are not just accidents. That's the way these things begin" (*Children*, 224). Likewise, for Sepha, the displacement of families in the violent gentrification is symbolic of an American empire that is as disappointing as the empire that Haile Selassie created in Ethiopia from which he fled.[41] The constant paralleling of Ethiopia's failed revolution with the fraught American lives and cities in the novel serves to demythologize America's infallibility. In fact, Sepha actually moved to Logan Circle because he "secretly loved the circle for what it had become: proof that wealth and power were not immutable and America was not always greater after all" (16).

Also in the novel, Frank Thomas, a longtime resident of Logan Circle, is presented as one of America's *exiles within*. He is forcefully displaced from his apartment and becomes homeless due to gentrification. To save the situation, he sets Judith's expensive house ablaze with the vain hope that Judith will be threatened enough to leave for another neighborhood. Unfortunately, he is caught and jailed, but Sepha, who knows him from a distance and shares with him the experience of displacement, remarks, "We could have passed for brothers" (*Children*, 225). This statement is a demonstration of some form of transnational Black solidarity in a translocal American city. But, more importantly, Sepha's personal experience of exile is what enables him to empathize with Frank. It is through this kind of empathy (and relationality) that the novel conveys the idea that experiences of displacement, intranational and transnational, follow a similar psychic logic. Another fascinating instance of "one world in relation"[42] is when Joseph, Sephas, and Kenneth sing the band T. Rex's "Children of the Revolution." That these three African immigrant friends are singing the song appeared to be a "misplaced enthusiasm" at first because the English rock band did not have them in mind when they wrote the song, but the lyrics of the song actually resonate with them because they are also "children of the revolution" in their respective historical and national contexts. Hence, "Children of the Revolution" as a song and as the title of the novel speaks to the universal aspects of human experience and the relationality of identities.

So far I have been concerned with how migrants' memories of home influence the formation of translocal spaces in migratory settings and how that process spotlights the relationality of identities and experiences. However, as Dorothy Driver cautions, to inhabit the translocal is not necessarily to be in a safe place.[43] In the case of Sepha, the experience of translocality more or less transmogrifies into a feeling of dislocation, which further aggravates his sense of loss. This feeling of dislocation also applies to his friends, Joseph and Kenneth, who continuously struggle to negotiate their sense of "placelessness" within the American cartography of belonging. This struggle impels Sepha to become so conversant with Washington, DC, that he lectures American citizens and tourists on its history and life. He tells the American couple who shop at his store that General Logan is a "hero to us all" (*Children*, 72). Joseph also follows America's politics so keenly that he knows all the "names and faces" of American politicians in the city (168). Sepha's act of space claiming and Joseph's political awareness can thus be interpreted as alternative practices of urban belonging that challenge Westphalian understandings of nationhood.

In addition, Sepha develops the habit of strolling through the city of Washington, DC, and, at times, reflects at the foot of the statute of General Logan, an American Civil War hero after whom Logan Circle was named. Kathy-Ann Tan interprets Sepha's reflections—on his immigrant life—at the statue as a form of resistant cosmopolitanism from below.[44] But in my view, it is misleading to frame Sepha and his friends as cosmopolitans, not least in Kwame Appiah's use of the term,[45] nor in the vocabulary of Afropolitanism in the writings of Achille Mbembe[46] or Taiye Selasi.[47] After all, Simon Gikandi argues that refugees and coerced migrants are the "mote in the eye of cosmopolitanism."[48] Therefore, in view of Gikandi's critique of cosmopolitanism, Sepha and his friends are underprivileged and vulnerable transnational subjects who strive, against all odds, for survival while hovering between a traumatic past in Africa and a traumatizing present in America.

Again, while America demands that migrants like Sepha put their pasts behind them, it also marginalizes them from its national memory narrative. Nevertheless, Sepha and his friends find ways of interpolating themselves into American national memory. For instance, Joseph memorizes the Gettysburg Address at the Lincoln Memorial (*Children*, 47) while Sepha develops the habit of standing in front of the Washington Monument in fearful awe (46). Sepha also invests in reading America's literature and history such that he confidently engages in a conversation with Judith, a professor of American history, about "America's repudiation of history and its antipathy towards anything that resembled the past" (56). These acts of positioning themselves within America's iconic sites of memory and engaging with America's history are demonstrations of memory citizenship,[49] even if such demonstrations remain monologic rather than dialogic.

Due to their absence from the national memory of America, Sepha and his friends become memory-makers themselves. This migrant memory-making move produces some form of migrant solidarity that their host nation may never understand.[50] That is, in addition to suturing themselves into America's national memory discourse, Sepha and his two African friends, Joseph of Zaire and Kenneth the Kenyan, construct their own memories of home (Africa) in America. Therefore, *Children of the Revolution* portrays the intricacies involved not only in the memory of migration but also in the migration of memory which, in the case of Sepha and his friends, leads to the production of an African transnational memory in a migratory setting. Put differently, Sepha, Kenneth, and Joseph form the habit of remembering together Africa's pasts whenever they are gathered in Washington, DC, America's capital. This enables them to escape the unwholesome effect of American capitalism, which individualizes memory economies and encourages the notion that memory is—and should always be—a private property.[51] But coming from different African countries, how exactly do these three immigrant friends "remember together" in America? This is what I attempt to think through in the next section of this chapter.

IN SEARCH OF AN AFRICAN TRANSNATIONAL MEMORY

Mengestu's trilogy, intentional or not, evinces Pan-African sensibilities; *Children of the Revolution* particularly provokes thoughts on the idea of an African transnational memory, especially in the way Africans of different nationalities remember communally in the novel. Before expanding on the traces of African transnational memory in the novel, I will elaborate on what I mean by "African transnational memory."

In the heydays of African nationalism, Ndabaningi Sithole noted that every African person needed to be detribalized before they could aspire nationally.[52] Fast-forward to the twenty-first century (a period that is arguably marked by a pressing need for intracontinental connectivity and collaboration), I argue that every African person needs to be denationalized to aspire continentally. This does not mean there were no transnational alliances in the nationalisms that spread through various parts of the continent in the mid-twentieth century, even though much of that history has been lost to collective amnesia. In fact, Frantz Fanon, in "The Pitfall of National Consciousness," instructs that the battle against colonialism did not initially run along the lines of nationalism. In the same vein, Toyin Falola observes that for the greater part of the twentieth century, transnationalism was expressed in Pan-Africanism, a political, cultural, and philosophical movement that underlay the clamor for the end of colonialism in Africa.[53] He also observes that the Pan-African ideology was behind the championing of the socioeconomic and political empowerment of Black people all over the world in the twentieth century. However, Falola's observation seems to conflate Pan-Africanism and African nationalism, which are not exactly the same, even if they share certain overlapping ideologies. That said, Black transnationalism has always been at the heart of Pan-Africanism long before the twentieth century.[54]

Pan-Africanism, as well as African nationalism, started to lose its appeal as African countries began to gain independence from the colonial overlords during the second half of the twentieth century. Its ideologies started to weaken as African leaders regressed into authoritarianism and as ethnic politics became the order of the day on the continent. Falola laments this decline of the Pan-African vision and contends that the challenge of the twenty-first century will be to return to this vision, even though he is quite pessimistic that such a return (as first advocated by W.E.B. Du Bois and Kwame Nkrumah) may no longer be possible.[55] Falola's submissions are pertinent even if his arguments are a little totalizing. The Pan-African vision, although weakened, has not died. Hence, a thorough mapping of Africa's sociopolitical landscape and a sufficient understanding of the zeitgeist of the present is needed in determining the solution to the "challenge" that Falola alludes to.

As I have indicated earlier, some of the main challenges of forwarding a common African future lie in our collective amnesia and the crisis in the culture of commemoration.[56] The transnational alliances in the African nationalist struggle that Fanon alludes to have been silently written out of many national narratives. A transnational African memory is therefore needed in reclaiming Africa's entangled histories, shared presents, and common futures. It is useful for understanding and commemorating Africa's common colonial pasts and for working through Africa's post-independence civil wars which are, in many cases, transnational. By amplifying Africa's cultural and historical legacies, an African transnational memory becomes a part of the Pan-African vision that refuses to die. It provides a conceptual and analytic framework for thinking about Africa as an imagined and real mnemonic community and helps to construct new structures of horizontal and vertical solidarities.[57] An African transnational memory work reimagines and reformulates Africa as one "thickened" community of memory.[58] It is also useful in challenging ultranationalism, arrogant provincialism, and ethnopolitical violence in this era of neo-imperial domination and neoliberal globalization.

It is well known that the idea of the nation-state is a by-product of colonial modernity and that it was created to meet certain political and economic needs of the colonial world. Benedict Anderson is clear about the nearly pathological character of nationalism although he is reluctant to embrace its diminishing importance in the age of globalization.[59] Eric Hobsbawm, on the other hand, is more open to embracing the decline of nationalism as a vector of historical change in today's world.[60] I am on the same page with Hobsbawm because it is quite evident that the decentralization of the nation-state is increasingly becoming ingrained into our consciousness and that more people live transnationally on a daily basis in today's world. However, this might not necessarily be the case on the African continent where colonialism successfully sold the idea of the nation-state as the most desirable form of political community. That said, recent developments such as the African Continental Free Trade Agreement (ACFTA), the introduction of a single currency for countries that are part of the Economic Community of West African States (ECOWAS), and several other initiatives by the African Union (AU) indicate that there is a silver lining in the sky for less rigid forms of nationalism on the continent. An African transnational memory culture is, therefore, potentially able to break the impervious political boundaries and national borders that have been put in place by colonialism. It can serve as a "soft factor" that helps facilitate a smooth negotiation of the "hard factors" of regional integration such as trade, migration, language, public policy, and so on.

Additionally, scholars in the field of memory studies are moving beyond methodological nationalism[61] because they reckoned that the nation-state can no longer be seen as the sole carrier of collective memory. In view of this, Alison Landsberg explains that in the wake of modernity and the exponential growth of mass media, memory is no longer exclusively reserved for organic communities but becomes available for adaptation and sharing across identity categories.[62] Yifat Gutman and her colleagues also maintain that while memory in the nineteenth and early twentieth centuries was put in the service of the nation-state, in today's world it is focused on an increasingly transnational future.[63] This move beyond the nation-state does not mean that a transnational memory imperative writes out national self-consciousness. Transnationality and nationality are mutually constitutive, not contradictory—that is, the nation is transnationally constituted.[64] Likewise, the term "transnational" implies that "even in the so called post-national age, the national itself as a framework for identity and memory-making is still a powerful one."[65] Therefore, a transnational memory work is cognizant of the agency and inflection of national memories. National memories are not necessarily discarded in the transnational memory framework; they are instead reshaped for better use. The idea of an African transnational memory sits well with the ongoing transnationalist temper in critical memory studies. It does not seek to homogenize Africa's pasts—and it is aware that ethical considerations are necessary for its sustainability. It embraces not only the similarities but also the contestations and peculiarities in the different national memory narratives in Africa. While I am not arguing for the erosion of national sovereignty in Africa nor for an African state, I reason along with Cheikh Anta Diop about the importance of recognizing individual histories of different nationalities in my thinking of memory without borders in Africa. Diop writes:

> A continental and multi-national state must be endowed with an ideological and cultural superstructure which will be one of the essential bulwarks of security. That means that this State, as a whole, must be conscious of the continent, embracing the individual histories of the different nationalities.[66]

An African transnational memory will, therefore, include the circulation of memory practices, cultures, and institutions across national and cultural formations within the continent. It may involve the creation of African transnational museums, monuments, and memorials. It is in a sense a decolonial work because it is aimed at deconstructing colonial—and received—ideas of nationhood and also challenging the temporal simultaneity upon which the idea of the nation-state is founded. It will strengthen intracontinental interactions and reconnection in a time of accelerating globalization and Western universalism.

The idea of an African transnational memory is not necessarily a new phenomenon, because there are many examples of collaborative cultural and commemorative projects among African countries. This book only seeks to reinforce and perhaps attract more intellectual attention to studying mnemonic materials and processes through the theoretical lens of African transnational memory. Therefore, in reclaiming the past and inventing the future, an African transnational memory work provokes these kinds of questions: How do we remember the role played by other African countries in the antiapartheid struggle? How have we remembered African nationalist heroes transnationally? How do we think about the commemoration of Winnie Mandela's death in Ghana or among African communities on social media? How do we think about the Rwandan genocide museum in Johannesburg? Or the African renaissance monument in Dakar? Or the Pan-African Museum in Ghana? How can we read Africa's digital platforms or events such as PANAFEST and FESTAC '77 as African transnational memory archives? What does it mean for a Kenyan to take on the memory of the Namibian genocide? Or how do I, as a high school student, explain my interaction with a film like *Sarafina*?[67] What is the history behind Solomon Mahlangu College in Tanzania? How is the past represented transnationally in African film, literature, and intracontinental music collaborations? These, among many others, are the concerns of an African transnational memory work.

A transnational memory that is distinctly African will challenge the politics of the global memory discourse that sometimes maintains the hegemony of the Holocaust memory and sometimes puts forward a homogenous idea and culture of memory. Susannah Radstone voices a similar concern as she writes that the idea of global memory politics replicates "too perfectly the neoliberal utopia of a globalized, borderless world."[68] Therefore, African transnational memory is a necessary—and not misplaced—provincial thinking in the age of multidirectional,[69] global,[70] cosmopolitan memories.[71] It is important to reiterate that an African transnational memory work does not remove Africa from global memory discourses; instead, it seeks to correct the exclusion of Africa within the global memory framework and to place its memories in conversation with other memories around the world. An African transnational memory work is needed in the negotiation of Africa's bearings within global memory discourses. Essentially, the transnational impetus in the African transnational memory hypothesis correlates with memory's constant bargaining between local, national and global spaces and temporalities. It rejects the blindness to the politics of national borders embraced by globalization scholars while, at the same time, recognizing that social relations transcend—and are also anchored within—the boundaries of the nation-state. It considers ways in which memory can be employed in forging a post-Westphalian order.

Back to *Children of the Revolution*, Chris Abani notes that the engine of the novel lies in the triangular friendship between Sepha, Joseph, and Kenneth.[72] Despite their challenges as underprivileged transnational subjects, they find comfort in one another's company. Their informal Tuesday meetings (*Children*, 1) can be interpreted as an African transnational memory meeting because of the memory game they always play.[73] In this game they "remember together" by discussing various civil wars in Africa, histories of colonialism in Africa, and the lives and times of African dictators. Sepha says about the game:

> So far we've named more than thirty different coups in Africa. It's become a game with us. Name a dictator and then guess the year and country. We've been playing the game for over a year now. We've expanded our playing field to include failed coups, rebellions, minor insurrections, guerrilla leaders and the acronyms of as many rebel groups as we can find—the SPLA, TPLF, LRA, UNITA—anyone who has picked up a gun in the name of revolution. No matter how many we named, there are always more, the names, dates, years multiplying as fast as we can memorise them so that at times we wonder, half-jokingly[,] if perhaps we ourselves aren't somewhat responsible. (98)

Each iteration of the game offers them a platform to do the work of remembering and makes them forever connected to Africa. The interminable mourning of their pasts in Africa enables them to forge this community of remembrance in a migratory setting (which is the United States). The African memory game is first mentioned when Kenneth walks over to the map of

Africa on the wall of Sepha's store. This presence of the map of Africa serves as an affirmation of the existence and legitimacy of African people (who embody African histories/memories) in a migratory space that constantly seeks to invisibilize them. It is important to reiterate that the African transnational memory in the novel transcends the nationalities of the three immigrant friends—that is, they remember across many countries and regions of Africa. However, despite the common/shared colonial and neocolonial histories, they remain attached to their individual countries and are conscious of the peculiarities of each country's history. To Mengestu's credit, the emphasis on the peculiarities of each migrant's home country may serve as a critique of the perception of Africa as a country within the American imaginary. In essence, Mengestu allows the migrant subjects in his novel to play out their minor transnationalism,[74] the one that forges a "relational discourse" among them.

Children of the Revolution becomes not only a site of Ethiopia's war memory but also a site of African transnational memory. It challenges nationalistic structures of memory by creating an African community of remembrance that transcends ethnic, national, and cultural boundaries—in a migratory setting. These three friends invoke memories and histories of war and colonization in Gabon, the Central African Republic, Uganda, Mauritania, Ethiopia, Kenya, Congo, and many more. They analyze—without much finesse—the (mis)demeanor of some controversial African figures like Mobutu Sese Seko, Jean-Bédel Bokassa, Joseph Kony, Ahmed Taya, Mengistu Haile Mariam, Idi Amin, Yusuf Lule, Godfrey Binaisa (*Children*, 184), Patrice Lumumba (170), Tito Okello, and Valentine Strasser (95) among others. In another instance, they open up a conversation on the involvement and integrity of the colonial government in the postcolonial atrocities in the Central African Republic. Joseph starts the conversation with Bokassa:

"Poor Bukassa. Emperor Bukassa. Minister of Defense, Education, Sports, Health, War, Housing, Land, Wildlife, Foreign Affairs, His Royal Majesty, King of the Sovereign World, and Not Quite But Almost the Lion of Judah Bukassa"

"He was a cannibal, wasn't he?" Kenneth asks Joseph.

"According to the French, yes. *But who can believe the French?* Just look at Sierra Leone, Senegal. Liars, all of them." (184; emphasis mine)

This conversation, as brief and light as it appears, provokes the need to revise some of the hegemonic colonial narratives on African wars and dictatorships. Apart from the sparseness of historical details in the African transnational memories brought to bear in the novel, another concern will be how to channel such memories toward social transformation so that they do not just end up as empty remembering. That said, the African transnational memory work in the novel is not unproductive; it allows for the three friends to perform a kind of deterritorialized nationalism and to insurgently inscribe themselves within America's national memory narrative. It also demonstrates the African diaspora's potential to challenge autocratic memory regimes back home because of their privilege of distance. It is important to note that Western metropolises like Paris, London, New York, and Washington, DC, are not the only sites of transnational movements. More importantly, while Mengestu's novel provides insights into how African transnational memory works in a diasporic space, it might even be more productive to think about how it may take shape on the African continent. For this reason, I explore, in the next chapter, the applicability of African transnational memory in an African setting. Overall, *Children of the Revolution* insightfully grapples with ideas around the interconnected mobilities of peoples, places, memories, times, and cultures. It mirrors the frictions that occur when immigratory and emigratory memories come into contact. It generates apparatuses for thinking about alternative forms of memory-making beyond the nation-state and suggests ways in which Africans can remember transnationally, albeit in a migratory setting.

CHAPTER 4

The Past Continues through Subject Positions

Memory, Subjectivity and Secondary Witnessing in *The Shadow of Imana*

> The past—or, more accurately, pastness—is a position. Thus, in no way can we identify the past as past.
> —Michel-Rolph Trouillot, *Silencing the Past: Power and the Production of History*

> The aftereffects of a traumatic event are not fully owned by anyone and, in various ways, affect everyone.
> —Dominick LaCapra, *Writing History, Writing Trauma*

> In the case of the Rwandan genocide—in which a number of skeletons were, when not exhumed, kept in a visible state—what is striking is the tension between, on the one hand, the petrification of the bones and their strange coolness and, on the other, their stubborn will to mean, to signify something.
> —Achille Mbembe, *Necropolitics*

AFRICAN TRANSNATIONAL MEMORY AND THE GENOCIDE AGAINST THE TUTSI IN RWANDA

Within a period of hundred days (April–June) in 1994, Rwanda experienced the gruesome death of about eight hundred thousand to one million people. In addition to this figure were the deaths arising from sicknesses and wounds months later.[1] This catastrophic event, which has come to be regarded as a genocide, involved the mass slaughter of the Tutsis (and moderate Hutus) by the Hutu majority in Rwanda. It was an anthropological oddity because the Hutus and Tutsis shared the same language and culture.[2] Anyone with some knowledge of Rwanda's history will recall that it was the Belgian colonizers who, in 1935, consolidated these identity labels on the prewar Rwandan psyche through the introduction of identity cards that placed people in fixed identity categories.[3] However, to assume that the genocide was a nation-bound event is to have an incomplete view of it. Mahmood Mamdani, stressing the transnationality of the genocide, writes:

> Since the genocide happened within the boundaries of Rwanda, there is a widespread tendency to assume that it must also be an outcome of processes that unfolded within the same boundaries. A focus confined to Rwandan state boundaries inevitably translates into a silence about regional processes that fed the dynamic leading to the genocide.[4]

Mamdani's argument about the silence on the regional processes that precipitated the genocide adds to its many complexities. Apart from the in/direct involvement of Rwanda's bordering nations—Tanzania, Uganda, Congo, and Burundi—in the genocide and its aftermath, there are other African transnational dimensions to this disastrous event. The war happened in 1994, around the same time that South Africa officially transitioned from apartheid to democracy. In view of that, Véronique Tadjo writes, "It was only several weeks after the slaughter had begun that the whole world really got to hear about it. The attention of the media, governments and the Organization of African Unity had been focused on the first democratic elections that were taking place in South Africa" (*The Shadow of Imana*; hereafter, *Shadow*, 33). Another transnational—or global—dimension of the genocide includes the various layers of complicity of Western superpowers such as Israel, France and America in the atrocity. There is no doubt about the deeply colonial roots of the genocide,[5] but during the genocide itself, Israel allegedly sold arms (guns, grenades, and bullets) to the Rwandan government.[6] France, in particular, is accused of supporting the dictatorial government of Juvénal Habyarimana, giving military training to Hutu militia members, and facilitating the escape of many genocidaires through its military operation called Opération Turquoise.[7] In addition, intelligence reports indicate that the American government was aware that there was a plan to kill the Tutsis but was more concerned with the evacuation of American citizens from the country than intervening in the killings. Bill Clinton would later admit that his failure to intervene in the genocide was his main foreign policy failure during his time as the president of the United States.[8] These transnational and global dimensions of the genocide corroborate the Caruthian notion that "history, like trauma, is never fully one's own. . . . It is precisely the way we are implicated in each other's trauma."[9] It is also one of the reasons why Tadjo avows that what happened in Rwanda was not about "one nation in the dark heart of Africa" but a result of a global "failure of empathy"[10] and the difficulty of imagining other people.[11]

However, what is quite striking is that for a period of time after the genocide, there was some sort of silence among African scholars and writers while, at the same time, the West experienced a proliferation of reports and writings that mostly propagated the single story of African ethnic violence.[12] This silence among African intellectuals was what propelled Maïmouna Coulibaly and Nocky Djedanoum's search for a distinctly African attempt to come to terms with this genocidal past, which eventually resulted in the "Rwanda: Écrire par Devoir de Memoire" (Rwanda: Writing as a Duty to Remember) initiative.[13] This initiative brought a group of ten African writers[14] from eight different countries to Rwanda's capital, Kigali, as part of the Fest'Africa project in 1998.[15] While in Kigali, these writers were enjoined to reflect upon—and write an imaginative response to—the genocide and its aftermath. Nine published texts emerged out of this initiative: four novels, two travel narratives, two essays, and a collection of poetry.[16] Being one of the first literary responses to the genocide by African writers, the initiative was very successful, and it went a long way in challenging the essentialization of post-genocide Rwanda in the global imagination.[17] Nocky Djedanoum captures the essence of the initiative in the following statement:

> True we acted four years after the genocide. But when I went to Rwanda, I realized to the full how much I had failed as a human being. It was necessary to show to Rwandans our solidarity as Africans and in our own way, through literature, fight against forgetting.[18]

From Djedanoum's statement, it is clear that "Rwanda: Writing as a Duty to Remember" is first and foremost a work of memory, and in view of this, many scholars have written about the various commemorative dimensions of the project.[19] For example, Nicki Hitchcott writes about the project's success in re-presenting the genocide via "a transnational commemorative approach that addresses a global consciousness."[20]

However, while "Rwanda: Writing as a Duty to Remember" as a collective commemorative initiative may be vital to global consciousness and memory, it is, more importantly, an African transnational memory project not merely because all the writers involved are Africans but specifically because of how it frames Africa as a "community of memory" with a "thick relationship."[21] The project is a demonstration of the continental ties that bind, ties of affiliation and affect borne out of shared histories of neo/colonial disillusionment as well as similarities of culture and affinities of ancestry. Put differently, while the genocide has become a common memory in the global public sphere, the "Rwanda: Writing as a Duty to Remember" project demonstrates how the genocide constitutes a shared—rather than a common—memory among Africans.[22] In addition, the word *devoir* (which translates as "duty" in English) has the same Latin root with another French word, *dette* (which translates as "debt" in English). And, as Paul Ricoeur reminds us, the idea of debt is inseparable from the notion of heritage.[23] Therefore, by participating in this "duty to remember or debt of memory," the non-Rwandan African writers in the project embrace the genocide as an African—not only a Rwandan—heritage. This debt of memory, as Myriam Bienenstock explains, does not necessarily lead to guilt or feelings of culpability but suggests *an indebtedness to the dead, an ancestral veneration.*[24] Hence, in *The Shadow of Imana*, one of the texts that came out of the project (which shall be discussed in more detail later in this chapter), we see a diviner telling post-genocide Rwandans that "what we must do now is bury the dead according to our rites, bury their desiccated bodies, their bones growing old in the open air, so that we keep of them nothing but their memory, heightened by respect. . . . We must bury the dead so that they may return to visit us in peace" (*Shadow*, 45). What this passage suggests is that within the debt of memory—or indebtedness to the dead—is a sense of responsibility or obligation to lay the dead to rest and, at the same time, keep their memory alive. This sense of responsibility is believed to ensure the prevention of resurgent violence. In other words, ingrained within the "Rwanda: Writing as a Duty to Remember" project is an ethico-political obligation that is not only geared toward remembering the past but also invested in safeguarding the future.

Memory, Avishai Margalit suggests, is constitutive of the notion of care. If we forget something or someone, it is likely because we do not really care about that thing or that person. "Caring is at the heart of our thick relation," and it is what enhances the distribution of genuine solidarities.[25] In the same spirit, Djedanoum notes that the "Rwanda: Writing as a Duty to Remember" project serves as "a testament of solidarity, a sharing of mourning," as well as a "moral solidarity of writers everywhere in Africa with the Rwandan people."[26]

In essence, the project, as an African transnational memory work, gravitates toward an African ethics of care and politics of mourning that produce lateral structures of solidarity among Africans. It is also anchored in the philosophy of Ubuntu because it is aimed at generating various formations of empathy and moral support for the genocide survivors.

What many of the texts that came out of the project provoke us to think about is the ethical dilemmas involved in doing memory work. Eight out of the ten writers are not Rwandan, which implies that they are not direct or firsthand witnesses to the atrocity and may not be directly affected by its aftermath. Therefore, the question is how this Pan-African solidarity and alliance will be carried out by these non-Rwandan Africans without laying claims to (vicarious) victimhood. How can they write about these events and eventualities without wounding the grief of the survivors? How can the survivors be given their personal space to mourn while ensuring that the genocide is mourned collectively? Where is the place of agency in these literary works that claim to give "the victims/survivors a face and a name?"[27] What are the ethical considerations that undergird this African transnational memory project?

In *The Ethics of Memory*, Avishai Margalit writes that ethics tells us how to regulate our "thick relations" while morality tells us how to regulate our "thin relations." He also notes that the ethics of memory is based on both microethics (ethics of the individual) and macro-ethics (ethics of the collective).[28] Since I am thinking of the "Rwanda: Writing as a Duty to Remember" project as one founded on thick relations rather than thin relations, the question of ethics rather than morality becomes very crucial. With this in view, I focus on one of the books that came out of the project in order to understand the ethics of the representation of other people's pain. In this chapter, I examine Véronique Tadjo's *The Shadow of Imana* as a work of secondary witnessing. I investigate how the text enhances our understanding of the multiple frictions involved in ethical witnessing. I also examine the limits and experimental possibilities of genre in the production of narratives about an/other's traumatic experience. I interrogate how, in the book, Tadjo interpolates herself into the memory of the genocide, especially during her visits to specific memorial sites, and I question whether those acquired memories could be regarded as prosthetic. Since empathy is said to be at the center of ethical relations,[29] I read the traces and precariousness of empathy in the text; I also give attention to instances where the author shows empathy without necessarily appropriating the experiences of the victims. I conclude the chapter with the idea that the past continues through subject positions—whether that of the victim, perpetrator, or secondary witness. As Michel-Rolph Trouillot (cited in this chapter's epigraph) writes, the past—or, more accurately, pastness—is a position that is mediated through different subjectivities. Hence, in *The Shadow of Imana*, the Rwandan genocidal past is mediated through Tadjo's subject position as a secondary witness. In other words, despite witnessing from the position of exteriority, Tadjo encounters, quite intimately, the continuity of the genocidal terror within the Rwandan memoryscape.

Tadjo is a Pan-African writer to the core; in fact, some critics have labeled her works as a particular kind of literary Pan-Africanism.[30] While originally an Ivorian, Tadjo has lived in Kenya, Nigeria, and South Africa at different points in her life—and her experiences of living in different African countries no doubt informed some of the Pan-African ethos that she weaves into her writings. It was in this same Pan-African spirit that she agreed to take part in the "Rwanda: Writing as a Duty to Remember" project, which ultimately led to her writing *The Shadow of Imana*, a multidimensional chronicle of the quotidian post-genocide Rwandan life. In the book, Tadjo makes her position as a post-genocide outsider-witness clear from the start. This already-known revelation went a long way in the overall reception and interpretation of the book. She says:

> When talking about my text on the Rwandan genocide, I always stress the fact that I wrote it as an outsider. Not as a direct witness. I had no link with the country prior to my trip. Notwithstanding this, I thought that it was my duty not to confine myself to the borders of my national identity.[31]

Here, Tadjo not only reveals her subject position as an outsider-witness, but she also justifies this position (of exteriority) by the fact of her Pan-African inclinations. Writing about the aftermath of the genocide was not simply another "literary project" or a "mere memory formula" but something she genuinely saw as a duty toward remembering. The writing of *The Shadow of Imana*, therefore, corroborates the idea that postcolonial memory narratives are not autotelic; instead, they serve moral, ideological, political, and, in this case, mnemonic functions.

Tadjo's subject position is what scholars in various contexts refer to as secondary witnessing,[32] intellectual witnessing,[33] indirect witnessing,[34] visiting witness-ing,[35] artist mediation,[36] mediated witnessing,[37] and witnessing from a belated position.[38] While I prefer to think of Tadjo as a "witness from a reflexive distance," I retain the term "secondary witnessing" in my analysis because it is an all-encompassing label for those who fall outside the survivor/direct witness category and also because of the idea of seconding—*not firsthand, accompanying, belated*. As I will show later in this chapter, Tadjo's positioning within her book allows us to think of secondary witnessing as a sacred act of listening to, and being touched by, the traumatic experiences of others. She begins the book with a commentary on the Rwandan memoryscape on her very first visit:

> From a distance, the city seems to have forgotten everything, digested everything, swallowed everything....
>
> Traces of war are rare in the town but people's memories are teeming with poisoned images. The vast majority of people carry their pain silently in their souls and find the unbelievable strength to live daily life as it begins again....
>
> The truth is revealed in people's eyes. Words have so little value. You need to get under people's skins. See what is inside. (*Shadow*, 11)

The "distance" that Tadjo refers to in this statement is not only physical but also positional and analytic. At first she points attention to what most outsiders and first-time visitors see: a city rebuilding itself, a palimpsestic memoryscape and a people breaking away from the shackles of their past. However, as a reflective outsider, she tears down the veil of silence in order to excavate repressed memories and expose histories that are hidden in plain sight. As a way of "getting under people's skins," she interacts closely with survivors, visits prisons, witnesses court proceedings, and also visits memorial sites, especially Ntarama and Nyamata churches.

Despite all of these, one cannot but notice in the book a sense of tension in the way Tadjo tries (not) to immerse herself into a traumatic memory that she, on the one hand, dreaded and, on the other, did not have familial or national ties with. However, it is through the domain of affect and the realm of the incorporeal that she mediates and navigates the complex triangulation of experience, memory, and positionality. Hence, through different kinds of subcutaneous engagements with the post-genocide Rwandan memoryscape, we see in *The Shadow of Imana* how viscerality is intricately tied to the formation of subjectivity. This brings me to the next section of this chapter where I examine Tadjo's affective interactions with the sites of memory in Rwanda. I engage with Alison Landsberg's concept of "prosthetic memory"[39] in order to understand Tadjo's mediated and autobiographical—which should not be conflated with survivors'—memories of the genocide. While I hesitate to regard Tadjo's memories as prosthetic because of the artificiality implied in the meaning of the term, Landsberg's idea (which I elaborate on in the next section) provides some insights on how individuals become sutured into memories they do not have direct historical links with.

SITES AND SUTURES OF MEMORY: VÉRONIQUE TADJO'S AFFECTIVE ENCOUNTERS

Embedded within the global memory imperative is the idea that the borders of memory are continuously expanding to such an extent that identity groups and nation-states can no longer lay exclusive claims to the memory of events. Memory has become "a common property threaded through dispersed networks of association even if corporations and nations attempt to copyright the past."[40] In light of this, Alison Landsberg argues that memory is no longer linked to "organic" communities but becomes available for creative adaptation and sharing across identity categories. This kind of memory, which she describes as "prosthetic," emerges at "the interface between a person and a historical narrative about the past, at an experiential site such as a movie theater or museum."[41] Put simply, someone who has no direct historical connection to an event can be attached to its memories through artistic mediation and cultural technologies of memory. Therefore, as Landsberg explains, in the moment of contact or encounter with an/other's history, an experience occurs through which a person sutures himself or herself into that history which is not "naturally" their own. Prosthetic memory, by and large, explains how one personalizes or takes on a deeply felt memory of a past event that one has not lived through but eventually shapes one's subjectivity and politics.

While many of the literary works that came out of the "Rwanda: Writing as a Duty to Remember" project can be read as acts of deterritorialization (and Africanization) of the memory of the genocide, the project, in and of itself, was not burdened by the question of ownership (of memory) which seems to be Landsberg's main preoccupation. In other words, the project was more concerned with the possibility and potentiality of employing narratives in the service of memory for both Rwandans and Africans. Be that as it may, Landsberg's idea about how conditions must be created for ethical thinking when suturing oneself to an/other's memory resonates with the project. These conditions particularly ring through in Tadjo's text, especially in the way her authorial voice constantly negotiates between her situatedness within the genocidal space of memory and the need for the recognition of her own alterity.

According to Landsberg, an "experiential museum," among other mass media of memory, constructs arenas in which people may take on prosthetic memories. Following a Freudian logic, she describes these memory sites as "transferential spaces" where people gain access to "processual, sensuously immersed knowledge" of an/other's past. Also in transferential spaces, people acquire memories as bodily symptoms that, on the one hand, propel anamnestic solidarity with the dead and, on the other, open doors for transnational relations of solidarities. The Nyamata and Ntarama churches, among other "experiential" sites of memory, are the transferential spaces through which Tadjo became somatically sutured into Rwanda's genocidal past. It was in those spaces that she truly saw, deeply felt, and distressingly imagined the rawness and horror of the genocide. In view of this, she writes:

> When we went to Rwanda in 1998, the sites of genocide which we visited housed the remains of the dead as they had been found on location or around the buildings where the victims had taken refuge. Some bodies had also been disinterred. What was striking was the fact that the remains had been left untouched (hence, the title of Boubacar Boris Diop's novel, *Murambi, the Book of Bones*). They were sprayed with lime but, otherwise, were not protected from the public. It was possible to touch them.[42]

It is also worthy of note that the "display" of the dead bodies in Nyamata and Ntarama churches at this time occurred with little or less mediation. Hence, the two sites become not only a transferential space of memory but also a "traumascape" where the past is reactivated, resulting in the elicitation of a whole palette of emotions in the visitors.[43] Still on her visit to Nyamata Church, Tadjo describes the state of the body of Mukandori, a twenty-five-year-old woman who was brutally raped before being axed to death, in the following:

> Her wrists are bound, and tied to her ankles. Her legs are spread wide apart. Her body is lying on its side. She looks like an enormous fossilised foetus....
> She has been raped. A pickaxe has been forced into her vagina. (*Shadow*, 11)

This excerpt enhances our understanding of the concrete way in which Tadjo comes proximately close to the Rwandan genocidal past as well as how the experiential knowledge she acquires on the spot makes her a witness not only to the aftermath of the genocide but to the genocide itself. A reader who is not aware of the context with which Tadjo writes may easily think that she was right there when Mukandori was being axed to death. This experiential—yet unlived—relationship with the past allows for an uncanny recrudescing of peoples and places from the past. With Tadjo's experience of a "flattened time"[44] in these transferential spaces, it becomes understandably inevitable that she uses the present tense to describe Mukandori in order to reinforce the seeming immediacy of that experience. Hence, after passing through the Nyamata memorial, Tadjo writes:

> But these dead are screaming still. The chaos remains palpable. The events are too recent. This is not a memorial but death laid bare, exposed in all its rawness. (*Shadow*, 12)

The experience of "death laid bare" and the "rawness" of the mnemonic objects transport Tadjo—imaginatively—into a genocidal space that transcends the material present. As part of this uncanny re-experiencing of the past and flattening of time, she almost literally hears the "screaming" of those who died in the genocide. This experience, perhaps, is what inspired one of the sections of the book, titled "The Wrath of the Dead," in which Tadjo gives agency to the dead and imagines them voicing their grievances to the living. She also observes:

> The bones of the skeleton-corpses are disintegrating before our very eyes. The stench infects our nostrils and settles inside our lungs, contaminates our flesh, and infiltrates our brains. Even later on, far away, this smell will linger in our bodies and our minds. (*Shadow*, 12)

It is quite interesting that it is when Tadjo describes the disintegrated state of the dead bodies that we start to become cognizant of the affective intensities circulating between her and the memorial sites. Tadjo's soaked-in-the-moment experience and the tactility of the memorial objects evoke heavy visceral responses that, again, point to the complex interplay of memory, affect, and spatiality. She invokes visual, olfactory, auditory—and all sorts of organic—imagery to convey her labyrinthine bodily sensations and to show how her body keeps the score of these memories. These imageries also provoke readers to imagine the unimaginable magnitude of the spectacles of death that swept through Rwanda within the space of three months. Likewise, the fact that the smell of the memorials will remain on Tadjo's body and mind long after she may have left Rwanda corroborates the idea that mediated memories can become part of one's bodily archive of unlived experiences.

After her experience at Ntarama Church, Tadjo writes: "My stomach is knotted with hunger. I haven't eaten since this morning, but I can swallow nothing. I do not want to put anything into my stomach" (*Shadow*, 17). It is quite striking that the impact of Tadjo's unsettling experiences at the memorial sites is also felt in her appetite. Even though she is hungry, she does not want to eat anything after all that she has witnessed. This refusal to eat may be construed as an early symptom of secondary trauma arising from an intimate encounter with the horrifying exhibition of death. However, it is worth reiterating that the experience of secondary trauma does not translate to victimhood although, according to Dori Laub, a secondary witness can become a co-owner of a traumatic event.[45] While I will not be quick to describe Tadjo as a co-owner of the trauma of the genocide, she certainly shares in it by the fact of the traumatic affects that were stirred in her at Nyamata and Ntarama churches and also because of the way in which her embodied experience—as I will explain in a moment—eventually shaped her outlook on life.

While spaces of memory are highly affective, the degree of the affect (and effect) on outsiders depends partly on how they open themselves to be affected. In other words, two people experiencing a site of memory may be sutured unevenly into that memory.[46] This makes one wonder if Tadjo's adoptive memory of the genocide would necessarily be different from that of a random outsider (especially a Westerner). It also calls for a sustained reflection on Tadjo's outsider-ness in relation to the memory of the genocide. As already established, Tadjo is an outsider by the virtue of her nationality; in fact, she was initially overcome with anxieties as to whether her "Ivorian nationality would be an advantage or a death sentence" (*Shadow*, 8). However, while she is more of a national outsider, she is less of a cultural outsider. She recounts how she was mistaken for a Rwandan by the survivors on her first trip and how, coming from a politically volatile country, she finds the Rwandan experience relatable. For instance, at some point in her account, Tadjo says, "Yes, I went to Rwanda but Rwanda is also here in my country" (37). That is, she sees similar patterns of colonial ethnic division and murderous identity framing at the heart of genocide also in Cote d'Ivoire. She concludes: "Everything is so similar to my home that it breaks my heart" (38). In essence, the attempt to suture oneself into an/other's memory opens up avenues for memory relationality and allows outsiders to mediate their outsider experiences within the insider and intimate spaces of memory.

Similarly, on her first journey, while she was about to disembark from the plane, Tadjo experienced a feeling of dread because the Rwanda of her imagination was a place of "nightmare and primal fear" (*Shadow*, 3). However, she invoked the memory (of the loss) of her mother as an anchor. She writes, "I think of my mother. I cannot believe that she is gone. I feel her close to me. I feel her still present beside me. I have the impression that she is with me, that she is holding my hand on this journey in which I am bound to meet death" (6). In that regard, Tadjo digs through her own archive of experience and holds tenaciously onto the memory of her late mother as a strategy for dealing with the apocalypse of death that she is about to meet in Rwanda. Her personal memory of loss becomes the foundation for her capacity to empathize with the survivors of the genocide. Therefore, while indisputably an outsider-witness, she is—by virtue of her connection to Rwanda based on a sense of affiliation and affect—an insider too. She can even be said to be witnessing from an outsider-insider position by the fact of her blackness and African-ness. Because of her locational proximity to Rwanda, she most likely possesses stronger flashbulb memories of the genocide than most non-Africans.[47] In short, Tadjo is not a spectator; neither is she a random outsider. She is an outsider within,[48] a proximate other, and an outsider with a "thickened" relationship founded on Pan-African ethics.

Furthermore, to visit a museum or listen to survivors' stories does not necessarily imply an automatic acquisition of their memories. There is a difference between becoming aware of a past that one did not live through and putting on the memories of that past. To be knowledgeable about an event is not necessarily the same as having an implicit understanding of it. Put differently, there is a difference between having a head knowledge of an event and acquiring a tacit or immersive knowledge of it. After all, historians, academics, and journalists may be knowledgeable about an event without necessarily acquiring its memory. Acquiring memory, as we have seen even in Tadjo's case, is more about an affective relationship with the past, and it comes with a strong sense of obligation and responsibility. Hence, she writes that "to forget Rwanda after the sound and the fury was like being blind in one eye, voiceless, handicapped. It was to walk in darkness, feeling your way with outstretched arms to avoid colliding with the future" (*Shadow*, 3). Apart from the fact that this statement indicates the extent to which Tadjo has embodied the genocide memory (especially in the way she constructs amnesia as analogous to bodily impairment), it also gestures toward futurity. Forgetting or forgetfulness, Tadjo implies, is tantamount to avoidance of the future. Her memories of, and affective encounters at, the genocidal sites went a long way in informing her politics of "never again" as well as her continuous works (post-1998) toward deconstructing patterns of division and reconstructing a livable future for Africa and the world at large. *The Shadow of Imana*, therefore, is a book not only about the memory of a genocidal past but also about the memory of a non-genocidal future. Tadjo concludes *The Shadow of Imana* with the following statement:

> I have not recovered from Rwanda. Rwanda cannot be exorcised. Danger is ever-present, lurking in the memory. . . . We need to understand, to analyse the mechanisms of hatred, the words that create division, the deeds that put the seal on treason, the actions that unleash terror. We need to understand. Our humanity is in peril. (*Shadow*, 118)

In my curiosity to evaluate the impact of the genocidal sites on Tadjo, I asked her, in an interview, if the memories of the genocide sites are still very vivid and raw, just exactly as she experienced them twenty years ago. And here is what she says: "Yes, it's been a long time and yet, 20 years is nothing at the scale of a country. The consequences of the genocide in Rwanda are still present. . . . The memory of the genocide sites will never disappear. They are still vivid. It was a truth that I did not wish to discover. The remains of the Dead force you to face it."[49] My point so far is that Tadjo's encounters at Rwandan genocidal sites demonstrate how traumatic affects circulate incorporeally at experiential sites of memory. Likewise, from her response to my question, it is evident that the Rwandan genocidal past has become stored as an implicit somatic memory within her. This is what continues to fuel her moral injunction to be responsible with—and for—memory, especially in her literary works.

MEMORY AND POSITIONALITY: AESTHETICS OF SECONDARY WITNESSING IN *THE SHADOW OF IMANA*

Since Tadjo's position as a secondary witness has already been established, it becomes pertinent to examine how she stylistically weaves this position into her narrative and how her duty to remember is reflected in her aesthetic commitment. *The Shadow of Imana* has generated a lot of division among critics who are trying to figure out the best way to classify it. Different critics have read the book as a travelogue,[50] a work of investigative journalism,[51] a collection of reported testimonies,[52] and an autobiographical reflection.[53] While its literariness is not in doubt, *The Shadow of Imana* refuses genre pigeonholing. It employs a montage of genres (travelogue, history, journaling, reporting, fiction, poetry, literary testimony, feature writing, documentary, magical realism, and folklore, among others) and a pastiche of styles as a way of underscoring the aesthetic friction that often emerges from imagining and narrativizing (other people's) trauma. In fact, in response to critics' attempt at deciphering her book's genre, Tadjo says, "I see my books more as a text . . . pieces of writings whose genres are not easily defined."[54] While the undefinability of the book's genre, on the one hand, suggests an embrace of a postmodernist temper on the part of Tadjo, it also speaks more broadly to the tension inherent in witnessing from a position of exteriority. This is not to say that Tadjo's positionality is extremely unique, because, to a large extent, most writers and artists, by their very nature, occupy a complicated positionality with the site of memory or history they explore in their works. However, as I will show, Tadjo's position as a secondary witness is quite valuable because it provides readers with the opportunity to see the genocide in a remarkably unique light.

Tadjo, at some points, complicates her positionality by inserting herself into the stories in the book. She sometimes plots the narrative in a way that revolves around the context of her own life, although she does this with some sort of narrative (self)consciousness. For instance, as indicated earlier in this chapter, Tadjo draws parallels between the ethnic divisions in Rwanda and her home country, Ivory Coast. She even goes further to say:

> I am afraid when, in my country, I hear people talk of who belongs there and who doesn't. Creating division. Creating foreigners. Inventing the idea of rejection. (*Shadow*, 37)

Instead of taking the position of an aloof observer, this statement above shows Tadjo's attempt to bring herself closer to the events she narrates; she uses what she understands to make sense of what she does not. By immersing herself into the narrative, she slightly dims the focus on alterity and accentuates a common belonging to shared humanity—the very commonality that the genocide has attempted to destroy.[55] In essence, by suturing herself into the narrative, Tadjo merges personal memories with collective memories and makes intimate memories public and public memories intimate. That said, Tadjo not only writes herself into the narrative; she also eclipses herself from the narrative.[56] By eclipsing herself, she gives agency to the victims and survivors and allows them to speak for themselves so that readers may feel the texture of their interiority.

Literature as an intricate mode of meta-witnessing[57]—or what Thomas Trezise calls "witnessing witnessing"[58]—provides the avenue for negotiating the impossibility as well as the necessity of bearing witness to historical truths that lie outside the experience of the writer[59] which, no doubt, hinges on the work of imagination. Hence, in writing *The Shadow of Imana*, Tadjo not only imaginatively situates herself in the genocidal temporality and space, but she also uses the imagination to shape the characters along with Rwanda's genocide and post-genocide landscape. However, she acknowledges the limits of the imagination in grappling with the genocide as she writes that "our imagination will never be able to get anywhere close to the reality" of what happened (*Shadow*, 15). This point is very important because it would be a mistake to assume that an active work of the imagination is all it takes to understand what happened during the genocide. The imagination only creates a sense—or paints an approximate picture—of what happened; no outsider can have a complete understanding of the gravity of the horror. However, it is precisely this fraught negotiation between literature, memory, and imagination that birthed Tadjo's admittedly finite grasp of the genocide encapsulated in *The Shadow of Imana*. It is also what allows Tadjo, as a neutral yet reflexive observer, to empathically represent the subjective experiences of the survivors without overidentifying with them. It is what allows for a balance between an objective detachment from, and an empathetic understanding of, what happened in Rwanda in 1994.

Tadjo's empathic response to the memorial sites and to the overall genocide is not simply an experimental empathy or merely a compassionate listening and writing; it is an unsettling empathic response.[60] We find this *unsettling* in the way she asks herself many self-reflexive questions throughout the text. For example, she writes: "What would I have done if I had been caught up in the spiralling violence of the massacre? Would I have resisted betrayal? Would I have been cowardly or brave?" (*Shadow*, 37). It is by asking these hypothetical yet self-searching rhetorical questions that Tadjo is able to imaginatively suture herself into the memory of the genocide. It is in those moments when she asks herself these questions that the problem of positionality becomes a little less consequential.

In light of the foregoing, Dominick LaCapra explains that responding to histories of violence by an outsider usually takes two turns. The first is an objective or distant reconstruction of the past while the second is an unchecked identification with the victims.[61] These two responses are not very exemplary because the first (objective response) falters on the ground that the victims' subjectively experienced traumatic memory is ignored while the second (vicarious response) is also flawed because it ends in some sort of facile "surrogate victimhood."[62] In view of the inherent problems with these responses, LaCapra coined the term "empathic unsettlement" to account for the liminal position that balances out these two seemingly extreme responses. Part of being an empathically unsettled listener/observer is that one remains close but distant—or distant but close—at the same time. This situation is exactly what Tadjo tries to give expression to when she writes, "That's what life is all about, we can't get close to people without them getting into our lives whether we like it or not" (*Shadow*, 36). She makes this statement after an encounter with Nelly, a dying survivor of the genocide. Nelly shows Tadjo around her crowded house and introduces her to her sickly family. But instead of feeling sorry for Nelly, Tadjo feels unsettled by her own empathic identification. She rushes out of Nelly's house because she is discomfited by what she has just witnessed, but while on her way out, Nelly tells her, "Remember Nelly. When I die, you must come to my funeral." Tadjo—pondering on Nelly's words—writes: "I know *very well* why she says this" (*Shadow*, 71; emphasis mine). From this conversation, we see that it is only in that moment of unsettled emotions—and empathy—that Tadjo becomes aware of what Nelly must have been through. This sentiment is echoed by one of the characters in the book who, like Tadjo herself, has come to Rwanda for the purpose of understanding and writing about the genocide. This character, who is generically referred to as "the writer" in the book, remarks that "[*unsettling*] emotion[s] can help us to understand what the genocide actually was *like*" (26; emphasis mine).

As LaCapra writes, empathic unsettlement often "upsets narrative voice and counteract[s] harmonizing narration."[63] That is, in the process of finding a middle ground between a critical and an affective stance, empathic unsettlement allows for certain "stylistic effects" in trauma narratives. As I will show next, Tadjo, in *The Shadow of Imana*, employs certain techniques that sometimes embrace and other times violate aesthetic and positional distance. These (un)distancing effects and affects contribute to the immersion of the readers into the events presented in the text while also making clear the fact that the events are beyond understanding. *The Shadow of Imana* is divided into two parts: "First Journey" and "Second Journey," both of which detail Tadjo's two travels into the heart of Rwanda. Each part has subsections with independent titles, making the text a polyphonic narrative. Some of these subsections take the shape of travel writing or diary keeping, except that they are not dated. On that account, Hitchcott construes Tadjo as a female Black African tourist who enacts a reversal of the grand narratives of discovery that characterize colonial travelogues.[64] While Hitchcott's reading is an important one, it might be a little reductionist because Tadjo's book, as I have already established, blatantly rejects genre pigeonholing. Tadjo cannot simply be read as a tourist, because by doing so, we fall easily into the trap of "trauma tourism"—or what Marita Sturken calls "tourist of history"[65]—even when it is very glaring that Tadjo does not respond to memory's call with the consumerist logic that underpins the fetishistic allure of thanatourism. Of course, there is a journey motif in the book, but its purpose is to help us understand how traveling is, in and of itself, a mode of witnessing.

Furthermore, Tadjo employs stylistic techniques such as fragmentation, shifting points of view, a montage of genres, an alternation between past and present, and self-reflexivity among others in order to allow for manifold interpretations of the genocide. These strategies of representation employed by Tadjo foreground the idea that a one-size-fits-all approach is inadequate to narrate what happened in Rwanda. In addition, the multiplicity of perspectives and polyphony of voices employed in telling the post-genocide story challenge hegemonic and homogenous accounts of the genocide. They allow Tadjo to objectively tell complicated stories of women perpetrators, Hutu victims, and the hidden crimes of the Rwandan Patriotic Front (RPF) during the genocide. Put differently, in the effort to paint a complex rather than a simplistic picture of the genocide, Tadjo writes and sees through the gazes of different post-genocide subjects—victim, perpetrator, the complicit, and the bystander, among others. Placing the voices of these subject positions side by side within the text is what allows for a productive narrative friction. In other words, the ethical and positional tensions associated with writing about other people's traumatic experiences contributed to the production of Tadjo's sublimely disharmonious narrative. It is also what enables the book to effectively mediate public and private memories as well as official and vernacular histories in post-genocide Rwanda.

Although there are no photographs in the book, Tadjo's cinematographic depictions and sometimes vivid visual imageries lead to what Susan Sontag describes as "an assault on the sensibility of the viewer [that is, readers]."[66] Tadjo's poetic language forces us out of our imaginative lethargy, brings us out of our emotional distance, and takes us along on a journey of empathic commitment. In light of this, Tadjo writes, "Rwanda is inside me, in you, in all of us" (*Shadow*, 37). In another instance, she says to her implied and implicated readers, "What happened there concerned us all" (3). More so, as a way of sensitizing her readers and bringing them into an affective community of memory, Tadjo constantly pluralizes personal pronouns. For example, she writes (to her readers), "We must all bear responsibility for this humanitarian failure" (34). In that regard, Sontag instructs that the pronoun "we" should not be taken for granted when looking at other people's pain. Therefore, the "we" in Tadjo's text is an empathic call to co-witnessing, collective responsibility, and reparative humanism.[67]

Tadjo's constant questioning of her subject position as a non-Rwandan is reflected in the overall structure of the narrative. In some instances, she writes about the experiences of survivors in the form of a reported speech, while in other instances, she documents her dialogic exchanges with them. This self-reflexive style of writing also manifests in the way the structure of each story in the book questions its own existence and sustainability in representing the unrepresentable. For instance, one of the stories in the first part of the book is titled "The Writer." In this story, an anonymous writer whom I alluded to earlier reflects on the most appropriate narrative form as well as the limit of (the fictive) genre in representing the genocide. The writer is quoted as saying, "Genocide is evil incarnate. Its reality exceeds any fiction. How can one write without mentioning the genocide that took place?" (*Shadow*, 26). In another story, titled "The Journalist," we come across an anonymous journalist who writes a feature story (in the passive voice) on the genocide. In yet another story in the book, titled "In Kigali, They Tell the Following Story," Tadjo's authorial voice interjects in the form of a (rhetorical) question, asking, "Is this a true story?" (37). All of these instances point to the tension between fact and fiction in the text, but, in the end, what matters is neither the fact nor the fiction but the emotional truth and affective authenticity of the heterogeneous stories.

The truth of the genocide against the Tutsis is stranger than fiction, and its reality exceeds what may be chronicled in any literary text. Therefore, as a way of grappling with the incomprehensibility and strangeness of the genocide, Tadjo gives primacy to the everyday stories of ordinary lives in her book. Some of the titles of the stories in the book are reflective of these ordinary lives. For instance, in the book we find stories with titles such as "The Lawyer from Kigali," "Consolate's Story," "The Man with a Mask," and "Seth and Valentine." In light of this, Tadjo explains that when "faced with the incomprehensible nature of the genocide, the mind shuts down and re-opens when brought back to the reality of daily life and past normality."[68] Overall, *The Shadow of Imana* amplifies the mundanity of the everyday and mediates the technologies of survival among ordinary lives in post-genocide Rwanda as a way of providing a glimpse into the obscenity of the genocide.

Despite the perceived advantages, bearing witness from a position of exteriority as well as listening to firsthand witnesses' stories is not always an easy task. Tadjo's first and second journeys to Rwanda are daunting. In the book she paints the picture of the burden of secondary witnessing when she says, "Occasionally, someone will reveal a secret to you that you have not asked to know. Then you are crushed under a burden of knowledge too heavy to bear" (*Shadow*, 8). However, it is exactly this burden that enables her and her colleagues (the other writers who participated in the "Rwanda: Writing as Duty to Remember" project) to extend their emotional and imaginative identifications beyond the confines of the self. It is exactly the same burden that Tadjo hopes to pass along to her readers so that they stay committed to the *duty to remember*. Tadjo concludes her book with the fact that she can never exorcise Rwanda. She says, "I have not recovered from Rwanda. Rwanda cannot be exorcised" (118). Interestingly, she begins the book with the pressing need to "exorcise Rwanda" (3), but having gone through the disrupting yet immersive process of empathic unsettlement, she discovers that it is better to sit with the survivors and allow mourning to take its course because a traumatic experience of such magnitude often rejects closure. Moreover, she realizes that while she is incapable of exorcising Rwanda, she is at least able to contribute to keeping the memory alive so that such an event never happens again. In view of this, she writes, "To remember. To bear witness is what remains for us in our attempt to combat the past" (85) and "dismantle the cycle of violence"

(34). Here again we see how remembering or misremembering the past is always at stake in the production of the future.

As a secondary witness, Tadjo feels strongly about the continuity of the past in the present as she writes, "Today, the conflicts continue. Sporadic but regular incursions on the part of the Hutu rebels. Attacks on and counter-attacks by the government in power" (*Shadow*, 34). Some of the characters in the book express similar concerns. For example, a character by the name of Consolate, a genocide survivor, notes that post-genocide Rwanda feels like "an interminable exile" (28). Another genocide survivor in the book laments that "when the war ended, we thought that everything could, at last, go back to normal, that we could start again on a better foundation, not make the same mistake again. But after a few years, everything seems to be settling back into place: corruption, impunity, uncertainty" (110). In other words, while the world is quick to celebrate Rwanda's success story, Tadjo and the genocide survivors in her book think that history, instead of moving forward, "is going into reverse" (100); they believe that the past has not really passed. And they might just be right because in Rwanda today, mass graves are still being discovered,[69] there are still conflicts surrounding how the history of the genocide is taught,[70] the country is still fighting border wars with its neighbors,[71] there are still cases of politically motivated assassinations,[72] and there are concerns about the state's policing of how the memory of the genocide is remembered in the public sphere.[73] In addition, as Tadjo confirms in my interview with her, her memories of the genocide memorial sites are still very vivid—twenty years later—and they may never go away. This proves that it is possible to open oneself to be affected by other people's traumatic memories and, by so doing, one can become connected with an/other. Therefore, as Anna-Marie de Beer suggests, allowing oneself to be unsettled and transformed by other people's stories and memories is the ultimate form of listening and, in this case, secondary witnessing.[74]

In this chapter, I have illustrated the ethical dimension to the notion of African transnational memory through my reading of Tadjo's *The Shadow of Imana*. While this ethical consideration largely focuses on literary commemoration, it can also apply to the curation of an African transnational museum or memorial as well as other media of memory. As we have seen with the Rwandan case, most civil conflicts in postcolonial Africa spread beyond the border of the nation-state; therefore, we will benefit immensely from thinking transnationally about the questions of justice, rehabilitation, reconciliation, and, most importantly, commemoration. Additionally, with the marginal presence of the continent in the enunciations of global memory, projects such as "Rwanda: Writing as a Duty to Remember" give visibility to Africa's sites of memory and transnationalize its memory cultures. One can only hope that more of such memory projects and collaborations emerge on the continent.

CHAPTER 5

The Past Continues in the Future

We must have the courage to invent the future, all that comes from man's imagination is realizable.
 —Thomas Sankara, *Thomas Sankara Speaks: The Burkina Faso Revolution*

The past and the future are part of the same space-time continuum.
 —David Staley, "A History of the Future"

Imagining the future is just another kind of memory.
 —Julie Beck, "Imagining the Future Is Just Another Kind of Memory"

In *Continuous Pasts*, I have examined the representations of memory in post-conflict African literature. I have looked at how fiction expands our understanding of the workings of memory in the postcolony. While some of the texts proved immensely productive when placed in dialogue with existing memory theories, others invite a rethinking of these theories, especially in a postcolonial African context. It is therefore pertinent at this point to take one last look at the threads that bind these texts together at both thematic and stylistic levels—and to reflect, holistically, on what they altogether provoke or suggest about memory friction and politics in postcolonial Africa.

In a post-conflict culture of repression, African fiction acts as a solid ground for the subversion of political silences and the negotiation of traumatic memories. This is the case with *The Memory of Love*, a novel that embodies the different shades of silence in post-conflict Sierra Leone. However, this artistic subversion of silence often comes with a cost, as is the case with *Half of a Yellow Sun*, a novel that, after its publication, ignited a lot of debates in post-conflict Nigeria. Overall, the frictions that the post-conflict African fiction of memory generates on either the aesthetic or political level are useful because they keep memories alive, revive conversations about repressed pasts, inspire new ways of thinking about conflicted pasts, and demonstrate how polarized pasts can be reconciled. In the same vein, the aesthetic friction in the writing of *The Shadow of Imana* is what enables Tadjo to narrativize the other's trauma without necessarily becoming a surrogate victim; it is also what allows her readers to appreciably grasp memory's complicated relationship with positionality. Similarly, it is in Adichie's use of multiperspectivity, polyvocality, and all kinds of epitextuality in *Half of a Yellow Sun* that she is able to overcome the oxymoronic impossibility and possibility of witnessing from a transgenerational distance. Also in Forna's *The Memory of Love*, we encounter frictions in individual acts of remembering, especially in the character of Elias Cole whose complicitous remembering of the war opens up conversations about memory's inherent fictiveness and plasticity. It is also the friction generated by the contact between emigratory and immigratory memories that created the possibility of an African transnational memory network in Mengestu's *Children of the Revolution*.

Perhaps the clearest point brought to bear by the four primary texts considered in this book is how the past remains an unfinished business—and how that informs the continued negotiation of the meaning of post-conflict nationhood in Africa. In each text we witness the continued presence of the past in the shapes of silence (*The Memory of Love*), structures of migration (*Children of the Revolution*), intergenerational transmissions (*Half of a Yellow Sun*), and memorial sites (*The Shadow of Imana*). This continuity of the past is indicative of a postcolonial politics of mourning that is interminable and a post-conflict temporality that does not follow a linear progression. In light of this, Kai, in *The Memory of Love*, draws our attention to how the Sierra Leonean Civil War rages on in the lives of the survivors even when it has been officially declared to be over. He notes, "They say it's over but it is not over" (*TML*, 304). "They" in Kai's statement obviously refers to the government as well as outsiders—especially Westerners—who are quick to ascribe terminality to postcolonial conflicts in a way that is not often in tandem with survivors' experiences. Similarly, Tadjo, while in Kigali, observes that "from a distance, the city seems to have forgotten everything. . . . You need to get under people's skin to see what is inside" (*Shadows*, 11). In other words, the post-conflict fictions of memory examined in this book invite us to think critically about the reversal of history in most post-conflict contexts in Africa. They show how—from Nigeria to Ethiopia—the past cannot be said to be over when the conditions for conflict and patterns of violence remain unchanged.

Apart from the fact that post-conflict fictions of memory in Africa depict the connection between an interminable mourning politics and a nonlinear configuration of phenomenological time, they also suggest that by framing time as chronological, we run the risk of framing reconciliation as smooth and straightforward. Therefore, in the selected post-conflict fictions of memory in this book, we witness—and are invited to reflect on—the jaggedness of reconciliation in post-conflict situations in the postcolony. These fictions depict the friction between the pursuit of justice and the scramble for survival in post-conflict African countries. The writing of *Half of a Yellow Sun*, for example, functions as a postgenerational cry against the flagrant denial of justice for the muted victims of Biafra, fifty years later. Similarly, the characters in *The Memory of Love* strive for survival in lieu of justice because of the fear of the resurgence of violence and also because of the postwar neoliberal (political) economy that creates the impression that remembering is too much of a price to pay. In Mamakay's observation of post-conflict Sierra Leone, she notices how "people think war is the worst this country has ever seen [but] they have no idea what peace is like" (*TML*, 282). This statement challenges our assumptions about irenology in postcolonial Africa; it construes peace as a complex political condition and a fragile illusion. In essence, post-conflict fictions of memory in Africa complicate the idea of peace as a mitigation of conflict and propel us to rethink our peace-making strategies amid the continued resonances of violence on the continent.

It should be noted that while post-conflict fictions of memory in Africa provide a glimpse into how our relationship with the past in the postcolony is full of ruptures, they also gesture toward futurity. In other words, the post-conflict fictions of memory in Africa are invariably about the future. In my reading of all four texts, I notice two approaches to the discourse of futurity. The first is in the idea that the future in the postcolony is under siege—that is, the spectral presence of the past, layered with injustices in the present, prevents survivors and victims from aspiring to a future. In view of this, one of the survivors in *The Shadow of Imana* says:

> "How can we envisage a future here? What future? Tomorrow seems a long way off to me. Plan what? So much can happen so quickly. From one day to the next, you have to begin all over again. When the war ended, we thought everything could go back to normal, that we could start again on a better foundation. But after a few years, everything seems to be settling back into place: corruption, impunity, uncertainty. . . .
>
> It seems nothing is moving forward, that gradually everything is falling into oblivion." (*Shadow*, 110–11)

This statement, which establishes the problem of an arrested future in the postcolony, is equally flagged in *The Memory of Love* when the narrator says about one of the survivors, "He tries to imagine a future, somewhere past this point but he cannot" (*TML*, 417). These examples altogether suggest that imagining the future is a kind of luxury that many victims and survivors of historical violence in the postcolony cannot afford. The failure or inability to remember the past (as a result of either trauma or state repression) is invariably the failure or inability to imagine the future—hence, where there is no memory, there is no futurity because the future is just another kind of memory.

It is precisely this despairing disposition toward the future and the inability to be consoled by history that the authors of the selected texts try to confront by diving into the past. In other words, they—like the mythical Sankofa bird known for simultaneously looking backward while moving forward—cling to the promise of a future by embracing and reflecting on the past. For instance, it is in the spirit of fostering a reparative future and redeeming the time for Rwandans and Africans in general that Tadjo agreed to participate in the "Rwanda: Writing as a Duty to Remember" project. Therefore, while her text depicts people who struggle to embrace the promises of a livable future, Tadjo writes with the hope that her work will contribute to the dismantling of structures of violence and open up the possibility of a future devoid of genocidal terror. In the same vein, while many survivors of the Nigeria-Biafra War gave a fatalistic shrug at the future, Adichie uses her "privilege of distance" to write *Half of a Yellow Sun* with the hope that it will serve as a "small act of repair"[1] for the survivors and that a reconciliatory future in Nigeria can be imagined. I will be a little prescriptive at this point and argue that studies and stories about Africa's tumultuous pasts need to be more future-oriented. Africa's histories of violence need to be studied in a way that is forward-looking and taught in a way that opens up conversations on how patterns of violence can be disrupted. The memory of the future and the future of memory need to take the primal place in the study of the past in—and on—Africa because "the opposite of the past is not the future but the absence of the future. The opposite of the future is not the past but the absence of the past. The loss of one is equivalent to the sacrifice of the other."[2]

Furthermore, one of the issues that also stands out in all of the texts is the deeply colonial root of the civil conflicts in the postcolony. From the Rwandan genocide to the Sierra Leonean Civil War, we see the inheritance of problematic structures of governance that contributed to the making of wounded democracies in the postcolony. These violent legacies of colonialism spill over to—and are deeply felt by—the succeeding generation; hence, the so-called children of the postcolony find themselves returning compulsively to the archive of the colonial encounter in order to make sense of the conflicts in the postcolonial present. For example, in my reading of *Half of a Yellow Sun*, I show how Adichie faults the bequests of British colonialism, which, she says, is the main catalyst of the Nigeria-Biafra War. Véronique Tadjo, in *The Shadow of Imana*, also lays out the ways in which Belgian colonialism is the root cause of the Rwandan genocide.

In addition, post-conflict fictions of memory in Africa often present the entanglement of familial and national histories; they often illustrate how there is only a thin line between public and private memories. After all, Veenas Das notes that the story of a life enmeshed in violence is the story of the nation.[3] And this is the case with Dinaw Mengestu, who merges personal and national histories in *Children of the Revolution* in a way that gives the novel a semiautobiographical feel. The story of the communist revolution in Ethiopia becomes the story of Mengestu's family's fracturing. This is also the case with Aminatta Forna, who fictionalizes the interconnectedness of her father's politically motivated assassination and the collapse of her country in *The Memory of Love*. In a similar vein, the post-conflict fictions of memory examined in this book are, in the psychoanalytic sense, a result of the persistent attachment to lost objects. Because the authors are in most of these cases personally affected—and sometimes traumatized—by the violent histories they are writing about, there is some sort of compulsion to return to those histories again and again in their works. For example, as I have shown in chapter 1, Adichie has been writing about Biafra (in the form of a play, poetry, and short story) since she was sixteen. The same thing can be said of Aminatta Forna, who had earlier written a memoir about her father and his connection to the political conflicts in Sierra Leone before writing *The Memory of Love*. Dinaw Mengestu also keeps returning to the memory of the revolution in all of his three novels to date. This repetitive compulsion—which, as shown in all the chapters, is not clinical morbidity—points to the aporia of finding closure to the aftereffects of trauma at the individual level as well as the diabolical continuity of violence on a national level in post-conflict situations in the postcolony.

Therefore, as non-redemptive narratives, post-conflict fictions of memory in Africa present an idea of coming to terms with the past that includes an interconnected mode of both *acting out* and *working through*. The four texts analyzed in *Continuous Pasts* prove, beyond doubt, that the postcolonial African narrative is a work of mourning. In their unique ways, they constitute a form of textual mourning. Put differently, the texts do not simply mourn or invite their readers to mourn; they are, by their very nature, constitutive of the process of mourning. They are part of the rituals of postcolonial mourning and contribute to the archive of postcolonial griefs and grievances. They portray the inextricable link between cultures of mourning, modes of writing and complexities of witnessing. For example, *Children of the Revolution* is not simply replete with grieving subjects; it is, intrinsically, a melancholic text because of the soulful narrative voice, elegiac tone, and overall jeremiad narrative flow. The same thing can be said of *Half of a Yellow Sun* and *The Shadow of Imana*, both of which serve as a kind of literary commemoration of the dead victims of the Nigeria-Biafra War and the Rwandan genocide, respectively. Therefore, as a kind of textual mourning,[4] it is not unanticipated that there are several instances of ancestral veneration and anamnestic solidarity with the dead in all of the narratives. *The Shadow of Imana* is dedicated "to all of those who are gone but who remain forever in our heart" (*Shadow*, x) while *Half of a Yellow Sun* is dedicated to the memory of Adichie's grandparents "who did not survive the war" (*Half of a Yellow Sun*, ix). *The Memory of Love* equally illustrates how we live in the penumbra of our ancestors' time and space. The moments of silence in the novel become, subliminally, the characters' moments of connection with their ancestors, far removed in time and space. In addition, in *Children of the Revolution*, we find instances where Sepha is seen conversing with his deceased father. Likewise, in *The Shadow of Imana*, we find instances where the dead are communicating with the living. Drawing from all of this, I conclude that the analyzed texts in *Continuous Pasts* showcase an African culture of mourning that recognizes the strong link between the dead and the living; they also, invariably, become spectral narratives that speak about the dead in the present tense.

Furthermore, the texts examined in *Continuous Pasts* invite critical reflections on the question of memory and distance. They suggest that we all come to memory—or witness the past—from different vantage points. Whether one is witnessing from a transgenerational (*Half of a Yellow Sun*, *The Memory of Love*), migratory (*Children of the Revolution*), or an outsider (*The Shadow of Imana*) position, the texts establish the fact that writers always occupy a complicated position with the site of memory they explore in their works. They also suggest that the presence of the past is felt not only by the participants in a traumatic event but that it can also be felt by outsiders and postgenerational witnesses. Distance—either critical, aesthetic, or positional—is very important in memory discourses because, in most cases, the imperative to bear witness could not be met during the actual occurrence of the traumatic event. Hence, with Adichie's privilege of distance, she is able to interrogate and demystify Biafra. In the same vein, Tadjo's distance as an outsider becomes quite advantageous because it enables the readers to see the genocide in a remarkably unique light. By the virtue of the complicated positionality these writers occupy, writing itself becomes an act of witnessing. For instance, as I have shown in chapter 1, it is in the writing and shaping of characters that Adichie really began to gain an affective knowledge of what happened in Biafra. Similarly, it is by writing *The Shadow of Imana* that Tadjo gets to grapple with the obscenity of understanding what happened in Rwanda. This entanglement of writing and witnessing makes the place of imagination in memory work even more crucial. As I have shown, Adichie had to put her imagination to work in order to recreate and reanimate the cultural signatures and daily lives in 1960s Nigeria. Tadjo also had to tap into the power of imagination so that the Rwandan memorial sites could come alive to her and her readers. Similarly, it is through imagination that Mengestu is able to find the courage to "go back and recreate what I don't know."[5] All of these, again, establish the importance of imagination in the work of memory. However, as shown in chapter 4, the imagination does have its limits when it comes to the portrayal of extremely traumatic events. Hence, it is when historicity is integrated into—instead of replacing—the work of imagination that writers are able to escape the trap of romanticizing memory and are able to deliver emotional truths about the past.

The question of witnessing and positionality, as presented in the selected texts, gives a nod to Caruth's statement that history—as well as memory—is never fully one's own but is precisely the way we are implicated in each other's trauma.[6] The post-conflict fictions of memory examined in this book invite unbounded readings of the sites of memory that they (re)present; they allow readers to stretch their imagination to various zones of relationality in Africa's post-conflict situations. To put it another way, while most post-conflict fictions of memory in Africa are put to the service of nation-building, they are not restrained by national and cultural boundaries. For instance, while a text like *Half of a Yellow Sun* invites a multidirectional way of thinking about the memory of the Nigeria-Biafra War (especially in the way it makes references to European colonialism and the Holocaust), *The Shadow of Imana* invites an African transnational reading of the Rwandan genocide. Likewise,

Children of the Revolution narrates the entanglement of America with the Ethiopian communist revolution as well as the relationality[7] of traumatic experiences/memories in a migratory setting. In other words, post-conflict fictions of memory in Africa are not insular, they are multi-scalar; they carry the potential for transnational and transcultural engagements.

Post-conflict fictions of memory in Africa create, in different ways, the space for imagining an African transnational memory imperative. For example, *The Shadow of Imana*, as I already mentioned, demonstrates the significance of the genocide in Africa's—not only Rwanda's—postcolonial memory. The "Rwanda: Writing as Duty to Remember" project itself promotes an African way of commemorating and mourning the genocide. This same African transnational mode of remembering (albeit in a migratory setting) is replicated in *Children of the Revolution*, where Sepha and his friends (Kenneth the Kenya and Joseph from Congo) form a habit of remembering Africa's violent histories in Washington, DC. While all the texts formulate different ways of thinking about a collective African memory archive, more thoughts still need to be given to the circulation of memory practices, cultures and institutions across national and cultural formations within the continent. This, as I have argued, will help to challenge the politics of memory that, in the name of globalization, universalizes memory cultures and positions certain memories at the margin. An African transnational memory culture will enhance the distribution of concrete structures of solidarity among Africans and also foster a collective effort at breaking the cycle of sociopolitical violence on the continent. In all, the texts studied in *Continuous Pasts* propel us to imagine how an African transnational memory imperative has the potential to unite African people and how it opens new epistemological and methodological possibilities in the study of memory in Africa.

Additionally, the texts studied in *Continuous Pasts* suggest that memory in the postcolony could be thought of as not simply the memory of a single event but also as an interconnected chain of events. For example, *Half of Yellow Sun* shows how the memory of the Nigeria-Biafra War cannot be divorced from the memory of colonialism and how colonial domination itself is a resultant effect of the transatlantic slave trade. *The Memory of Love* also suggests how the postwar silence in Sierra Leone could be traced back to centuries of violence that had taken place in the country. Therefore, considering the many histories of violence in the postcolony, we could think of the memories of slavery, colonialism, and post-independence wars as concatenated rather than differentiated or individuated. In other words, the postcolonial topography and body politic are constituted by an accumulation of histories and a layering of memories. African post-conflict fiction embodies a palimpsestic assemblage of histories and re-presents a repository of memories that academic historiography might be incapable of capturing all at once.

This book has only begun to scratch the surface of the depth of insights that postcolonial narratives have to offer on issues relating to memory. One aspect that I touched on but did not sustainedly explore in this book is the question of gender and memory in post-conflict Africa. This question is important because of the way some of the political conflicts on the continent are framed using a masculinist language and logic while, in the wake of such conflicts, it is mostly the women (as some of the selected texts reveal) who bear the burden of memory.[8] In addition, while postcolonial narratives present an understanding of a postcolonial formation that is posttraumatic, there is the need to exercise caution against the fetishization of suffering in our engagements with these narratives. After all, there is abounding study and evidence of resilience, hope, recovery, and posttraumatic growth in some of these narratives too.[9] Nonetheless, based on the findings from this book, it is safe to conclude that post-conflict fiction of memory in Africa funeralizes the dead, especially in situations where dead bodies are absent, missing, and, as a result, are not given a proper wake. They give the impression that memory-making processes in post-conflict African societies are still ongoing; the past, just as the future, is still under construction. They also depict a calibration of time that is based on a structure of mourning—a time of/in the wake.

In *Continuous Pasts*, I have managed to provide different conceptual apparatuses for thinking about memory in African post-conflict fiction. I have also shown the different kinds of frictions of memory that these fictions portray at the political and aesthetic levels. While I borrowed from established memory theories in my readings, I also focused on the ways in which post-conflict African fiction rejects such theories and, in turn, attracts alter/native reading methods. I showed how memory in the postcolony is transnational, transcultural, transgenerational, and transpersonal. I also explored how post-conflict African fiction promotes a notion of memory that is about being with the dead as well as how it invites a reading of memory as a kind of concatenation. Overall, in this book I have shown how post-conflict fictions of memory in Africa demonstrate the idea that the past is not only present but also continuous, threateningly rolling into the future.

NOTES

INTRODUCTION

1. Theodore W. Adorno, *Negative Dialectics*, 2004.
2. Richard Werbner, "Beyond Oblivion: Confronting Memory Crisis," 1998.
3. In the essay, "Forms of Forgetting," Aleida Assmann describes mnemocide as the act of "killing" the memory of an individual or a collective. Assman, "Forms of Forgetting," 2016.
4. Richard Werbner, "Beyond Oblivion," 1998, 7.
5. Michael Rothberg, *The Implicated Subject: Beyond Victims and Perpetrators*, 2019.
6. Errol A. Henderson, "When States Implode: The Correlates of Africa's Civil Wars, 1950–92," 2000.
7. Achille Mbembe, *On the Postcolony*, 2001, 62.
8. Terry Eagleton, *The Ideology of the Aesthetic*, 1990, 381.
9. Zoe Norridge, *Perceiving Pain in African Literature*, 2013.
10. Emeka Joseph Nwankwo, "White Eyes," 2020. Also see Oduor Oduku. "Poverty Porn: A New Prison for African Writers," 2017.
11. The year 2021, for example, has been declared the year of African Literature because the major literary prizes around the world (Nobel Prize, Booker Prize, International Booker Prize for Translated Novel, Jhalak Prize, PEN Pinter Prize, Prix Goncourt, Neustadt International Prize for Literature, and Prémio Camões, among others) went to African writers.
12. Andreas Huyssen, *Present Pasts: Urban Palimpsest and the Politics of Memory*, 2003, 22.
13. Jeffrey K. Olick, "Collective Memory: The Two Cultures," 1999, 338.
14. Maurice Halbwachs, *On Collective Memory*, 1992.
15. Pierre Nora, *Realms of Memory: Rethinking the French Past*, 1992.
16. Jan Assmann, "Communicative and Cultural Memory," 2008, 112.
17. Daniel Levy and Natan Sznaider, "Memory Unbound: The Holocaust and the Formation of Cosmopolitan Memory," 2002.
18. Alison Landsberg, *Prosthetic Memory: The Transformation of American Remembrance in the Age of Mass Culture*, 2004.

19. Michael Rothberg, *Multidirectional Memory: Remembering the Holocaust in the Age of Decolonization*, 2009.

20. Astrid Erll, "Travelling Memory," 2011.

21. Max Silverman, *Palimpsestic Memory: The Holocaust and Colonialism in French and Francophone Fiction and Film*, 2013.

22. Chiara De Cesari and Ann Rigney, *Transnational Memory: Circulation, Articulation, Scales*, 2014.

23. Anna Cento Bull and Hans Lauge Hansen, "On Agonistic Memory," 2016.

24. Anna Reading, "Memory and Digital Media: Six Dynamics of the Globital Memory," 2011.

25. Lucy Bond, Ben De Bruyn, and Jessica Rapson, *Planetary Memory in Contemporary American Fiction*, 2018.

26. While recent memory concepts and theories are reflective of the transculturality of memory, Astrid Erll argues that transcultural remembering actually goes way back. She notes that memory as a transcultural process has a long genealogy and that since ancient times, the content, forms, and technologies of memory have crossed the boundaries of time, space and social groups. Erll, "Travelling Memory."

27. Michael Rothberg, "Remembering Back: Cultural Memory, Colonial Legacies, and Postcolonial Studies," 2013, 5.

28. Frantz Fanon, *The Wretched of the Earth*, 1963, 98.

29. My idea of the "coloniality of memory" draws from Anibal Quijano's idea of the coloniality of knowledge, which is part of his broader theorization of the coloniality for power. Quijano sees the Western knowledge system as hegemonic and, as a result, critiques Eurocentric forms of knowing and exposes how the legacies of colonialism recalcitrantly survive within the domains of knowledge and knowledge production. Therefore, the coloniality of memory involves the ways in which colonialism erases the pasts of colonized people as well as how critical memory studies reproduces this colonial erasure through its existing theories, epistemologies, and methodologies. See Quijano, "Coloniality of Power and Eurocentrism in Latin America," 2000.

30. Sandra Greene, *West African Narratives of Slavery: Texts from Late Nineteenth- and Early Twentieth-Century Ghana*, 2011; Pumla Gqola, *What Is Slavery to Me? Postcolonial/Slave Memory in Post-Apartheid South Africa*, 2010.

31. V. Y. Mudimbe, *The Invention of Africa*, 1988; Richard Reid, "Past and Presentism: The Pre-Colonial and the Foreshortening of African History," 2011.

32. Walter Rodney, *How Europe Underdeveloped Africa*, 1972; Basil Davidson, *The African Past: Chronicles from Antiquity to Modern Times*, 1964; Mahmood Mamdani, *Citizen and Subject: Contemporary Africa and the Legacy of Late Colonialism*, 1996.

33. Frantz Fanon, *Toward the African Revolution*, 1964; Aimé Césaire, *Discourse on Colonialism*, 1953; Amilcar Cabral, *Return to the Sources*, 1973.

34. Premesh Lalu, *The Deaths of Hintsa: Postapartheid South Africa and the Shape of Recurring Pasts*, 2009.

35. Mbembe, *On the Postcolony*; Ngugi wa Thiong'o, *Decolonising the Mind*, 1986.

36. See Rick Crownshaw, *Transcultural Memory*, 2014; Jessica Rapson and Lucy Bond, *The Transcultural Turn: Interrogating Memory Between and Beyond Borders*, 2014.

37. The massive brain drain in Africa in the 1980s was mostly because of political instability and economic drought. See Colin I. Legum et al., *Africa in the 1980s: A Continent in Crisis*, 1979.

38. Rothberg, "Remembering Back," 359–79.

39. One prominent example of the works in postcolonial memory studies is an edited volume titled *Memory and Postcolonial Studies: Synergies and New Directions*, edited by Dirk Gottsche (2020). Richard Werbner's edited volume *Memory and the Postcolony* (1998) is another example. There is also Alec G. Hargreaves, *Memory, Empire, and Postcolonialism*, 2005.

40. There are so many examples to cite here. One could think of Paul Gilroy, *Postcolonial Melancholia*, 2005, which details Britain's struggle to deal with its imperial past. Another example is Brita Schilling, *Postcolonial Germany: Memories of Empire in a Decolonized Nation*, 2014, which focuses on the collective memory of German colonialism as well as the legacies of colonialism on Germany itself. Other examples include Paul Silverstein, *Postcolonial France: Race, Islam, and the Future of the Republic*, 2018; Étienne Achille et al., *Postcolonial Realms of Memory: Sites and Symbols in Modern France*, 2020; Gert Oostinie, *Postcolonial Netherlands: Sixty-Five Years of Forgetting, Commemorating, and Silencing*, 2011; Lars Jensen, *Postcolonial Denmark: Nation Narration in a Crisis Ridden Europe*, 2018; Goddeeris Idesbald, *Postcolonial Belgium: The Memory of the Congo*, 2015; and Cristian Lombardi-Diop and Caterina Romeo, *Postcolonial Italy: Challenging National Homogeneity*, 2012. There is even a whole journal by the name *Postcolonial Europe*.

41. There are so many examples to mention here. In fact, major memory conferences, debates, and lectures in the past few years have been about this subject. Because of the constraint of space, I will mention just two notable works here. First is Kristen Chick and Ryan Brown, "Art of the Steal: European Museums Wrestle with Returning African Art," 2019, and second is Claire Wintle, "Decolonizing the Museum: The Case of the Imperial and Commonwealth Institute," 2013. One might as well add Ann Rigney, "Why Monuments Matter (And When They Don't)," 2020.

42. Dipesh Chakraborty, "Postcoloniality and the Artifice of History: Who Speaks for 'Indian' Pasts?," 1992, 12.

43. David Scott, *Omens of Adversity: Tragedy, Time, Memory, and Justice*, 2013.

44. The use of the term "postcolonial" in context of this book refers to both a political/theoretical discourse of European colonial rule in Africa as well as the period following colonialism on the continent.

45. Gottsche, *Memory and Postcolonial Studies*, 12.

46. Filip De Boeck, "Beyond the Grave: Death, Body, and Memory in Postcolonial Congo/Zaire," 1998, 23.

47. Mahmood Mamdani, *Neither Settler nor Native: The Making and Unmaking of Permanent Minorities*, 2020.

48. Frantz Fanon, *Black Skin, White Masks*, 1952, 30.

49. The phrase is borrowed from Han Ruin, *Being with the Dead: Burial, Ancestral Politics and the Roots of Historical Consciousness*, 2019.

50. Sam Durrant, *Postcolonial Narrative and the Work of Mourning*, 2004.

51. Berber Bevernage, *History, Memory, and State-Sponsored Violence: Time and Justice*, 2012, 19.

52. Mamadou Diawara, Bernard Lategan, and Jorn Rusen, eds., *Historical Memory in Africa: Dealing with the Past, Reaching for the Future in an Intercultural Context*, 2010, 17.

53. See Rolf J. Kleber et al., *Beyond Trauma: Cultural and Societal Dynamics*, 1995. See Ann Rigney, "Remembering Hope: Transnational Activism beyond the Traumatic," 2018. See Tea Sinbaek Andersen and Jessica Ortner, "Memories of Joy," 2019; and Wulf Kansteiner, "Testing the Limits of Trauma," 2014.

54. For a discussion on postcolonial trauma, see Stef Craps, *Postcolonial Witnessing: Trauma Out of Bounds*, 2013.

55. Here, I draw from the work of Dominick LaCapra, who also draws from Freud's original ideas about mourning (working through) and melancholia (acting out). He notes, unlike Freud, that mourning and melancholia are two sides of the same coin. And that a more productive approach to thinking about collective memory and trauma is not to see acting out (melancholia) as a different kind of memory from working through (mourning) because they are intimately related part of the same process. See Dominick LaCapra, *Writing History, Writing Trauma*, 2001.

56. Durrant, *Postcolonial Narrative*.

57. Christina Sharpe, *In the Wake: On Blackness and Being*, 2016.

58. Avery Gordon, *Ghostly Matters*, 1997, 13.

59. Ogaga Ifowodo, *History, Trauma, and Healing in Postcolonial Narratives: Reconstructing Identities*, 2013.

60. D. Scott, *Omens of Adversity*.

61. D. Scott, *Omens of Adversity*, 15.

62. Rothberg, "Remembering Back."

63. Mbembe, *On the Postcolony*.

64. Walter Benjamin, "Theses on the Philosophy of History," 1968.

65. Jacques Derrida, *Spectres of Marx: The State of the Debt, the Work of Mourning, and the New International*, 1994.

66. Adorno, *Negative Dialectics*.

67. Huyssen, *Present Pasts*.

68. Luc Huyse, *All Things Pass, Except the Past*, 2009.

69. David Scott, "Black Futurities," 2018.

70. Ian Baucom, *Spectres of the Atlantic: Finance Capital, Slavery, and the Philosophy of History*, 2005.

71. Nora, *Realms of Memory*.

72. Benedict Anderson, *Imagined Communities. Reflections on the Origins and Spread of Nationalism*, 1983.

73. Mahmood Mamdani, *When Victims Become Killers. Colonialism, Nativism, and the Genocide in Rwanda*, 2001, 21.
74. Avishai Margalit, *The Ethics of Memory*, 2002.
75. Astrid Erll, "Regional Integration and (trans)Cultural Memory," 2010.
76. Erll, "Regional Integration," 312.
77. In their seminal book, *The Empire Writes Back: Theory and Practice in Postcolonial Literatures*, Bill Ashroft, Gareth Griffiths, and Helen Tiffin argue that writers and scholars from postcolonial countries are often engaged in the act of "writing back" to the colonial center. By this, they mean that postcolonial writers do not "write for" but "write against" the underlying assumptions of colonial discourses about colonized subjects. In other words, the trope of "writing back" in postcolonial literature is a subversive tool for questioning and revising problematic, hegemonic—and even racist—representations of the subjectivity of the colonized in colonial discourses. See Ashcroft, Griffiths, and Tiffin, *The Empire Writes Back: Theory and Practice in Postcolonial Literatures*, 1989.
78. Astrid Erll, *Memory in Culture*, 2011, 13.
79. Renate Lachmann, *Memory and Literature*, 1997.
80. Lachmann, *Memory and Literature*, 15.
81. See Erll, *Memory in Culture*, 13.
82. Erll, *Memory in Culture*, 25.
83. Ansgar Nünning, *Fictions of Memory*, 2003.
84. Cited in Chris Lorenz and Berber Bevernage, *Breaking Up Time: Negotiating the Borders between Present, Past, and Future*, 2013.
85. The works of Elizabeth Loftus and Daniel Schacter come to mind here. See Loftus, "The Fiction of Memory," 2013; and Schacter, *The Seven Sins of Memory: How the Mind Forgets and Remembers*, 2001. Sigmund Freud, in "Screen Memories" also argues that people unconsciously construct things in their memory, almost like the way we construct works of fiction. He notes that "there is in general no guarantee of the data produced by our memory." Freud, "Screen Memories," 1898/1953, 314.
86. Toni Morrison, "The Site of Memory," 1995.
87. Erll, *Memory in Culture*, 19.
88. Eleni Coundouriotis, *The People's Right to the Novel: War Fiction in the Postcolony*, 2014.
89. Antagonistic memory promotes antagonism among groups; it presents a past that causes a moral struggle between "us" and "them," where "them" is an enemy to overcome. On the other hand, agonistic memory rejects a single narrative about the past; it allows for different interpretations of the past as a step toward reconciliation. For more, see Bull and Hansen's "On Agonistic Memory."
90. Leela Gandhi, *Postcolonial Theory: A Critical Introduction*, 1998, 4.
91. Werbner, "Beyond Oblivion," 1998, 12.
92. Susan Andrade, *The Nation Writ Small: African Fictions and Feminisms, 1958–1988*, 2010, 1.
93. Harry Garuba, "The Unbearable Lightness of Being: Re-Figuring Trends in Recent Nigerian Poetry," 2005.

94. D. Scott, *Omens of Adversity*, 13.
95. Chris Ouma, *Childhood in Contemporary Diasporic African Literature*, 2020, 14.
96. Abdourahman Waberi, "Les enfants de la postcolonie: Esquisse d'une nouvelle génération d'écrivains francophones d'Afrique noire," 1998.
97. Dominic Thomas, "New Voices, Emerging Themes," 2010, 229.
98. F. Abiola Irele, "Perspectives on the African Novel," 2010, 4.
99. Anna Tsing, *Friction: An Ethnography of Global Connections*, 2004, 3.
100. Eileen Julien, "The Extroverted African Novel," 2006.
101. Olivia Laing, "Dream Catcher: A Review of *Children of the Revolution*," 2007.
102. Julia Creet, *Memory and Migration: Multidisciplinary Approaches to Memory Studies*, 2011.
103. Saidiya Hartman, *Scenes of Subjection: Terror, Slavery, and Self-Making in Eighteenth-Century America*, 1997, 11.
104. Mbembe, *On the Postcolony*, 12.
105. Paul Ricoeur, *Memory, History, Forgetting*, 2000.

1. THE PAST IS A CONTESTED TERRITORY

1. A. Dirk Moses and Lasse Heerten, *Postcolonial Conflict and the Question of Genocide: The Nigeria-Biafra War*, 2017.
2. In Paul Connerton's essay "Seven Types of Forgetting," he talks about forgetting as repressive erasure, which (totalitarian) governments use to cover up a scandalous past or deny a historical rupture. Connerton, "Seven Types of Forgetting," 2008.
3. Chimamanda Adichie, "Hiding from Our Past," 2014.
4. Pius Adesanmi and Chris Dutton, "Nigeria's Third Generation Writing: Historiography and Preliminary Theoretical Considerations," 2005.
5. Pius Adesanmi and Chris Dutton, "Introduction. Everything Good Is Raining: Provisional Notes on the Nigerian Novel of the Third Generation," 2008, viii.
6. Emmanuel Ngwira, "He Writes about the World That Remained Silent," 2012; Chris Ouma, *Childhood in Contemporary Diasporic African Literature*, 2020; Aghogho Akpome, "Focalisation and Polyvocality in Chimamanda Ngozi Adichie's *Half of a Yellow Sun*," 2013; Aghogho Akpome, "Intertextuality and Influence: Chinua Achebe's *Anthills of the Savannah* and Chimamanda Adichie's *Half of a Yellow Sun*," 2017; Heather Hewett, "Coming of Age: Chimamanda Ngozi Adichie and the Voice of the Third Generation," 2005; John Hawley, "Biafra as Heritage and Symbol: Adichie, Mbachau and Iweala," 2008.
7. "100 Notable Books of the Year," *New York Times*, December 4, 2005, https://archive.nytimes.com/www.nytimes.com/ref/books/review/20061203notable-books.html
8. "The 100 Best Books of the 21st Century," *The Guardian*, September 21, 2019, https://www.theguardian.com/books/2019/sep/21/best-books-of-the-21st-century/
9. "BBC Panel Aims to Spark Debate on the Novels That Shaped Our World with the Reveal of Their 100 Page-turners," BBC, November 5, 2019, https://www.bbc.co.uk/mediacentre/latestnews/2019/100-novels/

10. *Half of a Yellow Sun*, dir. Biyi Bandele, Slate Films and Shareman Media, 2013.

11. Chris Ouma, *Childhood in Contemporary Diasporic African Literature*, 2020; Olaoluwa Senayon, "Synmemory: Civil War Victimhood and the Balance of Tales in Adichie's *Half of a Yellow Sun* and Habila's *Measuring Time*", 2017.

12. Since I will be using the word "repair" a lot in this chapter, it is pertinent to provide a conceptual clarification from the outset. Repair on a national level, in my opinion, suggests a kind of ethico-political duty on the part of the Nigerian government to right the wrongs of the past (which may begin with a public acknowledgment of the enormous scale of violence brought on Biafra). But more importantly for this paper, repair as a postmemorial charge is more of a personal and psychic need. Marianne Hirsch and Leo Spitzer, drawing from the works of Melanie Klein, suggest that repair can be viewed as a psychoanalytic concept, an intrapsychic process of restoration. Accordingly, a reparative effort is more or less a kind of mourning, enabling one to work through a sense of loss. That said, the psychic need for repair can significantly inflect political needs for reparations. See Hirsch and Spitzer, "Small Acts of Repair: The Unclaimed Legacy of the Romanian Holocaust," 2016.

13. Dominick LaCapra, *Writing History, Writing Trauma*, 2001; Abraham and Torok, *The Shell and the Kernel: Renewals of Psychonanalysis*, 1994; Ellen Fine, "The Absent Memory: The Act of Writing in Post-Holocaust French Literature," 1998; Alison Landsberg, *Prosthetic Memory: The Transformation of American Remembrance in the Age of Mass Culture*, 2004; Henri Raczymow, "Memory Shot through with Holes," 1994; Pumla Gobodo-Madikizela, "Interrupting Cycles of Repetition," 2016.

14. Sigmund Freud, "Remembering, Repeating, and Working-Through," 1937/2001, 309.

15. W. G. Sebald, *On the Natural History of Destruction*, 1999.

16. Martha Minow, "Foreword," in *Memory, Narrative, and Forgiveness: Perspectives on the Unfinished Journeys of the Past*, 2009, 7.

17. Marianne Hirsch, "The Generation of Postmemory," 2008, 103.

18. Hirsch, "Generation of Postmemory," 105.

19. Marianne Hirsch, *Family Frames: Photography, Narrative, and Postmemory*, 1997, 22.

20. Ernst van Alphen, "Second-Generation Testimony, Transmission of Trauma, and Postmemory," 2006; Gary Weissman, *Fantasies of Witnessing: Postwar Efforts to Experience the Holocaust*, 2004; Guy Beiner, "Probing the Boundaries of Irish Memory: From Postmemory to Prememory and Back," 2014; Liz Stanley, *Mourning Becomes . . . Post/memory and Commemoration of the Concentration Camps of the South African War 1899–1902*, 2006.

21. Beiner, "Probing the Boundaries."

22. Stanley, *Mourning Becomes*.

23. Hirsch notes that postmemory is not limited to "the intimate embodied space of the family" but can be extended to "more distant, adoptive witnesses or affiliative contemporaries." Hirsch, "Generation of Postmemory," 105.

24. Lucy Bond, Stef Craps, and Pieter Vermeulen, "Introduction." In *Memory Unbound: Tracing the Dynamics of Memory Studies*, 2016, 11.

25. See Toni Morrison, 2014, "Toni Morrison Talks to Peter Florence on *Beloved*," https://www.youtube.com/watch?v=vtJFK_HtlQk

26. Marianne Hirsch, "Maternity and Rememory: Toni Morrison's *Beloved*," 1994, 94.

27. Chimamanda Adichie, "The Story behind the Book," *Half of a Yellow Sun*, 2006, 440.

28. Chimamanda Adichie, "Hard talk," 2014, https://www.youtube.com/watch?v=EsWfm0_xgkc

29. Jan Assmann makes a distinction between communicative and cultural memory. Communicative memory is the memory of a survivor passed down to the next generation mainly through the family. It comes about by daily interaction in the family. Cultural memory refers to institutionalized memories, which can be stored, transferred, and reincorporated across generations. It is formed by symbolic heritage embodied in texts, rites, monuments, celebrations, objects, sacred scriptures, and other media that serve as mnemonic triggers to initiate meanings associated the past. See J. Assmann, "Communicative and Cultural Memory," 2008, 109–88.

30. Chimamanda Adichie, "We Remember Differently," 2012.

31. Chimamanda Adichie, "The Right to Tell Your Story," 2013.

32. Chimamanda Adichie, "Conversation on Humanizing History with Ellah Allfrey," 2013.

33. Chimamanda Adichie, "African 'Authenticity' and the Biafran Experience," 2008, 44.

34. Adichie, "Conversation on Humanizing History."

35. Hirsch distinguishes between "familial" and "affiliative" postmemory. While the former describes the vertical transmission of traumatic events directly from parents to children, the latter is a horizontal transmission from the children of survivors to those of their generation who might also be oblivious of the past. Consequently, affiliative postmemory helps members of the "postgeneration connect with other members of the same postgeneration." See Hirsch, "Generation of Postmemory," 114.

36. Adichie, "Conversation on Humanizing History."

37. Chimamanda Adichie, "In the Shadow of Biafra," 2006, 423.

38. Ann Rigney, "Portable Monuments: Literature, Cultural Memory, and the Case of Jeanie Deans," 2004.

39. Jacques Derrida, *Spectres of Marx: The State of Debt, the Work of Mourning, and the New International*, 1994, 85.

40. Chimamanda Adichie, *For the Love of Biafra*, 1997.

41. Chimamanda Adichie, "Ghosts," 2004, and "That Harmattan Morning," 2002.

42. Chimamanda Adichie, *Decisions*, 1997.

43. Adichie, "Conversation on Humanizing History"; emphasis added.

44. Adichie, "African 'Authenticity,'" 47.

45. In "In the Shadow of Biafra," an addendum to the novel, Adichie explains how she hopes the novel's "emotional truth" will be its most recognizable quality. While she admits the difficulty of defining the concept of "emotional truth," she describes it as having a quality different from honesty and being more resilient than fact. Toni Morrison makes a similar argument in "The Site of Memory," where she notes that the difference should not be between fact and fiction but between fact and truth. This is because fact can exist without human intelligence but truth cannot. The strength of Adichie's postmemorial work therefore lies in her ability to portray emotional truths that are realized in her exploration of the interior lives of her characters. The idea of emotional truth relates to what many scholars, especially Lindsay Stonebridge, describe as narrative truth. Literature has the ability to provide narrative truths that facts cannot provide because narratives provide interiority and are rooted in the human experience. See Morrison, "Site of Memory," 1995; and Stonebridge, *Writing and Righting: Literature in the Age of Human Rights*, 2020.

46. The Aburi Accord was a peace agreement hosted by the Ghanaian general Joseph Ankrah, who had invited both Ojukwu and Gowon to Aburi, Ghana, in order to make an agreement that would ensure the unity of the Federal Republic of Nigeria.

47. Sam Durrant, *Postcolonial Narrative and the Work of Mourning: J. M. Coetzee, Wilson Harris, and Toni Morrison*, 2004, 37.

48. Here, I am drawing from and building on Linda Hutcheon's idea that the metatext is an essential quality of postmodern fiction. I also draw from Hayden White's idea that postmodernists believe that history is not an objective, scientific, or infallibly true account of the past, because it depends on written sources that were created from the imperfect and selective memories of their authors. White also opines that history writing retains the literary characteristics of fiction, including use of emplotments, character development, and tropes. See Hutcheon, *A Poetics of Postmodernism?*, 1983; H. White, *Metahistory: The Historical Imagination in the Nineteenth Century Europe*, 1973; and H. White, "Historical Fiction, Fictional History, and Historical Reality," 2005,147–57.

49. Dori Laub, "Memory and History from Past to Future: A Dialogue with Dori Laub on Trauma and Testimony," 2010.

50. A "people's history," as theorized by Raphael Samuel, is the writing of a history that represents "the people" and their subjectivities. It is a history written from "below." It is "oppositional" to the state narrative and its structures of power because it offers an alternative to the static and often elite history taught in schools. People's histories recover subjective experiences by looking at the everyday life of people. See Samuel, *People's History and Socialist Theory*, 1981.

51. Chris Ouma sees Ugwu as a vernacular intellectual because he started as a semi-literate houseboy who becomes immersed into the academic community in Nsukka. Ouma states that the phrase "vernacular intellectualism" can be regarded as an offshoot of Farred Grant's idea of "Black vernacular intellectuals," which is about intellectuals who in their critique of social justice stand both inside and outside of academic and conventional spheres. See Ouma, "Composite Consciousness and Memory of War in

Chimamanda Ngozi Adichie's *Half of a Yellow Sun*," 2011, 15–30; and Grant, *What's My Name?*, 2003.

52. Hutcheon, *Poetics of Postmodernism?*, 3.
53. Morrison, "Site of Memory."
54. Adichie, "The Story behind the Book," *Half of a Yellow Sun*, 2006, 440.
55. Ouma, "Composite Consciousness and Memories of War."
56. Adichie, "We Remember Differently."
57. Dori Laub, "Bearing Witness, or the Vicissitudes of Listening," 1992.
58. Ranjana Khanna, *Dark Continents: Psychoanalysis and Colonialism*, 2003, 255.
59. Rothberg, "Remembering Back," 5.
60. In "The Position of the Unthought," Saidiya V. Hartman, in conversation with Frank B. Wilderson III, describes how the European anti-slavery project came to legitimize the colonial project in Africa. In other words, the Europeans ended the slave trade in Africa only to begin the colonial rule. The Atlantic slave trade paved the way for colonialism in Africa. See Hartman and Wilderson, "The Position of the Unthought," 2003.
61. Amy Novak, "Who Speaks? Who Listens? The Problem of Address in Two Nigerian Novels," 2008, 13.
62. Chimamanda Adichie, "The Danger of a Single Story," 2009.
63. Mbembe, *On the Postcolony*, 12.
64. Novak, "Who Speaks? Who Listens?," 14.
65. Adichie, "Hardtalk."
66. In *Discourse on Colonialism*, Aimé Césaire writes that before Europeans were victims of Nazism, they were its accomplices. He explains that Nazism in the Third Reich was a situation of a chicken that came home to roost because Europeans had tolerated, cultivated, and legitimized Nazism—in the form of brutal colonial procedures—on non-European soils before it became inflicted on them. He notes, "[Hitler's crime is] the fact that he applied to European colonialist procedures which until then had been reserved exclusively for the Arabs of Algeria, the coolies of India, and the blacks of Africa." Césaire, *Discourse on Colonialism*, 1953/2000, 14. For more on the subject, see Michael Rothberg, *Multidirectional Memory: Remembering the Holocaust in the Age of Decolonization*, 2009; and Elizabeth Baer, *The Genocidal Gaze: From German Southwest Africa to the Third Reich*, 2017.
67. In describing prememory, Guy Beiner notes that "as an event is unfolding, it is understood and interpreted through reference to memories of previous events, which can be labelled prememory. In turn, traditions of prememory shape and influence the subsequent memory of the event." See Beiner, "Probing the Boundaries of Irish Memory," 154–70.
68. I am not arguing for the relativization of the Holocaust here; rather, what I am getting at is that the Nigeria-Biafra War, being the first post-independence war in Africa, relied on certain war schemata and modalities derived from the Second World War. It is also not impossible that there were soldiers who fought in both wars, as the Nigeria-Biafra War broke out only twenty-two years after the Second World War.

69. Akpome, "Intertextuality and Influence"; Hewett, "Coming of Age"; Chris Ouma, "Late Achebe: Biafra as Literary Genealogy," 2015.

70. The novel was adapted into a film of the same title by Biyi Bandele in 2013.

71. D'Banj, the popular Nigerian musician, did the soundtrack for the film. In 2014 he released the music video, which contains footages from the movie.

72. https://www.facebook.com/Half-of-a-Yellow-Sun-1793433037614760/

73. Gladys Rayborn, *Half of a Yellow Sun: An Audiobook*, 2014 https://www.youtube.com/watch?v=DEZYR77JYQs

74. Chimamanda Adichie, "To Instruct and Delight: A Case for Realist Literature," 2012.

75. Ouma, "Late Achebe," 53.

76. Hawley, "Biafra as Heritage and Symbol," 16.

77. Ayo Kehinde, "Intertextuality and the Contemporary African Novel," 2003, 6.

78. Over the years, there have been several debates on the possibility that Adichie plagiarized other people's works in *Half of a Yellow Sun*. For more on this, see Alison Flood, "Chimamanda Adichie Rejects Delusional Plagiarism Claim," 2020.

79. Adichie, "We Remember Differently."

80. As a blurb for the novel, Chinua Achebe is quoted saying, "We do not usually associate wisdom with beginners, but here is a new writer endowed with the gift of ancient storytellers. . . . Adichie came almost fully made."

81. It is interesting that even till today some Nigerians still refer to Kwashiorkor as Harold Wilson syndrome, named after the British prime minister during the Biafran war. It is one of the ways in which memory is encoded and continues in language use.

82. In the Fourth State edition of the novel, readers are told that the photos were taken by Susan Bachan in January 1970 and were given to Adichie while she was writing the novel.

83. Hirsch, *Family Frame*, 23.

84. Richard Crownshaw, "The Limits of Transference: Theories of Memory and Photography in W. G. Sebald's *Austerlitz*," 2009, 68.

85. Eleni Coundioritis, *The People's Right to the Novel: War Fiction in the Postcolony*, 2014, 12.

86. Zoe Norridge, drawing from the works of Primo Levi and Elie Wiesel, writes about how the ultimate witness is dead and how testimonies of survivors assert yet another absence—that of the ultimate witness. She stresses how it is not materially possible for the ultimate witness to survive. See Norridge, *Perceiving Pain in African Literature*, 2013.

87. Walter Benjamin, "Theses on the Philosophy of History," 1968, 60.

88. Chimamanda Adichie, "Capturing Biafra's Brief Day in the 'Yellow Sun': An NPR Interview," 2006.

89. I am using the pronoun "us" deliberately here because I belong to this postwar generation, although I am not sure about the shape that this responsibility will take. But I believe it begins with having a historical awareness and engaging in deliberate and informed conversations with others.

138 • Notes to Pages 44–50

90. Emmanuel Levinas, *Ethics and Infinity*, 1985.
91. Adichie, "In the Shadow of Biafra," 423.
92. Martijn van Gils, "In the Shadow of Biafra: Construction of War Memory in Adichie's *Half of a Yellow Sun*," 2016.
93. Chimamanda Adichie, "Nigerian Identity Is Burdensome," 2004.
94. Mahmood Mamdani, *Neither Settler nor Native: The Making and Unmaking of Permanent Minorities*, 2020.
95. Similar to Derrida's interminable mourning, Vamik Vodkan coined the term "perennial mourning" to describe the adult mourning that offers no symbolic closure. The mourner creates linking objects such as photographs, symbols, and other inanimate objects that emotionally connect him to the past or to the dead person. These linking objects tend to freeze the mourning process. In the case of Odenigbo, the Biafran flag is a linking object to the past. See Vodkan, "Not Letting Go: From Individual Perennial Mourners to Societies with Entitlement Ideologies," 2007.
96. Chimamanda Adichie, "Writing *Half of a Yellow Sun* Affected My Mental Health—Chimamanda Adichie," 2020.
97. Laura Murphy, "The Curse of Constant Remembrance: The Belated Trauma of the Slave Trade in Ayi Kwei Armah's *Fragments*," 2008.

2. THE PAST CONTINUES IN SILENCE

1. Lansana Gberie, *A Dirty War in West Africa: The RUF and the Destruction of Sierra Leone*, 2005.
2. While there are many critical works /nonfictions on the war, there is only a relatively small number of creative/literary works on the subject. Syl Cheney Coker, Casely Hayford, and Ambrose Massaquoi are critically acclaimed creative writers from Sierra Leone, but many of their literary outputs are not centered on the war. However, recently, Ishmeal Beah's *A Long Way Gone* (2007), Delia Jarrett-Macauley's *Moses, Citizen, and Me* (2005), and Sheikh Kamarah's *The Child of War* (2016) have engaged with the issue of child soldiers during the war. Also, Gary Stewart and John Amman's *Black Man's Grave: Letters from Sierra Leone* (2007) is a collection of letters written in Sierra Leone during the civil war. But Aminatta Forna has consistently written about the war, directly or indirectly, in many of her nonfiction works and in almost all of her fiction. Her works garner critical attention from all over the world. She continues to grant interviews and give talks on the subject.
3. Aminatta Forna, "My Country Had a Civil War," 2011.
4. Susan Suleiman refers to the 1.5 generation as different from the "born-after" generation because they were alive during an (atrocious) event even though they may be too young to have an adult understanding of what was happening. See Suleiman, *Crises of Memory and the Second World War*, 2006.
5. Carolyn Pedwell, "Affective Translation: Empathy and *The Memory of Love*," 2014; Irene Fernandez, "Emotional Unbelonging in Aminatta Forna's *The Memory of Love*," 2017.

6. Anne Gagiano, "Women Writing Nationhood Differently: Affiliative Critique in Novels by Forna, Attah, and Farah," 2013; Rosanne Kennedy, "Reparative Transnationalism: The Friction and Fiction of Remembering in Sierra Leone," 2018.

7. Dave Gunning, "Dissociation, Spirit Possession, and the Languages of Trauma in Some Recent African-British Novels," 2015.

8. Stef Craps, "Beyond Eurocentrism: Trauma Theory in the Global Age," 2014.

9. Zoe Norridge, "Sex as Synecdoche: Intimate Languages of Violence in Chimamanda Ngozi Adichie's *Half of a Yellow Sun* and Aminatta Forna's *The Memory of Love*," 2012.

10. The melancholic subject is trapped in a noncommunicable grief to the extent that s/he loses all interest in words, actions, and even life itself. See Julia Kristeva, *Black Sun: Depression and Melancholia*, 2008.

11. Aminatta Forna and Valeriu Nicolae, "Memory and Forgetting: Aminatta Forna and Valeriu Nicolae in Conversation," 2006.

12. My idea of a "chrono-trope" is a spin on Mikhail Bakhtin's chronotope and the cardiological idea of chronotropy. My argument is that there is an intrinsic temporal rhythm in the novel, and it can be measured in silence. This peculiar rhythm of time, which I call "silent time," becomes some kind of a trope throughout the novel. To put it simply, in *The Memory of Love*, there is a peculiar configuration/beat/trope of time (chrono-trope) that can be described as "silent time."

13. In his paper "Textual Silence and the Discourse of Homelessness," Thomas Huckin, with reference to the Prague school, explains that silence does have communicative dynamism because it conveys information from writer/speaker to reader/listener. See Huckin, "Textual Silence and the Discourse of Homelessness," 2002. For more on communicative dynamism, see Jan Firbas, "Carriers of Communicative Dynamism," 1984.

14. This is Trouillot (1995)'s idea cited in Leanne Munroe's "Negotiating Memories and Silences: Museum Narratives of Transatlantic Slavery in England," 2016.

15. Craps, "Beyond Eurocentrism."

16. Motsemme Nthabiseng, "The Mute Always Speaks: On Women's Silences at the Truth and Reconciliation Commission," 2014.

17. Pumla Gobodo-Madikizela, *A Human Being Died That Night*, 2003.

18. Kevin Quashie, *The Sovereignty of Quiet: Beyond Resistance in Black Culture*, 2012, 13.

19. Cathy Caruth, *Unclaimed Experience: Trauma, Narrative, and History*, 1996.

20. Dori Laub, "Bearing Witness, or the Vicissitudes of Listening," 1992.

21. Caruth, *Unclaimed Experience*.

22. Dominick LaCapra notes that "redemptive narrative is a narrative that denies the trauma that brought it into existence. And more experimental, non-redemptive narratives are narratives that are trying to come to terms with the trauma in a post-traumatic context, in ways that involve both acting-out and working-through. This is a way in which you can read a great deal of modern literature and art, as a kind of relatively safe

haven in which to explore post-traumatic effects." (From a 1998 interview with Dominick LaCapra at the SHOAH Resource Centre, www.yadvashem.org/.)

23. Kennedy, "Reparative Transnationalism."

24. Berber Bevernage, *History, Memory, and State-Sponsored Violence: Time and Justice*, 2012.

25. John Brewer argues that memories can become obstacles to post/conflict adjustment. He avers that memory is implicated in war as much as it is in peace. It can lead to renewed outbreaks of violence. Therefore, silence becomes a way of forgetting to remember and remembering to forget. See Brewer, "Memory, Truth, and Victimhood in Post-Trauma Societies," 2006.

26. While Forna speaks of the "silence of culture" as the third kind of silence observable in post-conflict Sierra Leone, her explanation actually suggests a "culture of silence," the kind of silence that occurs on a cultural level.

27. Paul Basu, "Confronting the Past? Negotiation a Heritage of Conflict in Sierra Leone," 2008.

28. Even before and after the settlement of the freed slaves in Freetown in 1787, there had been several histories of violence in the country we now know as Sierra Leone. Examples include the brutal Trans-Saharan slavery, which is traceable to as early as the sixth century, the Atlantic slave trade (fifteenth to mid-nineteenth century), the Mani invasion of the mid-sixteenth century, the Gbanka war of the nineteenth century, the Mende uprising of 1898, the Hut tax war of 1898, and the Manga Sewa and Mandinka army battle of 1884. D. J. Siddle estimates that there were actually over one thousand such wars in Sierra Leone. See Siddle, "War-Towns in Sierra Leone: A Study in Social Change," 1968.

29. Caruth, *Unclaimed Experience*.

30. Michael Jackson, *The Varieties of Temporal Experience: Travels in the Philosophical, Historical, and Ethnographic Time*, 2018.

31. Paul Connerton, "Seven Types of Forgetting," 2008.

32. I suppose what is "social" in this kind of forgetting is the fact that the people choose to forget as a collective, which does not necessarily equate with forgetting on a personal level. Social forgetting, Rosalind Shaw writes, "is a refusal to reproduce the violence by talking about it publicly. It involves the alternative memory practices that are incompatible with the verbal remembrance of the Sierra Leone Truth and Reconciliation Committee (SLTRC). It 'unmakes' past violence and 'remakes' ex-combatants as new social persons." See Shaw, "Rethinking Truth and Reconciliation Commissions. Lessons from Sierra Leone," 2015.

33. Oblivion, which means "take away" in its Latin root, is a state of mind, as opposed to forgetting, which takes place at various levels and includes daily life more easily than does oblivion. See Luisa Passerlini, "Memories between Silence and Oblivion," 2005.

34. Paul Ricoeur, in his book *Memory, History, and Forgetting*, argues that silence is inextricably connected to the processes of memory and forgetting. He introduces the

term *oubli de reserve* (forgetting as a reserve) to illustrate this complexity. He also argues that forgetting does not equal erasure, it is a latent archive that can be reactivated. Ricoeur, *Memory, History, and Forgetting*, 2000.

35. Ecclesiastes 3:7.
36. Passerlini, "Memories between Silence and Oblivion."
37. Following the end of the war, human and natural disasters continued to plague the country. A mudslide (on August 14, 2017) killed so many people that the president had to declare seven days of national mourning. More so, political violence continues to haunt the country. A recent example is the violence that erupted after the 2018 presidential elections. In addition, microaggressions closely tied with poverty (Sierra Leone is one of the poorest countries in the world), cultural misogyny in the form of female genital mutilation, and the Ebola outbreak (2014–16), among others, are some of the problems the country is confronted with. What is noticeable in all of these is the presence of silence manifesting in various forms. Raouf J. Jacob examines these conditions of silence in postwar Sierra Leone in his film *A Culture of Silence* (2014) and concludes that the various layers of human tragedy in the country remain unspoken.
38. Charles B. Stone, Alin Coman, Adam D. Brown, Jonathan Koppel, and William Hirst, "Toward a Science of Silence: The Consequence of Leaving a Memory Unsaid," 2012.
39. See Stone, et al., "Toward a Science of Silence."
40. Homi Bhabha, "Even the Dead Have Human Rights" (2018), 714.
41. Edward Casey, *Remembering: A Phenomenological Study*, 1987/2000.
42. Zoe Norridge, "Ways of Knowing Civil War: Human Rights and the Traction of Complicity in Aminatta Forna's *The Hired Man*," 2014.
43. Forna and Nicolae, "Memory and Forgetting."
44. Mark Sanders, *Complicities: The Intellectual and Apartheid*, 2002.
45. Debarati Sanyal, *Memory and Complicity: Migrations of Holocaust Remembrance*, 2015.
46. Michael Rothberg, *The Implicated Subject: Beyond Victims and Perpetrators*, 2019.
47. Hannah Arendt, "Collective Responsibility," 1987.
48. Mark Sanders, *Complicities: The Intellectual and Apartheid*, 2002.
49. Christopher Kutz, *Complicity*, 2000.
50. Adam Lebor, *Complicity with Evil: The United Nations in the Age of Genocide*, 2006.
51. Caruth, *Unclaimed Experience*.
52. Homi Bhabha, "DissemiNation: Time, Narrative, and the Margins of the Modern Nation," 1995, 233.
53. See Jane Guyer, "Prophecy and the Near Future: Thoughts of Macroeconomic, Evangelical, and Punctuated Time," 2007.
54. Lawrence Langer, "Uses and Misuses of a Young Girl's Diary: If Anne Frank Could Return from among the Murdered, She Would be Appalled," 2000.
55. Achille Mbembe, *On the Postcolony*, 2001.

56. In *Time and Narrative*, vol. 1, Paul Ricoeur reflects on cosmological and phenomenological times. He notes that we experience time as linear succession; we experience the passing hours and days and the progression of our lives from birth to death—this is what he describes as "cosmological time." "Phenomenological time," on the other hand, is a time experienced in terms of the past, present, and future—that is, as self-aware embodied beings, we not only experience time as linear succession, but we are also oriented to the succession of time in terms of what has been, what is, and what will be. In other words, phenomenological time is the time experienced in the form of past, present, and future, while cosmological time is the linear succession of time in terms of minutes and hours. See Ricoeur, *Time and Narrative*, vol. 1, 1984.

57. Unforgetting relates with the default state of oblivion. See Ann Rigney, "Remembrance as Remaking: Memories of the Nation Revisited," 2018.

58. Caruth, *Unclaimed Experience*.

59. Juliet Rogers, "Rethinking Remorse," 2016.

60. Besides its clinical meaning, fugue is a contrapuntal piece of music wherein a particular melody is played in a number of voices, each voice introduced in turn by playing the melody, but, more generally, fugue is any work of art (literature, film, painting) that has an elaborate complexity of structure and form.

61. Michael Ignatieff, "The Nightmare from Which We Are Trying to Awake," 1998, 166–90.

62. Ricoeur's concept of human time is expressive of a complex experience where phenomenological time and cosmological time are integrated. See Ricoeur, *Time and Narrative*.

63. Daniel Levy and Natan Sznaider, "Cosmopolitan Memory and Human Rights," 2011.

64. Paul Connerton, *The Spirit of Mourning: History, Memory, and the Body*, 2011.

65. After the relative failure of the SLTRC, Fambul Tok (Krio for family talk), a local and community-led reconciliation initiative, was introduced in 2007. The initiative is rooted in the local Sierra Leonean "family talk" traditions and is created with the aim of bringing victims and perpetrators together to talk, reconcile, and heal.

3. THE PAST CONTINUES IN ANOTHER COUNTRY

1. Rob Nixon, "African, American," 2007. See also James Lasdun, "How to Read the Air. A Review," 2010; and Chris Abani, "Divided Hearts," 2007.

2. It is noteworthy that while, in the United Kingdom, the novel is titled *Children of the Revolution*, it was released as *The Beautiful Things That Heavens Bear* in America. This is because the US publisher felt that the original title "sounded too political." Prospero, "Dinaw Mengestu, Novelist," *The Economist*, 2011. https://www.economist.com/prospero/2011/04/26/dinaw-mengestu-novelist/

3. Diane Kresh, "Author Dinaw Mengestu Speaks at the Arlington Public Library," 2013. https://www.youtube.com/watch?v=afEj_SJwj9w

4. The title of the novel is a reference to the "children," like Dinaw Mengestu himself, born during and after the Ethiopian revolution and, by extension, other revolutions that swept across Africa in the 1970s and 1980s.

5. There is a tradition of reading African literature through the lens of childhood and childhood memories. For example, Abdourahman Waberi describes the African writers born after the end of colonialism as "Children of the Postcolony," Binyavanga Wainaina also speaks of the African "Children of the Cold War," and Sefi Atta (writes about the "Children of the Oil Boom" in Nigeria. See Waberi, "Les enfants de la postcolonie: Esquisse d'une nouvelle génération d'écrivains francophones d'Afrique noire," 1998; Wainaina, *One Day I will Write about this Place*, 2011; and Atta, *Everything Good Will Come*, 2005. For more on this, see Chris Ouma, *Childhood in Contemporary Diasporic African Literature*, 2020.

6. Alison Landsberg argues against ethnic particularism and compartmentalization of experience in America by maintaining that technologies of mass culture make it possible for anyone, regardless of race, ethnicity, or gender, to share collective memories of others, to assimilate as personal experience historical events that they themselves have no direct historical connection to, and to take on other people's memories prosthetically. See Landsberg. *Prosthetic Memory: The Transformation of American Remembrance in the Age of Mass Culture*, 2004.

7. James Arnett, "No Place Like Home: Failures of Feeling and the Impossibility of Return in Dinaw Mengestu's *The Beautiful Things That Heavens Bear*," 2016, 107.

8. Anne Shulock, "Interview with Dinaw Mengestu," *The Rumpus*, 2010; emphasis mine.

9. Svetlana Boym, "On Diasporic Intimacies," 1998.

10. David Eng and Shinhee Han, "A Dialogue on Racial Melancholia," 2003.

11. Caren Irr, *Toward the Geopolitical Novel: U.S. Fiction in the Twenty-First Century*, 2013.

12. Inci Tebis Picard, "Migratory Grief," 2016.

13. Sigmund Freud, "Mourning and Melancholia," 1917/1953.

14. Richard Sennett, "Disturbing Memories," 2012.

15. Karwin Klein, "On the Emergence of Memory in Historical Discourse," 2000, 127–50.

16. Freud, "Mourning and Melancholia," 1917, 246.

17. Freud, "Mourning and Melancholia," 1917, 250

18. David Eng and David Kazanjian, eds., "Introduction," in *Loss: The Politics of Mourning*, 2003.

19. James Scott, *Weapons of the Weak: Everyday Forms of Peasant Resistance*, 1985.

20. Slavoj Žižek, "Melancholy and the Act," 2000, 660.

21. Linking objects are the inanimate objects that connect a mourner to the past or to a dead person. Vamik Vodkan, "Not Letting Go: From Individual Perennial Mourners to Societies with Entitlement Ideologies," 2007.

22. Kajsa Henry theorizes textual mourning as a "formalized process that exists once

we understand the connections between rituals of mourning, functions of writing and the modes of witnessing and testifying." In other words, in textual mourning, the text itself is a part of mourning ritual and a site of mourning as the writing (and reading) processes become extensions of mourning practices. Henry, "A Literary Archaeology of Loss: The Politics of Mourning in African American Literature," 2006.

23. See Jay Winter, "Introduction," in *History, Memory, and Migration: Perceptions of the Past and the Politics of Incorporation*, 2012.

24. Riverhead Books, "How to Read the Air by Dinaw Mengestu," July 13, 2010, https://www.youtube.com/watch?v=xZteshCUKOk

25. Melancholy of no return is simply the melancholic feeling that accompanies the realization that one will not return to one's home country. See Zofia Rosinska, "Emigratory Experience: The Melancholy of No Return," 2011.

26. Opeyemi Ajibola, "Representation of Female Migrants in Selected Nigerian Migrant Narratives," 2018.

27. Michelle Fine regards the "exile within" as the minority groups within America who face day-to-day discrimination and "spiky violence" based on their race, class, sexual orientation, or religion. See Fine, *Just Research in Contentious Times: Widening the Methodological Imagination*, 2018.

28. Trymaine Lee, "As Black Population Declines in Washington D.C., Little Ethiopia Thrives," *Huffington Post*, April 8, 2012, https://www.huffpost.com/entry/black-population-declies-dc-little-ethiopia-thrives_n_846817/

29. See Elizabeth Chacko, "Africans in Washington, DC: Ethiopia Ethnic Institutions and Immigrant Adjustment," 2010.

30. Arjun Appadurai, *Modernity at Large*, 1996, 171.

31. The slogan "America: A Nation of Immigrants" was popularized through John F. Kennedy's book (1958) of the same title. However, the term had appeared earlier in 1874 in the *Daily State Journal of Alexandria*, where, in a bid to encourage the European immigrant, it stated, "We are a nation of immigrants and immigrants' children." The problem with this view is that by framing America as an immigrant nation, it erases indigenous presence and sovereignty.

32. Murat Aydemir and Alex Rotas, eds. "Introduction," in *Migratory Settings*, 2008, 5.

33. Aydemir and Rotas, "Introduction," 7.

34. Abani, "Divided Hearts."

35. Oscar Handlin, *The Uprooted*, 1973.

36. Linda Basch, Nina Glick-Schiller, and Cristina Szanton-Blanc, eds., *Nations Unbound: Transnational Projects, Postcolonial Predicaments, and Deterritorialized Nation-States*, 1994.

37. Derek Attridge, "No Escape from Home: History, Affect, and Art in Zoe Wicomb's Translocal Coincidences," 2017.

38. Julia Creet, *Memory and Migration: Multidisciplinary Approaches to Memory Studies*, 2011.

39. Astrid Erll, "Homer: A Relational Mnemohistory," 2018.

40. In her essay "Setting, Intertextuality, and the Resurrection of the Postcolonial Author," Zoe Wicomb applies the literary concept of intertextuality (relationship between texts) to physical spaces. That is, just as texts are shaped by one another, places can also be interconnected, especially in the perspective of the people that navigate them. See Wicomb, "Setting, Intertextuality, and the Resurrection of the Postcolonial Author," 2005.

41. Abani, "Divided Hearts."

42. "One world in relation" is a reference to Manthia Diawara's documentary *Edouard Glissant: One World in Relation*, K'a Yéléma Productions, 2010. The documentary itself is a reference to Glissant's *Poetics of Relation* and an elaboration on Glissant's problematization of national and cultural boundaries in his works.

43. Dorothy Driver, "Troubling the Politics of Location," 2017.

44. Kathy-Ann Tan, *Reconfiguring Citizenship and National Identity in North American Imagination*, 2015.

45. Kwame Appiah, *Cosmopolitanism: Ethics in a World of Strangers*, 2006.

46. Achille Mbembe, "Afropolitanism," 2007.

47. Taiye Selasi, "Bye-Bye Babar, or What Is an Afropolitan?," 2005.

48. Simon Gikandi, "Between Roots and Routes: Cosmopolitanisms and the Claims of Locality," 2010, 27.

49. Michael Rothberg and Yasemin Yildiz suggest that performances of memory can function as "acts of citizenship." Their use of the phrase "acts of citizenship" owes its meaning to the political theorist Engin Isin, who maintains that acts of citizenship are deeds that take place regardless of legal citizenship, which usually comes with civil responsibilities such as voting and paying taxes. In other words, an act of citizenship is the performance of citizenship outside the boundaries of normative practices that formal citizens undertake. See Rothberg and Yildiz, "Memory Citizenship: Migrant Archive of Holocaust Remembrance in Contemporary Germany," 2011.

50. Irial Glynn and Olaf Kleist, *History, Memory, and Migration: Perceptions of the Past and the Politics of Incorporation*, 2012.

51. Ricard Sennett argues that the goal of capitalism is that people do not remember together or remember well. He notes that while the liberal hope of collective memory is that there are social structures of remembering, the neoliberal hope of memory is mnemonic individualism. Using America as an example, he argues that modern capitalism encourages us to see memory as a private property. See Sennett, "Disturbing Memories."

52. Ndabaningi Sithole, *African Nationalism*, 1959, 23.

53. Toyin Falola, *The African Diaspora: Slavery, Modernity, and Globalization*, 2013.

54. Pan-Africanism has a much longer history than African nationalism. It, arguably, dates back to the eighteenth century in London when Ottobah Cuguano led the Sons of Africa political group. Modern Pan-Africanism sometimes seeks political and economic federation of African nation-states. African nationalism, however, was based on national self-determination of African countries, especially after the Second World War.

It inspired the formation of nationalist political parties across Africa and also the clamor for decolonization. It was never a single movement, although it was framed purely in opposition to colonial rule and was therefore frequently unclear or contradictory about its other objectives. The relation between African nationalism and Pan-Africanism was ambiguous because many nationalist leaders professed Pan-African loyalties but refused to commit to supranational unions. However, today Pan-Africanism (with uppercase "P") is generally understood as a political movement, a kind of African (by extension, Black) political self-determination, while pan-Africanism (with a lowercase "p") is more of cultural movement that pays attention to the cultural memories and ties that bind Africa and the Black world in general. See Robert Rotberg, "African Nationalism: Concept or Confusion," 1966; and Basil Davidson, *Let Freedom Come: Africa in Modern History*, 1978.

55. Falola, *African Diaspora*.

56. By "collective amnesia," I am referring to a kind of (African) continental forgetting in which all the transnational alliances in the struggle for independence have been written out of memory books. With a few exceptions, most histories of the struggles for independence in Africa have become highly nationalized. This also links to what I mean by crisis in the culture of commemoration which Richard Werbner addresses in his book, *Memory and the Postcolony*, 1998.

57. "Horizontal solidarity—a solidarity created for us by the colonial, semi-colonial or para-colonial situation imposed upon us from without. Vertical solidarity—a solidarity in time, due to the fact that we started from an original unity, the unity of African civilization." Aimé Césaire, "Culture and Colonisation," 1956, 199.

58. Avishai Margalit distinguishes between thick and thin relations in the act of remembering. "Thick relation" is more intimate; it connects those who have a shared past. He notes that memory is the cement that holds thick relations together, and communities of memory are the obvious habitats for thick relations. On the other hand, "thin relations" connect those who are strangers or remote to each other. See Margalit, *The Ethics of Memory*, 2002.

59. See Benedict Anderson, *The Spectres of Comparisons: Nationalism, Southeast Asia, and the World*, 1998.

60. Eric Hobsbawm, *Nations and Nationalism since 1780: Programme, Myth, and Reality*, 1990, 162.

61. Andreas Wimmer and Nina Glick Schiller, "Methodological Nationalism and Beyond: Nation-State Building, Migration, and the Social Sciences," 2002.

62. Landsberg, *Prosthetic Memory*.

63. Yifat Gutman, Adam Brown, and Amy Sodaro, eds., *Memory and the Future: Transnational Politics, Ethics, and Society*, 2010.

64. Chiara de Cesari and Ann Rigney, *Transnational Memory: Circulation, Articulation, Scales*, 2014.

65. De Cesari and Rigney, *Transnational Memory*, 31.

66. Cheikh Anta Diop, "The Cultural Contribution and Prospects of Africa," 1956, 347.

67. Darrell Roodt, dir., 1992, *Sarafina!* Produced by Hollywood Pictures, written by Ngema and William Nicholson.

68. Susanah Radstone, "What Place Is This? Transcultural Memory and the Locations of Memory Studies," 2011.

69. See Michael Rothberg, *Multidirectional Memory: Remembering the Holocaust in the Age of Decolonization*, 2009.

70. See Aleida Assmann and Sebastian Conrad, eds., *Memory in a Global Age: Discourses, Practices, and Trajectories*, 2010.

71. See Daniel Levy and Natan Sznaider, "Memory Unbound: The Holocaust and the Formation of Cosmopolitan Memory," 2002.

72. Abani, "Divided Hearts."

73. There is now an African Memory Game initiative founded in the United States with the aim of equipping children of African immigrants with the knowledge and history of Africa. It is not clear if this initiative was inspired by the African Memory Game in Mengestu's novel.

74. Shu-mei Shih and Francoise Lionnet put forward the concept of minor transnationalism in order to move beyond the limitations of postcolonial theory and global and ethnic studies. They note that transnational studies often capitalize on the interaction between minor culture and mainstream society, overlooking the lateral or vertical relationship among minority groups. They argue that minor transnationalism pays attention to the interactions and exchanges among minority groups in a transnational/multicultural setting. This eventually gives legitimacy to minority subjects and produces new possibilities. See Shih and Lionnet, *Minor Transnationalism*, 2005.

4. THE PAST CONTINUES THROUGH SUBJECT POSITIONS

1. Véronique Tadjo, "Genocide: The Changing Landscape of Memory in Rwanda," 2010.

2. In his 2001 book, *When Victims Become Killers: Colonialism, Nativism, and the Genocide in Rwanda*, Mahmood Mamdani argues that many accounts of the genocide, academic or popular, are ahistorical. He notes that many writers wrote about the genocide as if it had no historical precedents. Hence, the Rwandan genocide "appears as an anthropological oddity," which gives rise to the temptation to dismiss it as exceptional. However, Mamdani instructs that even if the genocide cannot be understood as rational, we need to understand it as thinkable. Mamdani, *When Victims Become Killers*, 2001, 7.

3. Identity categories were common in precolonial Rwanda but were not always fixed. For instance, it was possible for a wealthy Hutu to become a Tutsi; however, with the identity cards introduced by the Belgian government, these identity categories became fixed. See Philip Gourevitch, *We Wish to Inform You That Tomorrow We Will Be Killed with Our Families*, 1998.

4. Mamdani, *When Victims Become Killers*, 12.

5. After the Berlin conference in 1884, Germany ruled Rwanda through indirect rule. During this period, Germany favored the Tutsis by assigning administrative roles to them. This propagated the idea that the Tutsis were racially superior because they descended from Ethiopia, while the Hutus were Bantu descendants. After the First World War, Belgium took over from Germany and continued to propagate ideas about the anatomical and ancestral difference between the Hutus and the Tutsis. By the end of the Second World War, the Tutsi elites had begun to clamor for independence. The clamor did not sit well with the colonial government, who would, as a result, lend more political and moral support to the Hutu majority. See Tadjo, "Genocide."

6. Uri Misgav, "The Israeli Guns That Took Part in the Rwanda Genocide," 2015.

7. Tadjo, "Genocide."

8. Rory Carrol, "The US Chose to Ignore Rwanda Genocide," *Guardian*, April 1, 2004.

9. Cathy Caruth, *Unclaimed Experience: Trauma, Narrative, and History*, 1996, 16.

10. Susan Sontag, *Regarding the Pain of Others*, 2003.

11. See Elaine Scarry, "The Difficulty of Imagining Other People," 1996, 98–110.

12. Boris Boubacar Diop, "Denial through Silence," 2016.

13. These two France-based African artists are the brain behind the initiative. See "Interview of Nocky Djedanoum by Chaacha Mwita." *Daily Nation*, June 25, 2000. http://www.nationaudio.com/News/DailyNation/25062000/Features/LS1.htm (page removed).

14. The writers were Abdourahman Waberi from Djibouti; Boubacar Boris Diop from Senegal; Monique Ilboudo from Burkina Faso; Tierno Monemembo from Guinea; Nocky Djedanoum and Koulsy Lamko, both from Chad; Jean-Marie V. Rurangaw and Vénuste Kayimahé, both from Rwanda; Meja Mwangi from Kenya; and Véronique Tadjo from Côte d'Ivoire.

15. "Fest'Africa" is an annual African arts and literature festival that Nocky Djedanoum and Maïmouna Coulibaly began in the French city of Lille in 1992. It was as part of the festival in 1998 that ten African writers went to Rwanda with the view to write an imaginative response to the genocide.

16. See Nicki Hitchcott, "A Global African Commemoration—Rwanda: Écrire par devoir de mémoire," 2009.

17. See Hitchcott, "Global African Commemoration."

18. "Certes, nous avons reagi quatre ans après le genocide. Mais au Rwanda, j'ai bu mon échec d'homme jusqu'à la lie. Il était nécessaire de montrer aux Rwandais notre solidarité d'Africains. Et de lutter contre l'oubli, à notre façon, avec l'écriture." Nocky Djedanoum, "Interview" 2000. Cited and translated into English by Tadjo in "Genocide."

19. Hitchcott, "Global African Commemoration"; Anna-Marie de Beer, "Ubuntu and the Journey of Listening to the Rwandan Genocide Story," 2015; Audrey Small, "The Duty of Memory. A Solidarity of Voices after the Rwandan Genocide," 2007.

20. See Hitchcott, "Global African Commemoration," 9.

21. According to Avishai Margalit, in *The Ethics of Memory*, a community of memory as a political concept is more significant and weightier than the notion of the nation because memory is the cement that holds thick relations together, and communities of memory are the obvious habitats for thick relations. Margalit, *The Ethics of Memory*, 2002.

22. Avishai Margalit, also in *The Ethics of Memory*, makes a distinction between shared and common memory. He notes that a common memory is an aggregate notion. Common memory "aggregates the memories of all those people who remember a certain episode which each of them experienced individually. If the rate of those who remember the episode in a given society is above a certain threshold (say, most of them, an overwhelming majority of them, more than 70 percent, or whatever), then we call the memory of the episode a common memory." On the other hand, a shared memory is not a simple aggregate of individual memories. "A shared memory integrates and calibrates the different perspectives of those who remember the episode—for example, the memory of the people who were in the square, each experiencing only a fragment of what happened from their unique angle on events—into one version." Margalit, *Ethics of Memory*, 51.

23. Paul Ricoeur, *Memory, History, Forgetting*, 2004.

24. Myriam Bienenstock, "Is There a Duty to Remember?," 2010.

25. Margalit, *Ethics of Memory*.

26. Interview with Nocky Djedanoum, 2000, http://www.nordnet.fr/festafrica/rwanda2.htm (page removed).

27. Boubacar Boris Diop, whose book, *Murambi, The Book of Bones*, was part of the literary works that came out of the project, said that the project served to give the victims and survivors a face and a name. He made this statement while in a conversation with Véronique Tadjo at a literary festival in Johannesburg in 2010. For more see *Mail & Guardian*, "Literary Festival: Writers Respond to *Murambi, The Book of Bones*," 2010. https://www.youtube.com/watch?v=4i0Pmmxkuf8

28. Margalit, *Ethics of Memory*.

29. Namwali Serpell, "The Banality of Empathy," 2019.

30. Kate Kelsal, "Veronique Tadjo's Literary Pan Africanism," 2017.

31. Tadjo, "Genocide."

32. Lawrence Langer, *Holocaust Testimonies: The Ruins of Memory*, 1991.

33. Geoffrey Hartman, "Shoah and the Intellectual Witness," 2006.

34. Alexandre Dauge-Roth, *Writing and Filming the Genocide of the Tutsis in Rwanda: Dismembering and Remembering Traumatic History*, 2010.

35. Zoe Norridge, *Perceiving Pain in African Literature*, 2013.

36. De Beer, "Ubuntu and the Journey of Listening," 2015.

37. Emily Keightley and Michael Pickering, *The Mnemonic Imagination: Remembering as Creative Practice*, 2012.

38. Martina Kopf, "Ethics of Fiction: African Writers on the Genocide in Rwanda," 2012.

39. Landsberg, *Prosthetic Memory*.

40. Michael Rothberg, "Multidirectional Memory: Entangled Narratives, Implicated Subjects," 2016.

41. Landsberg, *Prosthetic Memory*, 16.

42. Tadjo, "Genocide."

43. Maria Tumarkin, *Traumascapes: The Power and Fate of Places Transformed by Tragedy*, 2015.

44. Alison Landsberg describes how prosthetic memories produces "the effect of collapsing the past into the present, of flattening time." Landsberg, *Prosthetic Memory*, 18.

45. Dori Laub, "Bearing Witness, or the Vicissitude of Listening," 1992.

46. Landsberg, *Prosthetic Memory*.

47. In R. Brown and J. Kulik's study on "flashbulb memories," they propose that certain groups or persons often have the ability to recall certain events of the past in great detail and even recall circumstances surrounding such events more than others because of the strong emotional arousal they had when the events happened, as well as the level of consequentiality of such events in their lives. Brown and Kulik, "Flashbulb Memories," 1977.

48. I am aware that Patricia Collins coined the term to explain the difficulties black women scholars face in the academia but I'm more interested in the way Katherine Hite recycles the term within the discourse of memory. In her essay "Empathic Unsettlement and the Outsider within Argentine Spaces of Memory," Hite examines how outsiders (Americans) engaged (or did not engage with) "narratives and representations" "within" an Argentine memorial site. The term "outsider within" applies to Tadjo's outsider-insider position. Even though she is not Rwandan, she is African (and Black) and therefore is connected by sense of "affiliation and affect" in ways that a non-African, non-Black subject will probably not. See Collins, "Learning from the Outsider Within: The Sociological Significance of Black Feminist Thought," 1986; and Hite, "Empathic Unsettlement and the Outsider within Argentine Spaces of Memory," 2015.

49. This is from an email interview that I had with Tadjo on December 3, 2018.

50. Hitchcott, "Global African Commemoration."

51. Hitchcott, "Global African Commemoration."

52. Norridge, *Perceiving Pain in African Literature*.

53. Norridge, *Perceiving Pain in African Literature*.

54. Véronique Tadjo, "Writing for Life: *The Shadow of Imana*," 2014.

55. Dauge-Roth, *Writing and Filming the Genocide*.

56. Dauge-Roth, *Writing and Filming the Genocide*.

57. I define "meta-witnessing" as the process of witnessing—critically and affectively—a firsthand witness's account.

58. See Thomas Trezise, *Witnessing Witnessing: The Reception of the Holocaust Survivor Testimony*, 2014.

59. Martina Kopf, "Ethics of Fiction: African Writers on the Genocide in Rwanda," 2012.

60. In explaining the inadequacy of compassionate listening, Bjorn Krondorfer writes, "A compassionate attitude has the tendency to erase some of the objective differences of agency vis-à-vis traumatic history. In the name of a common humanity, compassion too quickly glosses over the ethical difference between harm inflicted and harm endured, presenting all sides as victims of circumstances they could not control." In lieu of compassionate listening, he suggests unsettling empathy as a better approach. He states that an "unsettling empathy requires the risk of vulnerability, of courage, of being shaken in one's foundation and assumptions about the world and the other. . . . [It] calls us into the presence of objective differences without negating the vitality of human interaction, whereas compassion may tempt us to erase some of the objective differences in the name of a common humanity." See Krondorfer, "Unsettling Empathy," 2016, 99–100.

61. Dominick LaCapra, *Writing History, Writing Trauma*, 2001.

62. Krondorfer, "Unsettling Empathy."

63. LaCapra, *Writing History, Writing Trauma*, 109.

64. Nicki Hitchcott, "Travels in Inhumanity: Véronique Tadjo's Tourism in Rwanda," 2009.

65. Marita Sturken regards tourists of history people who approach tragic sites of memory like comfort-seeking consumers as opposed to deeply reflective mourners. See Sturken, *Tourists of History: Memory, Kitsch, and Consumerism from Oklahoma City to Ground Zero*, 2007.

66. Sontag, *Regarding the Pain of Others*, 12.

67. Pumla Gobodo-Madikizela coined the term "reparative humanism" as a vocabulary of rehumanization that is capable of forging the restoration of human bonds in the wake of a violent history. Reparative humanism is capable of opening up possibilities of a shared vision of empathy and solidarity for the suffering of the other. See Gobodo-Madikizela, "Interrupting Cycles of Repetition," 2016.

68. Tadjo, "Genocide," 5.

69. Melody Schreiber, "Rwanda's Genocide Ended 26 Years Ago: Survivors Are Still Finding Mass Graves," NPR, July 16, 2020.

70. National Post, "New Seeds of Conflict," 2014.

71. Tom Collins, "Rwanda-Uganda Conflict: Is the End in Sight?," 2020.

72. Alex Ngarambe, "Rwanda's Opposition Rattled by Killings and Disappearance of Members," 2019.

73. Some of the scholars who have raised such concerns either directly or indirectly in their works include Judi Rever, in her book *In Praise of Blood: The Crimes of the Rwandan Patriotic Front* (2018); Michela Wrong, in her book, *Do Not Disturb: The Story of a Political Murder and an African Regime Gone Bad* (2021); Jennie Burnet, in her work,

Genocide Lives in Us: Amplified Silence and the Politics of Memory in Rwanda (2005) and Susan Thomson, in her book, *Rwanda: From Genocide to Precarious Peace* (2018).

74. Anna-Marie de Beer, "Ubuntu, Reconciliation in Rwanda and the Returning to Personhood through Collective Narrative," 2019.

5. THE PAST CONTINUES IN THE FUTURE

1. Marianne Hirsch and Leo Spitzer, "Small Acts of Repair: The Unclaimed Legacy of the Romanian Holocaust," 2016.

2. Elie Wiesel, "Hope, Despair, and Memory," 1986.

3. Veena Das, *Life and Worlds: Violence and the Descent into the Ordinary*, 2007.

4. For more on textual mourning, see Kajsa K. Henry, "A Literary Archaeology of Loss: The Politics of Mourning in African American Literature," 2006.

5. Anne Shulock, "Interview with Dinaw Mengestu," 2010.

6. Cathy Caruth, *Unclaimed Experience: Trauma, Narrative, and History*, 1996.

7. Here I am drawing on Astrid Erll's concept of "mnemonic relationality" in which she explains how the connective structure of cultural memory creates social and temporal linkages. She notes that mnemonic relationality is toward "acts of connecting and blending, co-constructions and negotiations that are necessary for bringing heterogenous mnemonic elements into meaningful relations with one another." Erll, "Homer: A Relational Mnemohistory," 2018, 5.

8. I am aware that scholars are producing some fantastic works in this area. For example, in the context of Rwanda, there is Jennie Burnet, *Genocide Lives in Us: Women, Memory and Silence in Rwanda*, 2012; and Catherine Gilbert, *From Surviving to Living: Voice, Trauma, and Witness in Rwandan Women's Writings*, 2018; but more needs to be done in the area of gender and memory, especially in other post-conflict contexts in Africa.

9. Caroline Williamson has done a lot of work on post-traumatic growth in Rwanda. See, for example, *Rwanda After Genocide: Gender, Identity and Post-Traumatic Growth*, 2018; and "Towards a Theory of Collective Posttraumatic Growth in Rwanda: The Pursuit of Agency and Communion," 2014.

REFERENCES

PRIMARY TEXTS

Adichie, Chimamanda. 2006. *Half of a Yellow Sun*. London: Fourth Estate.
Forna, Aminatta. 2010. *The Memory of Love*. London: Bloomsbury.
Mengestu, Dinaw. 2007. *Children of the Revolution*. London: Jonathan Cape.
Tadjo, Véronique. 2010. *The Shadow of Imana: Travels in the Heart of Rwanda*. Portsmouth: Heinemann African Writers Series.

SECONDARY TEXTS

Abani, Chris. 2007. Divided Hearts. *Los Angeles Times*. http://articles.latimes.com/2007/mar/04/books/bk-abani4
Abraham, Nicolas, and Maria Torok. 1994. *The Shell and the Kernel: Renewals of Psychoanalysis*. New York: University of Chicago Press.
Achille, Étienne, Charles Forsdick, and Lydie Moudileno. 2020. *Postcolonial Realms of Memory: Sites and Symbols in Modern France*. Liverpool: Liverpool University Press.
Adesanmi, Pius, and Chris Dutton. 2005. Nigeria's Third Generation Writing: Historiography and Preliminary Theoretical Considerations. *English in Africa* 32, no. 1: 7–19.
Adesanmi, Pius, and Chris Dutton. 2008. Introduction. In Everything Good Is Raining: Provisional Notes on the Nigerian Novel of the Third Generation. *Research in African Literatures* 32, no. 1: vii–xii.
Adichie, Chimamanda. 1997. *For the Love of Biafra*. Ibadan: Spectrum Books.
Adichie, Chimamanda. 1997. *Decisions*. London: Minerva Press.
Adichie, Chimamanda. 2002. That Harmattan Morning. In *Zoetrope: All-Story* (out of print).
Adichie, Chimamanda. 2004. Ghosts. In *Zoetrope: All-Story* 8.4 (winter).
Adichie, Chimamanda. 2006. The Story behind the Book: Q&A with the Author. *Half of a Yellow Sun*. London: Fourth Estate, 440–46.
Adichie, Chimamanda. 2006. Capturing Biafra's Brief Day in the "Yellow Sun": An NPR Interview. September 17. https://www.npr.org/templates/story/story.php?storyId=6088156/

Adichie, Chimamanda. 2006. In the Shadow of Biafra. In *Half of a Yellow Sun*, 420–30. London: Fourth Estate.

Adichie, Chimamanda. 2008. African "Authenticity" and the Biafran Experience. *Transition* 99: 42–53.

Adichie, Chimamanda. 2009. The Danger of a Single Story. *Ted Global*. https://www.ted.com/talks/chimamanda_adichie_the_danger_of_a_single_story

Adichie, Chimamanda. 2012. To Instruct and Delight: A Case for Realist Literature. Commonwealth Lecture. https://www.youtube.com/watch?v=vmsYJDP8g2U

Adichie, Chimamanda. 2012. We Remember Differently. *Premium Times*, November 23. https://www.premiumtimesng.com/entertainment/108378-chinua-achebe-at-82-we-remember-differently-by-chimamanda-ngozi-adichie.html

Adichie, Chimamanda. 2013. Conversation on Humanizing History with Ellah Allfrey. London: The Royal Society for the Encouragement of Arts. https://www.youtube.com/watch?v=vmsYJDP8g2U

Adichie, Chimamanda. 2013. The Right to Tell Your Story. Louisiana Channel. Louisiana Museum of Art. https://channel.louisiana.dk/video/chimamanda-adichie-right-tell-your-story

Adichie, Chimamanda. 2014. Hiding from Our Past. *The New Yorker*, May 1. https://www.newyorker.com/culture/culture-desk/hiding-from-our-past

Adichie, Chimamanda. 2014. Conversation with Ted Hodgkinson. June 1. Hay Festival. https://www.hayfestival.com/p-8301-chimamanda-ngozi-adichie-talks-to-ted-hodgkinson.aspx?skinid=16

Adichie, Chimamanda. 2014. Hardtalk. https://www.youtube.com/watch?v=EsWfm0_xgkc

Adichie, Chimamanda. 2017. Chimamanda Ngozi Adichie with Nicola Sturgeon at the Edinburgh International Book Festival. September 4. https://www.youtube.com/watch?v=y-UTBS-vrF8/

Adichie, Chimamanda. 2020. Writing *Half of a Yellow Sun* Affected My Mental Health—Chimanda Adichie. May 30. Sahara TV. https://www.youtube.com/watch?v=_NsELe67UxM

Adichie, Chimamanda, and Wale Adebanwi. 2004. Nigerian Identity Is Burdensome. Nigeria Village Square—Marketplace of Ideas, 11 May. http://www.nigeriavillagesquare.com/book-reviews/nigerian-identity-is-burdensome-the-chimamanda-ngozi-adichie-interview.html (page removed).

Adorno, Theodore. 2004. *Negative Dialectics*. Translated by E. B. Ashton. London: Routledge.

Agamben, Giorgio. 1999. *Remnants of Auschwitz: The Witness and the Archive*. Translated by Daniel Heller-Roazen. New York: Zone Books.

Ajibola, Opeyemi. 2018. Representation of Female Migrants in Selected Nigerian Migrant Narratives. In *Literary and Linguistic Perspectives on Orality, Literacy, and Gender Studies*, edited by Ayo Osisanwo, Kazeem Adebiyi-Adelabu, and Adebayo Mosobala, 170–85. Ibadan: Kraft Books.

Akpome, Aghogho. 2013. Focalisation and Polyvocality in Chimamanda Ngozi Adichie's *Half of a Yellow Sun*. *English Studies in Africa* 56, no. 2 :25–35.

Akpome, Aghogho. 2017. Intertextuality and Influence: Chinua Achebe's *Anthills of the Savannah* and Chimamanda Adichie's *Half of a Yellow Sun*. *Journal of Postcolonial Writing* 53, no. 5: 530–42.

Anderson, Benedict. 1983. *Imagined Communities: Reflections on the Origins and Spread of Nationalism*. London: Verso.

Anderson, Benedict. 1998. *The Spectres of Comparisons: Nationalism, South East Asia, and the World*. London: Verso.

Anderson, Tea Sinbaek, and Jessica Ortner. 2019. Memories of Joy. *Memory Studies* 12, no. 1: 5–10.

Andrade, Susan. 2010. *The Nation Writ Small: African Fictions and Feminisms, 1958–1988*. Durham: Duke University Press.

Appadurai, Arjun. 1996. *Modernity at Large*. Minneapolis: University of Minnesota Press.

Appiah, Kwame. 2006. *Cosmopolitanism: Ethics in a World of Strangers*. New York: W.W. Norton.

Arendt, Hannah. 1987. Collective Responsibility. In *Amor Mundi*, Boston College Studies in Philosophy, Vol. 26, edited by S. J. James W. Bernauer, 43–51. Dordrecht: Springer.

Arnett, James. 2016. No Place Like Home: Failures of Feeling and the Impossibility of Return in Dinaw Mengestu's *The Beautiful Things That Heavens Bear*. *African Literature Today* 34: 103–22.

Ashcroft Bill, Gareth Griffiths, and Helen Tiffin. 1989. *The Empire Writes Back: Theory and Practice in Postcolonial Literatures*. London: Routledge.

Assmann, Aleida. 2016. *Formen des Vergessens* [Forms of Forgetting]. Göttingen: Wallstein.

Assmann, Aleida, and Sebastian Conrad, eds. 2010. *Memory in a Global Age: Discourses, Practices, and Trajectories*. Basingstoke: Palgrave Macmillan.

Assmann, Jan. 2008. Communicative and Cultural Memory. In *Cultural Memory Studies: An International and Interdisciplinary Handbook*, edited by Astrid Erll and Ansgar Nünning, 109–88.OBerlin: De Gruyter.

Atkinson, Meera, and Michael Richardson, eds. 2013. *Traumatic Affect*. Cambridge: Cambridge Scholars.

Atta, Sefi. 2005. *Everything Good Will Come*. Massachusetts: Interlink Publishing.

Attridge, Derek. 2017. No Escape From Home: History, Affect, and Art in Zoe Wicomb's Translocal Coincidences. In *Zoe Wicomb and the Translocal: Scotland and South Africa*, edited by Kai Easton and Derek Attridge, 49–63. London: Routledge.

Aydemir, Murat, and Alex Rotas, eds. 2008. Introduction. In *Migratory Settings*. Leiden: Brill, 7–32.

Baer, Elizabeth. 2017. *The Genocidal Gaze: From German Southwest Africa to the Third Reich*. Detroit: Wayne State University Press.

Bandele, Biyi, dir. 2013. *Half of a Yellow Sun*. Written by Chimamanda Adichie. Produced by Slate Films and Shareman Media.

Basch, Linda, Nina Glick-Schiller, and Cristina Szanton-Blanc, eds. 1994. *Nations Unbound: Transnational Projects, Postcolonial Predicaments, and Deterritorialized Nation-States*. Amsterdam: Gordon and Breach Science.

Basu, Paul. 2008. Confronting the Past? Negotiating a Heritage of Conflict in Sierra Leone. *Journal of Material Culture* 13, no. 2: 233–47.

Baucom, Ian. 2005. *Spectres of the Atlantic: Finance Capital, Slavery, and the Philosophy of History*. Durham: Duke University Press.

Beah, Ishmeal. 2007. *A Long Way Gone*. New York: Farrar, Straus, and Giroux.

Beck, Julie. 2017. Imagining the Future Is Just Another Kind of Memory. *The Atlantic*, October 17. https://www.theatlantic.com/science/archive/2017/10/imagining-the-future-is-just-another-form-of-memory/542832/

Beiner, Guy. 2014. Probing the Boundaries of Irish Memory: From Postmemory to Prememory and Back. *Irish Historical Studies* 39: 154–70.

Benjamin, Walter. 1968. Theses on the Philosophy of History. In *Illuminations*, edited by Hannah Arendt, 253–64. New York: Schocken Books.

Bevernage, Berber. 2012. *History, Memory, and State-Sponsored Violence: Time and Justice*. London: Routledge.

Bhabha, Homi. 1995. DissemiNation: Time, Narrative, and the Margins of the Modern Nation. In *The Post-Colonial Studies Reader*, edited by Bill Ashcroft, Gareth Griffiths, and Helen Tiffin, 230–54. New York: Routledge.

Bhabha, Homi. 2018. Even the Dead Have Human Rights (in conversation with Frank Schulze-Engler, Pavan Malreddy, and John Njenga-Karugia). *Journal of Postcolonial Writing* 54, no. 5: 702–16.

Bienenstock, Myriam. 2010. Is There a Duty to Remember? *Modern Judaism: A Journal of Jewish Ideas and Experience* 30, no. 3: 332–47.

Bond, Lucy, Ben De Bruyn, and Jessica Rapson. 2018. *Planetary Memory in Contemporary American Fiction*. London: Routledge.

Boym, Svetlana. 1998. On Diasporic Intimacies. *Critical Inquiry* 24, no. 2: 498–524.

Brewer, John D. 2006. Memory, Truth, and Victimhood in Post-Trauma Societies. In *Sage Handbook of Nations and Nationalism*, edited by Gerard Delanty and Krishan Kumar, 214–24. London: Sage.

Brown, R., and J. Kulik. 1977. Flashbulb Memories. *Cognition* 5: 73–79.

Bull, Anna Cento, and Hans Lauge Hansen. 2016. On Agonistic Memory. *Memory Studies* 9, no. 4: 390–404.

Burnet, Jennie. 2012. *Genocide Lives in Us: Women, Memory and Silence in Rwanda*. Madison: University of Wisconsin Press.

Cabral, Amilcar. 1973. *Return to the Sources*. New York: New York University Press.

Carrol, Rory. 2004. The US Chose to Ignore Rwanda Genocide. *The Guardian*, April 1. https://www.theguardian.com/world/2004/mar/31/usa.rwanda

Caruth, Cathy. 1996. *Unclaimed Experience: Trauma, Narrative, and History*. Baltimore: Johns Hopkins University Press.
Casey, Edward. (1987) 2000. *Remembering. A Phenomenological Study*. Bloomington: Indiana University Press.
Césaire, Aimé. (1953) 2000. *Discourse on Colonialism*. Translated by Joan Pinkham. New York: Monthly Review Press.
Césaire, Aimé. 1956. Culture and Colonization. *Presence Africaine: Cultural Journal of the Negro World* 8 (June–November): 193–207.
Chacko, Elizabeth. 2010. Africans in Washington, DC: Ethiopia Ethnic Institutions and Immigrant Adjustment. In *The African Diaspora in the US and Canada at the Dawn of the 21st Century*, edited by John Frazier and Nora Henry, 140–63. New York: SUNY Press.
Chakraborty, Dipesh. 1992. Postcoloniality and the Artifice of History: Who Speaks for "Indian" Pasts? *Representations* 37: 1–26.
Chick, Kristen, and Ryan Brown. 2019. Art of the Steal: European Museums Wrestle with Returning African Art. *Christian Science*, April 30. https://www.csmonitor.com/World/Africa/2019/0430/Art-of-the-steal-European-museums-wrestle-with-returning-African-art
Collins, Patricia. 1986. Learning from the Outsider Within: The Sociological Significance of Black Feminist Thought. *Social Problem* 33, no. 6:14–32.
Collins, Tom. 2020. Rwanda-Uganda Conflict. Is the End in Sight? *African Business*, March 23. https://african.business/2020/03/economy/rwanda-uganda-conflict-is-the-end-in-sight/
Connerton, Paul. 2008. Seven Types of Forgetting. *Memory Studies* 1, no. 1: 59–71.
Connerton, Paul. 2011. *The Spirit of Mourning: History, Memory, and the Body*. Cambridge: Cambridge University Press.
Coundouriotis, Eleni. 2014. *The People's Right to the Novel: War Fiction in the Postcolony*. New York: Fordham University Press.
Craps, Stef. 2013. *Postcolonial Witnessing: Trauma Out of Bounds*. Basingstoke: Palgrave Macmillan.
Craps, Stef. 2014. Beyond Eurocentrism: Trauma Theory in the Global Age. In *The Future of Trauma Theory: Contemporary Literary and Cultural Criticism*, edited by Gert Buelens, Sam Durrant, and Robert Eaglestone, 417–42. Abingdon: Routledge.
Creet, Julia. 2011. *Memory and Migration: Multidisciplinary Approaches to Memory Studies*. Toronto: University of Toronto Press.
Crownshaw, Richard. 2009. The Limits of Transference: Theories of Memory and Photography in W. G. Sebald's *Austerlitz*. In *Mediation, Remediation, and the Dynamics of Cultural Memory*, edited by Astrid Erll and Ann Rigney, 68–90. Berlin: De Gruyter.
Crownshaw, Richard. 2014. *Transcultural Memory*. London: Routledge.
Das, Veena. 2007. *Life and Worlds: Violence and the Descent into the Ordinary*. Los Angeles: University of California Press.

Davidson, Basil. 1964. *The African Past: Chronicles from Antiquity to Modern Times*. Boston: Little, Brown.

Davidson, Basil. 1978. *Let Freedom Come: Africa in Modern History*. Boston: Little, Brown.

Dauge-Roth, Alexandre. 2010. *Writing and Filming the Genocide of the Tutsis in Rwanda: Dismembering and Remembering Traumatic History*. Lanham, MD: Lexington Books.

De Beer, Anna-Marie. 2015. Ubuntu and the Journey of Listening to the Rwandan Genocide Story. *Verbum et Ecclesia* 36, no. 2: 74–91.

De Beer, Anna-Marie. 2019. Ubuntu, Reconciliation in Rwanda, and the Returning to Personhood through Collective Narrative. In *Ubuntu and the Reconstitution of Community*, edited by James Ogude, 185–205. Bloomington: University of Indiana Press.

De Boeck, Filip. 1998. Beyond the Grave: Death, Body, and Memory in Postcolonial Congo/Zaire. In *Memory and the Postcolony: African Anthropology and the Critique of Power*, edited by Richard Werbner, 23–35. Chicago: University of Chicago Press.

De Certeau, Michel. 1992. *The Writing of History*. Cambridge: Cambridge University Press.

De Cesari, Chiara, and Ann Rigney, eds. 2014. *Transnational Memory: Circulation, Articulation, Scales*. Berlin: De Gruyter.

Derrida, Jacques. 1994. *Specters of Marx: The State of the Debt, the Work of Mourning, and the New International*. Translated by Peggy Kamuf. New York: Routledge.

Derrida, Jacques. 1997. *The Politics of Friendship*. New York: Verso.

Diawara, Mamadou, Bernard Lategan, and Joon Rusen, eds. 2010. *Historical Memory in Africa: Dealing with the Past, Reaching for the Future in an Intercultural Context*. New York: Berghahn.

Diawara, Manthia (dir.). 2010. *Edouard Glissant: One World in Relation*. K'a Yéléma Productions.

Diop, Boubacar Boris. 2016. Denial through Silence. *Contemporary French and Francophone Studies* 20, no. 2: 243–54.

Diop, Cheikh Anta. 1956. The Cultural Contribution and Prospects of Africa. *Presence Africaine: Cultural Journal of the Negro World* 8 (June–November): 347–54.

Djedanoum, Nocky. 2000. Interview. *Humanité quotidien*, 3 June. http://www.nordnet.fr/festafrica/rwanda2.htm (page removed).

Driver, Dorothy. 2017. Troubling the Politics of Location. In *Zoe Wicomb and the Translocal: Writing Scotland and South Africa*, edited by Kai Easton and Derek Attridge, 8–33. London: Routledge.

Durrant, Sam. 2004. *Postcolonial Narrative and the Work of Mourning: J. M. Coetzee, Wilson Harris, and Toni Morrison*. New York: SUNY Press.

Eagleton, Terry. 1990. *The Ideology of the Aesthetic*. Oxford: Basil Blackwell.

Eng, David. 1999. Melancholy/Postcoloniality: Loss in the Floating Life. *Qui Parle* 11, no. 2: 137–50.

Eng, David, and David Kazanjian, eds. 2003. Introduction. In *Loss: The Politics of Mourning*, 1–25. Berkeley: University of California Press.

Eng, David, and Shinhee Han. 2003. A Dialogue on Racial Melancholia. In *Loss: The Politics of Mourning*, edited by David Eng and David Kazanjian, 343–71. Berkeley: University of California Press.

Erll, Astrid. 2010. Regional Integration and (trans)Cultural Memory. *Asia Europe Journal* 8: 305–15.

Erll, Astrid. 2011. *Memory in Culture*. Basingstoke: Palgrave Macmillan.

Erll, Astrid. 2011. Travelling Memory. *Transcultural Memory. Parallax* 17, no. 4: 4–18.

Erll, Astrid. 2018. Homer: A Relational Mnemohistory. *Memory Studies* 11, no. 3: 274–86.

Falola, Toyin. 2013. *The African Diaspora: Slavery, Modernity, and Globalization*. New York: University of Rochester Press.

Fanon, Frantz. 1952. *Black Skin, White Masks*. Translated by Charles Lam Markmann. New York: Grove Press.

Fanon, Frantz. 1963. *The Wretched of the Earth*. Translated by Constance Farrington. New York: Grove Press.

Fanon, Frantz. (1964) 1994. *Toward the African Revolution*. New York: Grove Press.

Fernandez, Irene. 2017. Emotional Unbelonging in Aminatta Forna's *The Memory of Love*. *Complutense Journal of English Studies* 25: 209–21.

Fine, Ellen. 1998. The Absent Memory: The Act of Writing in Post-Holocaust French Literature. In *Writing and the Holocaust*, edited by Berel Lang, 41–57. New York: Holmes and Meier.

Fine, Michelle. 2018. *Just Research in Contentious Times: Widening the Methodological Imagination*. New York: Teachers College Press.

Firbas, Jan. 1984. Carriers of Communicative Dynamism. *Prague Studies in English* 18, no. 84: 63–73.

Flood, Alison. 2020. Chimamanda Adichie Rejects Delusional Plagiarism Claim. *The Guardian*, 18 March, https://www.theguardian.com/books/2020/mar/18/chimamanda-ngozi-adichie-rejects-delusional-plagiarism-claim

Forna, Aminatta. 2011. My Country Had a Civil War. It Would Be Extraordinary Not to Want to Write about That. *The Independent*. https://www.independent.co.uk/news/people/profiles/aminatta-forna-my-country-had-a-war-it-would-be-extraordinary-not-to-want-to-write-about-that-2291536.html

Forna, Aminatta, and Valeriu Nicolae. 2006. Memory and Forgetting: Aminatta Forna and Valeriu Nicolae in Conversation. *Index on Censorship* 35 no. 2: 74–81.

Freud, Sigmund. (1898) 1953. Screen Memories. *The Standard Edition of the Complete Psychological Works of Sigmund Freud*. Vol. 3, edited by James Strachey, 303–22. London: Hogarth.

Freud, Sigmund. (1917) 1953. Mourning and Melancholia. *The Standard Edition of the Complete Psychological Works of Sigmund Freud*. Vol. 14, edited by James Strachey, 243–58. London: Hogarth.

Freud, Sigmund. (1937) 2001. Remembering, Repeating, and Working-Through. *The*

Standard Edition of the Complete Psychological Works of Sigmund Freud. Vol. 12, edited by James Strachey, 145–56. London: Vintage.
Gagiano, Anne. 2013. Women Writing Nationhood Differently: Affiliative Critique in Novels by Forna, Attah, and Farah. *Ariel: A Review of International English Literature* 44, no. 1: 45–72.
Gandhi, Leela. 1998. *Postcolonial Theory: A Critical Introduction.* New York: Columbia University Press.
Garuba, Harry. 2005. The Unbearable Lightness of Being: Re-Figuring Trends in Recent Nigerian Poetry. *English in Africa* 32, no. 1: 51–72.
Gberie, Lansana. 2005. *A Dirty War in West Africa: The RUF and the Destruction of Sierra Leone.* Bloomington: Indiana University Press.
Gikandi, Simon. 2010. Between Roots and Routes: Cosmopolitanisms and the Claims of Locality. In *Rerouting the Postcolonial*, edited by Janet Wilson, Christina Şandru, and Sarah Lawson-Welsh, 22–35. London: Routledge.
Gilbert, Catherine. 2018. *From Surviving to Living: Voice, Trauma, and Witness in Rwandan Women's Writings.* Montpellier: Presses Universitaires de la Méditerranée.
Gilroy, Paul. 2005. *Postcolonial Melancholia.* New York: Columbia University Press.
Glissant, Edouard. 1997. *Poetics of Relation.* Ann Arbor: University of Michigan Press.
Glynn, Irial, and Olaf Kleist. 2012. *History, Memory, and Migration. Perceptions of the Past and the Politics of Incorporation.* Basingstoke: Palgrave Macmillan.
Gobodo-Madikizela, Pumla. 2003. *A Human Being Died That Night: A South African Story of Forgiveness.* New York: Houghton Mifflin.
Gobodo-Madikizela, Pumla. 2016. Interrupting Cycles of Repetition. In *Breaking Intergenerational Cycle of Repetition: A Global Dialogue on Historical Trauma and Memory*, edited by Pumla Gobodo-Madikizela, 65–89. Leverkusen: Barbara Budrich.
Gordon, Avery. 1997. *Ghostly Matters.* Minneapolis: University of Minnesota Press.
Gottsche, Dirk. 2019. *Memory and Postcolonial Studies: Synergies and New Directions.* New York: Peter Lang.
Gourevitch, Philip. 1998. *We Wish to Inform You That Tomorrow We Will Be Killed with Our Families: Stories from Rwanda.* New York: Farrar, Straus and Giroux.
Gqola, Pumla. 2010. *What Is Slavery to Me? Postcolonial/Slave Memory in Post-apartheid South Africa.* Johannesburg: Wits University Press.
Grant, Farred. 2003. *What's My Name?* Minneapolis: University of Minnesota Press.
Greene, Sandra. 2011. *West African Narratives of Slavery: Texts from Late Nineteenth- and Early Twentieth-Century Ghana.* Bloomington: Indiana University Press.
Gunning, Dave. 2015. Dissociation, Spirit Possession, and the Languages of Trauma in Some Recent African-British Novels. *Research in African Literatures* 46, no. 4: 119–32.
Gutman, Yifat, Adam Brown, and Amy Sodaro, eds. 2010. *Memory and the Future: Transnational Politics, Ethics, and Society.* London: Palgrave Macmillan.
Guyer, Jane. 2007. Prophecy and the Near Future: Thoughts of Macroeconomic, Evangelical, and Punctuated Time. *American Ethnologist* 43, no. 3: 23–40.

Halbwachs, Maurice. 1992. *On Collective Memory*. Translated by Lewis A. Coser. Chicago: University of Chicago Press.

Handlin, Oscar. 1973. *The Uprooted*. Boston: Little, Brown.

Hartman, Saidiya. 1997. *Scenes of Subjection: Terror, Slavery, and Self-Making in Eighteenth-Century America*. Oxford: Oxford University Press.

Hartman, Saidiya, and Frank B. Wilderson III. 2003. The Position of the Unthought: An Interview with Saidiya Hartman Conducted by Frank B. Wilderson III. *Qui Parle* 13, no. 2: 189–90.

Hartman, Geoffrey. 2006. Shoah and the Intellectual Witness. *Reading On* 1, no. 1: 1–8.

Hawley, John. 2008. Biafra as Heritage and Symbol: Adichie, Mbachau, and Iweala. *Research in African Literatures* 39, no. 2: 15–26.

Hargreaves, Alec. 2005. *Memory, Empire, and Postcolonialism: Legacies of French Colonialism*. Washington, DC: Lexington Books.

Henderson, Errol A. 2000. When States Implode: The Correlates of Africa's Civil Wars, 1950–92. *Studies in Comparative International Development* 35, no. 2: 28–47.

Henry, Kajsa K. 2006. A Literary Archaeology of Loss: The Politics of Mourning in African American Literature. PhD Thesis, Department of English, Florida State University.

Hewett, Heather. 2005. Coming of Age: Chimamanda Ngozi Adichie and the Voice of the Third Generation. *English in Africa* 32, no. 1: 73–97.

Hirsch, Marianne. 1994. Maternity and Rememory: Toni Morrison's Beloved. In *Representations of Motherhood*, edited by Donna Bassin, Margaret Honey, and Meryle Mahrer Kaplan, 92–110. New Haven: Yale University Press.

Hirsch, Marianne. 1997. *Family Frames: Photography, Narrative, and Postmemory*. Cambridge: Harvard University Press.

Hirsch, Marianne. 2008. The Generation of Postmemory. *Poetics Today* 29, no. 1: 103–28.

Hirsch, Marianne, and Leo Spitzer. 2016. Small Acts of Repair: The Unclaimed Legacy of the Romanian Holocaust. In *Memory Unbound: Tracing the Dynamics of Memory Studies*, edited by Lucy Bond, Stef Craps, and Pieter Vermeulen, 67–89. New York: Berghahn.

Hirst, William, and Elizabeth A. Phelps. 2016. Flashbulb Memories. *Current Directions in Psychological Science* 25, no. 1: 36–41.

Hitchcott, Nicki. 2009. A Global African Commemoration—Rwanda: Écrire par devoire de mémoire. *Forum for Modern Language Studies* 45, no. 2: 151–61.

Hitchcott, Nicki. 2009. Travels in Inhumanity: Véronique Tadjo's Tourism in Rwanda. *French Cultural Studies* 20, no. 2: 147–64.

Hite, Katherine. 2015. Empathic Unsettlement and the Outsider within Argentine Spaces of Memory. *Memory Studies* 8, no. 1: 24–38.

Hobsbawm, Eric. 1990. *Nations and Nationalism since 1780: Programme, Myth, and Reality*. New York: Cambridge University Press.

Hutcheon, Linda. 1983. *A Poetics of Postmodernism?* Baltimore: Johns Hopkins University Press.

Huyse, Luc. 2009. *All Things Pass, Except the Past*. Kalmthout, Belgium: Pelckmans.
Huyssen, Andreas. 2003. *Present Pasts: Urban Palimpsest and the Politics of Memory*. Stanford: Stanford University Press.
Idesbald, Goddeeris. 2015. Postcolonial Belgium: The Memory of the Congo. *Interventions* 17, no. 3: 434–51.
Ifowodo, Ogaga. 2013. *History, Trauma, and Healing in Postcolonial Narratives: Reconstructing Identities*. New York: Palgrave Macmillan.
Ignatieff, Michael. 1998. The Nightmare from Which We Are Trying to Awake. In *The Warrior's Honor: Ethnic War and the Modern Conscience*, 170–89. New York: Metropolitan Books.
Irele, F. Abiola. 2010. Introduction: Perspectives on the African Novel. In *The Cambridge Companion to the African Novel*, edited by F. Abiola Irele, 1–14. Cambridge: Cambridge University Press.
Irr, Caren. 2013. *Toward the Geopolitical Novel: U.S. Fiction in the Twenty-First Century*. New York: Columbia University Press.
Jackson, Michael. 2018. *The Varieties of Temporal Experience: Travels in Philosophical, Historical, and Ethnographic Time*. New York: Columbia University Press.
Jacob, Raouf J. dir. 2014. *A Culture of Silence*. Produced by Worldwide Cinema Frames.
Jarrett-Macauley, Delia. 2005. *Moses, Citizen, and Me*. London: Granta.
Jensen, Lars. 2018. *Postcolonial Denmark: Nation Narration in a Crisis Ridden Europe*. London: Routledge.
Julien, Eileen. 2006. The Extroverted African Novel. In *The Novel: History, Geography, and Culture*. Vol. 1., edited by Franco Morretti, 667–702. Princeton: Princeton University Press.
Kamarah, Sheikh. 2016. *The Child of War*. Freetown: Sierra Leonean Writers Series.
Kansteiner, Wulf. 2004. Testing the Limits of Trauma: The Long-Term Psychological Effects of the Holocaust on Individuals and Collectives. *History of Human Sciences* 17, no. 2: 97–123.
Kehinde, Ayo. 2003. Intertextuality and the Contemporary African Novel. *Nordic Journal of African Studies* 12, no. 3: 372–86.
Keightley, Emily, and Michael Pickering, 2012. *The Mnemonic Imagination: Remembering as Creative Practice*. Basingstoke: Palgrave Macmillan.
Kelsall, Kate. 2017. Veronique Tadjo's Literary Pan Africanism. *The Culture Trip*. https://theculturetrip.com/africa/ivory-coast/articles/veronique-tadjo-s-literary-pan-africanism/
Kennedy, Rosanne. 2018. Reparative Transnationalism: The Friction and Fiction of Remembering in Sierra Leone. *Memory Studies* 11, no. 3: 342–54.
Khanna, Ranjana. 2003. *Dark Continents: Psychoanalysis and Colonialism*. Durham: Duke University Press.
Kleber, Rolf J., Charles R. Figley, and Berthold P. R. Gersons, eds. 1995. *Beyond Trauma: Cultural and Societal Dynamics*. New York: Springer.

Klein, Karwin. 2000. On the Emergence of Memory in Historical Discourse. *Representations* 69, no. 1: 127–50.

Kopf, Martina. 2012. Ethics of Fiction: African Writers on the Genocide in Rwanda. *Journal of Literary History* 6, no. 1: 45–67.

Kresh, Diane. 2013. Author Dinaw Mengestu Speaks at the Arlington Public Library. April 26. https://www.youtube.com/watch?v=afEj_SJwj9w

Kristeva, Julia. 1989. *Black Sun: Depression and Melancholia*. Translated by Leon S. Roudiez. New York: Columbia University Press.

Krondorfor, Bjorn. 2016. Unsettling Empathy. In *Breaking Intergenerational Cycle of Repetition: A Global Dialogue on Historical Trauma and Memory*, edited by Pumla Gobodo-Madikizela, 89–111. Leverkusen: Barbara Budrich.

Kutz, Christopher. 2000. *Complicity*. Cambridge: Cambridge University Press.

LaCapra, Dominick. 1998. An Interview with Dominick LaCapra. Jerusalem: Shoah Resource Centre. www.yadvashem.org

LaCapra, Dominick. 2001. *Writing History, Writing Trauma*. Baltimore: Johns Hopkins University Press.

Lachmann, Renate. 1997. *Memory and Literature*. Minneapolis: University of Minnesota Press.

Laing, Olivia. 2007. Dream Catcher: A Review of the *Children of the Revolution*. *The Guardian*. June 2. https://www.theguardian.com/books/2007/jun/02/featuresreviews.guardianreview32/

Lalu, Primesh. 2009. *The Deaths of Hintsa: Postapartheid South Africa and the Shape of Recurring Pasts*. Cape Town: HSRC Press.

Landsberg, Alison. 2004. *Prosthetic Memory: The Transformation of American Remembrance in the Age of Mass Culture*. New York: Columbia University Press.

Langer, Lawrence. 1991. *Holocaust Testimonies: The Ruins of Memory*. New Haven: Yale University Press.

Langer, Lawrence. 2000. Uses and Misuses of a Young Girl's Diary: If Anne Frank Could Return from among the Murdered, She Would Be Appalled. In *Anne Frank: Reflections on Her Life and Legacy*, edited by Hyman A. Enzer and Sandra Solotaro Enzer, 203–5. Urbana: University of Illinois Press.

Lasdun, James. 2010. How to Read the Air. A Review. *The Guardian*. January 1. https://www.theguardian.com/books/2011/jan/01/dinaw-mengestu-read-air-review

Laub, Dori. 1992. Bearing Witness, or the Vicissitudes of Listening. In *Testimony: Crisis of Witnessing in Literature, Psychoanalysis, and History*, edited by Shoshana Felman and Dori Laub, 57–74. New York: Routledge.

Laub, Dori. 2010. Memory and History from Past to Future: A Dialogue with Dori Laub on Trauma and Testimony. In *Memory and the Future: Transnational Politics, Ethics, and Society*, edited by Yifat Gutman, Adam Brown, and Amy Sodaro, 50–65. Basingstoke: Palgrave Macmillan.

Lebor, Adam. 2008. *Complicity with Evil: The United Nations in the Age of Genocide*. New Haven: Yale University Press.

Legum, Colin, I. William Zartman, Steven Langdon, and Lynn K. Mytelka. 1979. *Africa in the 1980s: A Continent in Crisis*. New York: McGraw-Hill.

Levinas, Emmanuel. 1985. *Ethics and Infinity*. Translated by Richard Cohen. Pittsburgh: Duquesne University Press.

Levy, Daniel, and Natan Sznaider. 2002. Memory Unbound: The Holocaust and the Formation of Cosmopolitan Memory. *European Journal of Social Theory* 5, no. 1: 87–106.

Levy, Daniel, and Natan Sznaider. 2011. Cosmopolitan Memory and Human Rights. In *The Ashgate Research Companion to Cosmopolitanism*, edited by Maria Rovisco and Madgalena Nowicka, 195–209. London: Routledge.

Loftus, Elizabeth. 2013. The Fiction of Memory. *Ted Global*, June 11. https://blog.ted.com/tk-elizabeth-loftus-at-tedglobal-2013/

Lombardi-Diop, Cristian, and Caterina Romeo. 2012. *Postcolonial Italy: Challenging National Homogeneity*. New York: Palgrave Macmillan.

Lorenz, Chris, and Berber Bevernage. 2013. *Breaking Up Time: Negotiating the Borders between Present, Past, and Future*. Gottingen: Vandehoeck and Ruprecht.

Mamdani, Mahmood. 1996. *Citizen and Subject: Contemporary Africa and the Legacy of Late Colonialism*. Princeton: Princeton University Press.

Mamdani, Mahmood. 2001. *When Victims Become Killers. Colonialism, Nativism, and the Genocide in Rwanda*. Princeton: Princeton University Press.

Mamdani, Mahmood. 2020. *Neither Settler nor Native: The Making and Unmaking of Permanent Minorities*. Cambridge: Harvard University Press.

Margalit, Avishai. 2002. *The Ethics of Memory*. Cambridge, MA: Harvard University Press.

Mbembe, Achille. 2001. *On the Postcolony*. Berkeley: University of California Press.

Mbembe, Achille. 2007. Afropolitanism. In *Africa Remix*, edited by Simon Njami and Lucy Durán. Johannesburg: Jacana Media.

Mbembe, Achille. 2019. *Necropolitics*. Durham: Duke University Press.

Minow, Martha. 2009. Foreword. In *Memory, Narrative and Forgiveness: Perspectives on the Unfinished Journeys of the Past*, edited by Pumla Gobodo-Madikizela and Chris Van Der Merwe, 7. Newcastle upon Tyne: Cambridge Scholars Publishing.

Misgav, Uri. 2015. The Israeli Guns That Took Part in the Rwanda Genocide. *Haaretz*, April 10. https://www.haaretz.com/.premium-the-israeli-guns-in-the-rwanda-genocide-1.5355564/

Morrison, Toni. 1995. The Site of Memory. In *Inventing the Truth: The Art and Craft of Memoir*, ed. William Zinsser, 83–102. Boston: Houghton Mifflin.

Morrison, Toni. 2014. Toni Morrison Talks to Peter Florence on *Beloved*. Hay Festival https://www.youtube.com/watch?v=vtJFK_HtlQ

Moses, Dirk, and Lasse Heerten. 2017. *Postcolonial Conflict and the Question of Genocide: The Nigeria-Biafra War*. London: Routledge.

Mudimbe, V. Y. 1988. *The Invention of Africa*. Bloomington: Indiana University Press.

Munroe, Leanne. 2016. Negotiating Memories and Silences: Museum Narratives of Transatlantic Slavery in England. In *Beyond Memory: Silence and the Aesthetics of*

Remembrance, edited by Winter Jay and Alexandre Dessingué. 170–83. London: Routledge.
Murphy, Laura. 2008. The Curse of Constant Remembrance: The Belated Trauma of the Slave Trade in Ayi Kwei Armah's *Fragments*. *Studies in the Novel* 40, no. 1: 52–71.
National Post. 2014. New Seeds of Conflict. April 14. https://nationalpost.com/news/new-seeds-of-conflict-20-years-post-genocide-there-are-fears-than-rwandan-schools-ferment-hate
Ngarambe, Alex. 2019. Rwanda's Opposition Rattled by Killing and Disappearance of Members. *DW*, September 26. https://www.dw.com/en/rwandas-opposition-rattled-by-killings-and-disappearances-of-members/a-50596049/
Ngwira, Emmanuel. 2011. He Writes about the World That Remained Silent: Witnessing Authorship in Chimamanda Adichie's *Half of a Yellow Sun*. *English Studies in Africa* 55, no. 2: 43–53.
Nicholas, Abraham, and Maria Torok. 1994. Secrets and Posterity: The Theory of the Transgenerational Phantom. In *The Shell and the Kernel*, edited by Nicholas Rand, 165–71. Chicago: University of Chicago Press.
Nixon, Rob. 2007. African, American. *New York Times*. https://www.nytimes.com/2007/03/25/books/review/Nixon.t.html
Nora, Pierre. 1992. *Realms of Memory: Rethinking the French Past*. Edited by Lawrence D. Kritzman. Translated by Arthur Goldhammer. New York: Columbia University Press.
Norridge, Zoe. 2012. Sex as Synecdoche: Intimate Languages of Violence in Chimamanda Ngozi Adichie's *Half of a Yellow Sun* and Aminatta Forna's *The Memory of Love*. *Research in African Literatures* 43, no. 2: 18–39.
Norridge, Zoe. 2013. *Perceiving Pain in African Literature*. Basingstoke: Palgrave Macmillan.
Norridge, Zoe. 2014. Ways of Knowing Civil War: Human Rights and the Traction of Complicity in Aminatta Forna's *The Hired Man*. *Critical Quarterly* 56, no. 4: 91–114.
Novak, Amy. 2008. Who Speaks? Who Listens? The Problem of Address in Two Nigerian Trauma Novels. *Studies in the Novel* 40, no. 1–2: 31–51.
Nthabiseng, Motsemme. 2014. The Mute Always Speaks: On Women's Silences at the Truth and Reconciliation Commission. *Current Sociology* 52, no. 5: 909–932.
Nünning, Ansgar. 2003. "Editorial: New Directions in the Study of Individual and Cultural Memory and Memorial Cultures." *Fictions of Memory*. Edited by Ansgar Nünning. *Journal for the Study of British Cultures* 10, no. 1: 3–9.
Nwankwo, Emeka Joseph. 2020. White Eyes. *Africa Is a Country*, July 27. https://africasacountry.com/2020/07/white-eyes
Oduku, Oduor. 2017. Poverty Porn: A New Prison for African Writers. *Brittle Paper*. April 24. https://richardoduor.wordpress.com/2017/04/24/poverty-porn-a-new-prison-for-african-writers/
Olick, Jeffrey K. 1999. Collective Memory: The Two Cultures. *Sociological Theory* 17, no. 3: 333–48.

Oostinie, Gert. 2011. *Postcolonial Netherlands: Sixty-Five Years of Forgetting, Commemorating, and Silencing*. Amsterdam: Amsterdam University Press.

Ouma, Chris. 2011. Composite Consciousness and Memories of War in Chimamanda Ngozi Adichie's *Half of a Yellow Sun*. *English Academy Review* 28, no. 2: 15–30.

Ouma, Chris. 2015. Late Achebe: Biafra as Literary Genealogy. In *Chinua Achebe's Legacy: Illuminations from Africa*, edited by James Ogude, 70–78. Oxford: African Books Collective.

Ouma, Chris. 2020. *Childhood in Contemporary Diasporic African Literature*. Basingstoke: Palgrave Macmillan.

Passerlini, Luisa. 2005. Memories between Silence and Oblivion. In *Memory, History, and Nation*, edited by Susannah Radstone and Katherine Hoddgkin, 45–63. New Brunswick: Transaction.

Pedwell, Carolyn. 2014. Affective Translation: Empathy and *The Memory of Love*. In *Affective Relations: Thinking Gender in Transnational Times*, edited by Pedwell Carolyn, 119–35. London: Palgrave Macmillan.

Picard, Inci Tebis. 2016. Migratory Grief. *British Psychological Society* 29, no. 1: 886–93.

Putuma, Koleka. 2017. *Collective Amnesia*. Cape Town: uHlanga.

Quashie, Kevin. 2012. *The Sovereignty of Quiet: Beyond Resistance in Black Culture*. New Brunswick: Rutgers University Press.

Quijano, Anibal. 2000. Coloniality of Power and Eurocentrism in Latin America. *International Sociology* 15, no. 2: 215–32.

Raczymow, Henri. 1994. Memory Shot through with Holes. Translated by Alan Astro. *Yale French Studies* 85, no. 1: 98–106.

Radstone, Susannah. 2011. What Place Is This? Transcultural Memory and the Locations of Memory Studies. *Parallax* 17, no. 4: 109–23.

Rapson, Jessica, and Lucy Bond. 2014. *The Transcultural Turn: Interrogating Memory Between and Beyond Borders*. Berlin: De Gruyter.

Rayborn, Gladys. 2014. *Half of a Yellow Sun: An Audiobook*. December 6. https://www.youtube.com/watch?v=DEZYR77JYQs

Reading, Anna. 2011. Memory and Digital Media: Six Dynamics of the Globital Memory. In *On Media Memory: Collective Memory in a New Media Age*, edited by Motti Neiger, Oren Meyers, and Eyal Zandberg. New York: Palgrave Macmillan.

Reid, Richard. 2011. Past and Presentism: The Pre-Colonial and the Foreshortening of African History. *Journal of African History* 52, no. 2: 135–55.

Rever, Judi. 2018. *In Praise of Blood: The Crimes of the Rwandan Patriotic Front*. Toronto: Random House.

Ricoeur, Paul. 1984. *Time and Narrative*. Vol. 1. Translated by Kathleen McLaughlin and David Pellauer. Chicago: University of Chicago Press.

Ricoeur, Paul. 2000. *Memory, History, Forgetting*. Translated by Kathleen McLaughlin and David Pellauer. Chicago: University of Chicago Press.

Rigney, Ann. 2004. Portable Monuments: Literature, Cultural Memory, and the Case of Jeanie Deans. *Poetics Today* 25, no. 2: 361–96.

Rigney, Ann. 2018. Remembering Hope: Transnational Activism beyond the Traumatic. *Memory Studies* 11, no. 3: 368–80.
Rigney, Ann. 2018. Remembrance as Remaking: Memories of the Nation Revisited. *Nations and Nationalism* 24, no. 2: 43–60.
Rigney, Ann. 2020. Why Monuments Matter (And When They Don't). *Remembering Activism*, June 30. https://rememberingactivism.eu/2020/06/30/why-monuments-matter-and-when-they-dont/
Riverhead Books. 2010. How to Read the Air by Dinaw Mengestu. July 13. https://www.youtube.com/watch?v=xZteshCUKOk
Rodney, Walter. 1972. *How Europe Underdeveloped Africa*. London: Bogle-L'Ouverture.
Rogers, Juliet. 2016. Rethinking Remorse. In *Breaking the Intergenerational Cycle of Repetition: A Global Dialogue on Historical Trauma and Memory*, edited by Pumla Gobodo-Madikizela, 55–75. Leverkusen: Barbara Budrich.
Rosinska, Zofia. 2011. Emigratory Experience: The Melancholy of No Return. In *Memory and Migration: Multidirectional Approaches to Memory Studies*, edited by Julia Creet and Andreas Kitzmann, 88–103. Toronto: University of Toronto Press.
Rotberg, Robert. 1966. African Nationalism: Concept or Confusion. *The Journal of African Modern Studies* 4.1:33–46.
Rothberg, Michael. 2009. *Multidirectional Memory: Remembering the Holocaust in the Age of Decolonization*. Stanford: Stanford University Press.
Rothberg, Michael. 2011. From Gaza to Warsaw: Mapping Multidirectional Memory. *Transcultural Negotiations of Holocaust Memory*. Special issue, edited by Stef Craps and Michael Rothberg. *Criticism: A Quarterly for Literature and the Arts* 53, no. 4: 523–48.
Rothberg, Michael. 2013. Remembering Back: Cultural Memory, Colonial Legacies, and Postcolonial Studies. *The Oxford Handbook of Postcolonial Studies*, edited by Graham Huggan, 359–79. Oxford: Oxford University Press.
Rothberg, Michael. 2016. Multidirectional Memory: Entangled Narratives, Implicated Subjects. Tagung Erinnerungsorte. Vergessene und verwobene Geschichten. Judisches Museum Berlin. https://www.youtube.com/watch?v=xs75PTmbtts
Rothberg, Michael. 2019. *The Implicated Subject. Beyond Victims and Perpetrators*. Stanford: Stanford University Press.
Rothberg, Michael, and Yasemin Yildiz. 2011. Memory Citizenship: Migrant Archive of Holocaust Remembrance in Contemporary Germany. *Parallax* 17, no. 4: 32–48.
Ruin, Han. 2019. *Being with the Dead: Burial, Ancestral Politics, and the Roots of Historical Consciousness*. Stanford: Stanford University Press.
Samuel, Raphael. 1981. *People's History and Socialist Theory*. London: Routledge.
Sanders, Mark. 2002. *Complicities: The Intellectual and Apartheid*. Durham: Duke University Press.
Sankara, Thomas. 1988. *Thomas Sankara Speaks: The Burkina Faso Revolution*. Atlanta: Pathfinder Press.

Sanyal, Debarati. 2015. *Memory and Complicity: Migrations of Holocaust Remembrance*. New York: Fordham University Press.
Scarry, Elaine. 1996. The Difficulty of Imagining Other People: Debating the Limit of Patriotism. In *For Love of Country: Debating the Limits of Patriotism.*, edited by Martha Nassbaum, 98–110. Boston: Beacon.
Schacter, Daniel. 2001. *The Seven Sins of Memory: How the Mind Forgets and Remembers*. New York: Houghton Mifflin.
Schilling, Brita. 2014. *Postcolonial Germany: Memories of Empire in a Decolonized Nation*. Oxford: Oxford University Press.
Schreiber, Melody. 2020. Rwanda's Genocide Ended 26 Years Ago: Survivors Are Still Finding Mass Graves. *NPR*, July 16, https://www.npr.org/2020/07/16/891815028/rwandas-genocide-ended-26-years-ago-survivors-are-still-finding-mass-graves
Scott, David. 2014. *Omens of Adversity. Tragedy, Time, Memory, and Justice*. Durham: Duke University Press.
Scott, David. 2018. Black Futurities. *Colonial Repercussions* event. Akademie der Kunste. https://www.youtube.com/watch?v=OlzDe2rgfzs&t=3s/
Scott, James. 1985. *Weapons of the Weak: Everyday Forms of Peasant Resistance*. New Haven: Yale University Press.
Sebald, W. G. 1999. *On the Natural History of Destruction*. Munich: Carl Hanser Verlag.
Selasi, Taiye. 2005. Bye-Bye Babar, or What Is an Afropolitan? *Lip Magazine*, March 3. https://thelip.robertsharp.co.uk/2005/03/03/bye-bye-barbar/
Senayon, Olaoluwa. 2017. Synmemory: Civil War Victimhood and the Balance of Tales in Adichie's *Half of a Yellow Sun* and Habila's *Measuring Time*. *Social Dynamics* 43, no. 1: 19–31.
Sennett, Richard. 2012. Disturbing Memories. In *Memory*, edited by Patricia Fara and Karalyn Patterson, 10–26. Cambridge: Cambridge University Press.
Serpell, Namwali. 2019. The Banality of Empathy. *New York Review*, March 2. https://www.nybooks.com/daily/2019/03/02/the-banality-of-empathy/
Sharpe, Christina. 2016. *In the Wake: On Blackness and Being*. Durham: Duke University Press.
Shaw, Rosalind. 2015. Rethinking Truth and Reconciliation Commissions. Lessons from Sierra Leone. (A Report Written for the United States Institute of Peace, Washington). https://www.usip.org/publications/2005/02/rethinking-truth-and-reconciliation-commissions-lessons-sierra-leone
Shih, Shu-mei, and Francoise Lionnet. 2005. *Minor Transnationalism*. Durham: Duke University Press.
Shulock, Anne. 2010. Interview with Dinaw Mengestu. *The Rumpus*. https://therumpus.net/2010/10/the-rumpus-interview-with-dinaw-mengestu/
Siddle, D. J. 1968. War-Towns in Sierra Leone: A Study in Social Change. *Africa* 38, no. 1: 47–56.
Silverman, Max. 2013. *Palimpsestic Memory: The Holocaust and Colonialism in French and Francophone Fiction and Film*. New York: Berghahn.

Silverstein, Paul. 2018. *Postcolonial France: Race, Islam, and the Future of the Republic*. London: Pluto Books.

Sithole, Ndabaningi. 1959. *African Nationalism*. Cape Town: Oxford University Press.

Small, Audrey. 2007. The Duty of Memory. A Solidarity of Voices after the Rwandan Genocide. *Paragraph* 30, no. 1: 85–100.

Sontag, Susan. 2003. *Regarding the Pain of Others*. New York: Farrar, Straus and Giroux.

Soyinka, Wole. 2000. *The Burden of Memory, the Muse of Forgiveness*. Oxford: Oxford University Press.

Staley, David. 2002. A History of the Future. *History and Theory* 41, no. 4: 72–89.

Stanley, Liz. 2006. *Mourning Becomes . . . Post/memory and Commemoration of the Concentration Camps of the South African War 1899–1902*. Manchester: University of Manchester Press.

Stewart, Gary, and John Amman. 2007. *Black Man's Grave: Letters from Sierra Leone*. Washington, DC: Cold Run Books.

Stonebridge, Lindsay. 2020. *Writing and Righting: Literature in the Age of Human Rights*. Oxford: Oxford University Press.

Stone, Charles B., Alin Coman, Adam D. Brown, Jonathan Koppel, and William Hirst. 2012. Toward a Science of Silence: The Consequences of Leaving a Memory Unsaid. *Perspectives on Psychological Science* 7, no. 1: 39–53.

Sturken, Marita. 2007. *Tourists of History: Memory, Kitsch, and Consumerism from Oklahoma City to Ground Zero*. Durham: Duke University Press.

Suleiman, Susan Rubin. 2006. *Crises of Memory and the Second World War*. Cambridge: Harvard University Press.

Tadjo, Véronique. 2010. "Genocide: The Changing Landscape of Memory in Kigali." *African Identities* 8, no. 4: 379–88.

Tadjo, Véronique. 2014. Writing for Life: *The Shadow of Imana*: Travels in the Heart of Rwanda. Columbia Maison Française. October 28. https://www.youtube.com/watch?v=mFwGhwy_tL0

Tan, Kathy-Ann. 2015. *Reconfiguring Citizenship and National Identity in North American Imagination*. Detroit: Wayne State University Press.

Thomas, Dominic. 2010. New Voices, Emerging Themes. In *The Cambridge Companion to the African Novel*, edited by Abiola Irele, 229. Cambridge: Cambridge University Press.

Thomson, Susan. 2018. *Rwanda: From Genocide to Precarious Peace*. New Haven: Yale University Press.

Trezise, Thomas. 2014. *Witnessing Witnessing: The Reception of the Holocaust Survivor Testimony*. New York: Fordham University Press.

Trouillot, Michel-Rolph. 1995. *Silencing the Past: Power and the Production of History*. Boston: Beacon Press.

Tsing, Anna. 2004. *Friction: An Ethnography of Global Connections*. Princeton: Princeton University Press.

Tumarkin, Maria. 2015. *Traumascapes: The Power and Fate of Places Transformed by Tragedy*. Carlton, Victoria: Melbourne University Publishing.
Van Alphen, Ernst. 2006. Second-Generation Testimony, Transmission of Trauma, and Postmemory. *Poetics Today* 27, no. 2: 473–88.
Van Gils, Martijn. 2016. In the Shadow of Biafra: Construction of War Memory in Adichie's *Half of a Yellow Sun*. BA Thesis, Department of English, Radboud University, 1–211.
Vinitzky-Seroussi, Vered, and Chana Teeger. 2010. Unpacking the Unspoken: Silence in Collective Memory and Forgetting. *Social Forces* 88, no. 3: 1103–22.
Vodkan, Vamik D. 2007. Not Letting Go: From Individual Perennial Mourners to Societies with Entitlement Ideologies. In *On Freud's 'Mourning and Melancholia'*, edited by F. Glocer, T. Bokanowski, and Y. Lewkowics, 90–101. London: Routledge.
Waberi, Abdourahman. 1998. Les enfants de la postcolonie: Esquisse d'une nouvelle génération d'écrivains francophones d'Afrique noire. *Notre librairie* 135, no. 11: 8–15.
Wainaina, Binyavanga. 2011. *One Day I will Write about This Place*. Minneapolis: Graywolf Press.
Wa Thiong'o, Ngugi. 1986. *Decolonising the Mind: The Politics of Language in African Literature*. Cambridge: Cambridge University Press.
Weissman, Gary. 2004. *Fantasies of Witnessing: Postwar Efforts to Experience the Holocaust*. Ithaca: Cornell University Press.
Werbner, Richard. 1998. Beyond Oblivion: Confronting Memory Crisis. In *Memory and the Postcolony: African Anthropology and the Critique of Power*. Chicago: University of Chicago Press.
White, Hayden. 1973. *Metahistory: The Historical Imagination in Nineteenth-Century Europe*. Baltimore: Johns Hopkins University Press.
White, Hayden. 2005. Historical Fiction, Fictional History, and Historical Reality. *Rethinking History* 9: 147–57.
Wicomb, Zoe. 2005. Setting, Intertextuality, and the Resurrection of the Postcolonial Author. *Journal of Postcolonial Writing* 41, no. 2: 144–55.
Wiesel, Elie. 1986. Hope, Despair, and Memory. Nobel Lecture. www.nobelprize.org/peace/laureate/1986/wiesel-lecture.html/
Williams, Adebayo. 1997. The Postcolonial Flaneur and Other Fellow-Travelers: Conceits for a Narrative of Redemption. *Third World Quarterly* 18, no. 5: 821–41.
Williamson, Caroline. 2014. Towards a Theory of Collective Posttraumatic Growth in Rwanda: The Pursuit of Agency and Communion. *Traumatology* 20, no. 2: 91–102.
Williamson, Caroline. 2018. *Rwanda After Genocide: Gender, Identity and Post-Traumatic Growth*. Cambridge: Cambridge University Press.
Wimmer, Andreas, and Nina Glick Schiller. 2002. Methodological Nationalism and Beyond: Nation-State Building, Migration, and the Social Sciences. *Global Networks* 2, no. 4: 301–334.

Winter, Jay. 2012. Introduction. In *History, Memory, and Migration: Perceptions of the Past and the Politics of Incorporation*, edited by Irial Glynn and J. Olaf Kleist, 1–11. New York: Palgrave Macmillan.

Wintle, Claire. 2013. Decolonizing the Museum: The Case of the Imperial and Commonwealth Institute. *Museum & Society* 11, no. 2: 185–201.

Wrong, Michela. 2021. *Do Not Disturb: The Story of a Political Murder and an African Regime Gone Bad*. New York: Public Affairs.

Yeoh, Brenda, Michael Charney, and Tong Kiong. 2003. *Approaching Transnationalism: Studies on Transnational Societies, Multicultural Contacts, and Imaginings of Home*. New York: Springer.

Žižek, Slavoj. 2000. Melancholy and the Act. *Critical Inquiry* 26, no. 4: 657–81.

INDEX

absent memory, 34
Aburi Accord, 32, 135n46
Achebe, Chinua, 16, 41, 45, 137n80
acting-in-complicity, 67
Addis Ababa, Ethiopia. *See Children of the Revolution* (Mengestu)
Adesanmi, Pius, 25
Adichie, Chimamanda, 3, 121; "Stories of Africa," 28–30, 34, 40; as a vicarious witness, 28–31. *See also Half of a Yellow Sun* (Adichie)
Adichie, David, 40
Adorno, Theodore, 11
affect: affective authenticity, 114; affective community of memory, 113; affective encounters, 103–8
African Continental Free Trade Agreement (ACFTA), 90
Africanism, 8; Pan-Africanism, 89–90, 92, 100, 101, 145n54
Africanization, 103
African Memory Game initiative, 147n73
African nationalism, 89, 92, 145n54
African renaissance monument, in Dakar, 92
African transnational memory (ATM), 5, 12–13, 17–18, 39–40, 89–95, 118, 124–25; immigrant melancholia, 20–21, 74–83; "Rwanda: Writing as a Duty to Remember" project, 21, 98–101, 103, 114, 116, 120, 124, 148n14, 149n27; Tutsis, genocide against, and, 96–103, 115–16. *See also Children of the Revolu-*

tion (Mengestu); *The Shadow of Imana* (Tadjo)
African Union (AU), 90
Afropolitanism, 88
Agamben, Giorgio, 79–80
agency, 2, 91, 100, 105, 151n60
agonistic memory, 7, 15, 131n89
Akpan, Uwem, 25
All Our Names (Mengestu), 75
alterity, 104, 110; outsider within, 107, 150n48. *See also* secondary witnessing
American dream, 78. *See also* United States of America
Amin, Idi, 94
amnesia, 16, 58, 76, 78; collective, 48, 89, 90, 146n56; institutionalized, 2, 15, 24. *See also* forgetting
anamnestic solidarity, with the dead, 10, 43, 104, 122
Ancestor Stone (Forna), 49
ancestral memory, 45–46, 57
ancestral veneration, 99, 122
anchoring, 54, 78, 93, 100, 107
Anderson, Benedict, 12
Andrade, Susan Z., 16–17
anonymity, 82
antagonistic memory, 15, 131n89
Appiah, Kwame, 88
archaic inheritance, 26
archival memory, 30
archival silences, 3, 33
Armah, Ayi Kwei, 17
Arnett, James, 76

173

artist mediation. *See* secondary witnessing
Assmann, Aleida, 7, 127n3
Assmann, Jan, 7, 134n29
autobiographical reflection, 109

Baer, Elizabeth, 39
Basu, Paul, 57
Baucom, Ian, 12
The Beautiful Things That Heavens Bear (Mengestu), 142n2. *See also Children of the Revolution* (Mengestu)
The Beautyful Ones Are Not Yet Born (Armah), 17
Beck, Julie, 117
Beiner, Guy, 27, 136n67
being-in-time, 70
Belgium, role in Rwandan genocide, 97, 121, 147n3, 148n5
belonging, alternative practices of, 83–88
Benjamin, Walter, 11, 43
Benson, Bobby, 34
Bergson, Henri, 7
Bevernage, Berber, 10, 56
Bhabha, Homi, 62
Biafra, 19; *Biafra and Other Poems* (Achebe), 41; *The Biafra Story* (Forsyth), 34; Biafra Zionist Movement (BZM), 45; Movement of the Actualization of the Sovereign State of Biafra (MASSOB), 45; postmemory and the possibility of justice for, 43–45; the shadow of, 23–26, 28, 135n45. *See also Half of a Yellow Sun* (Adichie)
Bienenstock, Myriam, 99
Binaisa, Godfrey, 94
Black vernacular intellectuals, 135n51
Bokassa, Jean-Bédel, 94
"born-after" generation, 138n4
Britain, 72; British Broadcasting Corporation (BBC), 25–26; role in Nigeria-Biafra War, 36–40, 43, 121. *See also Half of a Yellow Sun* (Adichie)
The Burden of Memory, The Muse of Forgiveness (Soyinka), 1, 23

canonization, 14
capitalism, 2, 4, 77–79, 88, 145n51
Caruth, Cathy, 55, 56, 57, 123
censorship. *See* state repression of memory
Central African Republic, 94–95
Césaire, Aimé, 8, 39, 136n66
Chakraborty, Dipesh, 9
Chana, Teeger, 58–59
children, 42, 74–75; "children of the postcolony," 17–18, 19, 121, 143n5; child soldiers, 138n2; child witnesses, 49. *See also* transgenerational memory narratives; transgenerational trauma
Children of the Revolution (Mengestu), 3–4, 5, 20–21, 118–25, 142n2, 143n4; African Transnational Memory, in search of, 89–95; "Children of the Revolution" (T. Rex), 87; immigrant melancholia, 74–83; memory, translocalities, and alternative practices of belonging in, 83–88
chronotopes, 15, 72, 139n12
chrono-trope, silent time as, 52, 72–73, 139n12
citizenship, acts of, 88, 145n49
civil war, 5. *See also Half of a Yellow Sun* (Adichie)
class, 2, 6, 24–25, 42, 79–80, 82, 141n37
coerced collaboration, 68
collective amnesia, 89, 90, 146n56; *Collective Amnesia* (Putuma), 48
collective memory, 7, 16, 91, 110, 130n55, 143n6, 145n51
collective ownership, network of, 41
collective responsibility, 113
collective silence, 61–62
colonialism, 12, 25, 89, 93–94, 120–21, 124–25; colonial gaze, 38, 94–95; coloniality of memory, 7–10, 37, 128n29; decolonization, 8–9, 36–37, 129n41, 146n54. *See also* postcolonialism
commemoration, 98–99, 115–16, 122, 124; culture of, 90, 92, 146n56; elitist memorialism, 2. *See also* sites of memory

common memory, 149n22
communicative dynamism, 52, 139n13
communicative memory, 134n29
communist revolution, 5, 75, 77, 121, 124. See also *Children of the Revolution* (Mengestu)
community of memory, 90, 99, 113, 149n21
compassionate listening, 151n60
complicity, 20, 62–63, 64–68, 69–73
composite consciousness, 35
concatenated memory, 12, 22, 45–46, 124–25
conflict, memories of, and conflicts of memory, 1–6
Connerton, Paul, 48, 57, 132n2
cosmological time, 142n56
cosmopolitanism from below, resistant, 87–88
Cote d'Ivoire, 107, 109, 148n14
Coulibaly, Maïmouna, 98, 148n15
Coundouriotis, Eleni, 43
counter-narrative, 36–37
co-witnessing, 113
Craps, Stef, 50
critical memory studies, 3
crying wound, 55
cultural memory, 7, 14, 84–88, 134n29, 152n7
cultural pluralism, 84
culture of silence, 57–58, 140n26, 141n37
"The Curse of Constant Remembrance" (Murphy), 23

Das, Veenas, 121
de Beer, Anna-Marie, 115
de Boeck, Filip, 9
debt of memory, 99
de Certeau, Michel, 1
decolonization, 8–9, 36–37, 129n41, 146n54. See also colonialism
Derg revolution, 21, 75, 76. See also *Children of the Revolution* (Mengestu)
Derrida, Jacques, 11, 31, 48, 138n95
Destination Biafra (Emecheta), 41

deterritorialization, 95, 103
The Devil That Danced on Water (Forna), 49
diamond industry, 5, 64. See also *The Memory of Love* (Forna)
Diawara, Mamadou, 10
Diop, Boubacar Boris, 104, 148n14, 149n27
Diop, Cheikh Anta, 91–92
Discourse on Colonialism (Césaire), 8, 136n66
disjunctive temporality, 69–73. See also temporality
dislocation, 21, 60, 86–87
distance, relationship to memory, 22, 122–23; privilege of distance, 35, 120
Djedanoum, Nocky, 98, 99, 148n14, 148n15
Driver, Dorothy, 87
Du Bois, W.E.B., 89
Durkheim, Émile, 7
Dutton, Chris, 25

Eagleton, Terry, 6
Ebola outbreak, 141n37
eclipsing, narrative, 110
Economic Community of West African States (ECOWAS), 90
Ejiofor, Chiwetel, 26
embodied memory, 44–45; prosthetic memory, 22, 100, 102–4, 107–8, 150n44
Emecheta, Buchi, 41
emotional truth, 123, 135n45
empathy, 50, 98, 100, 107, 110–11, 113; empathic unsettlement, 111–12, 114, 151n60; global ethics of care, 39
empty remembering, 95
Eng, David, 74
Erll, Astrid, 13, 14, 128n26, 152n7
ethical dilemmas, in doing memory work, 100–101, 115–16; *The Ethics of Memory* (Margalit), 100, 149nn21–22; micro-ethics, 100
Ethiopia, 3. See also *Children of the Revolution* (Mengestu)

exiles within, 86–87, 144n27
experiential museums, 104–6
exteriority, 22, 101, 109, 114–15. *See also* secondary witnessing
extratextuality, 26

Falola, Toyin, 89–90
Fambul Tok (family talk), 142n65
Fanon, Frantz, 8, 10, 39, 89–90
fatalism, 50
female genital mutilation, 141n37
feminism, 38
FESTAC '77, 92
Fest'Africa project, 98, 148n15
fiction, historicity of, 31–33, 123
fiction of memory, 2–3, 6, 14–15, 16–18, 117–25, 131n85. *See also Children of the Revolution* (Mengestu); frictions of memory; *Half of a Yellow Sun* (Adichie); *The Memory of Love* (Forna); *The Shadow of Imana* (Tadjo)
flashbulb memories, 107, 150n47
flattened time, 105, 150n44
forgetting, 58–64, 108; fibrillation of remembering-forgetting, 62, 140n25; oblivion, 58, 140n33; *oubli de reserve* (forgetting as a reserve), 57, 140n34; as repressive erasure, 132n3; social forgetting, 57–58, 140n32; "will to forget," 16, 24. *See also* amnesia; remembering; silence
Forna, Aminatta, 3, 49, 121, 138n2. *See also The Memory of Love*
Forsyth, Frederick, 34
fragmentation, 112
France, role in Rwandan genocide, 97
Franco, Francisco, 58
Freetown, Sierra Leone, 72, 140
Freud, Sigmund, 7, 55, 78, 79, 130n55, 131n85
frictions of memory, 2, 13–16, 18, 117–25. *See also Children of the Revolution* (Mengestu); fiction of memory; *Half of a Yellow Sun* (Adichie); *The Memory of Love* (Forna); *The Shadow of Imana* (Tadjo)

fugue, 59–60, 70–71, 142n60
futurity, 11–12, 22, 108, 119–20, 125

Gaddafi, Muammar, 64
Gandhi, Leela, 16
Garuba, Harry, 17
Gbanka war, in Sierra Leone, 140n28
gender, memory and, 125, 152n8; feminism, 38; phallocentric narratives, 38. *See also* women
genetic memory, 46
genocide, 92; Holocaust memory, 2–3, 7, 13, 20, 28, 39, 46, 73, 92, 136n66, 136n68; "Rwanda: Writing as a Duty to Remember" project, 21, 98–101, 103, 114, 116, 120, 124, 148n14, 149n27. *See also The Shadow of Imana* (Tadjo)
genre pigeonholing, refusal of, 14–16, 109–13
gentrification, 82, 86–87
Germany: colonial history of, 129n40, 148n5; Holocaust memory, 2–3, 7, 13, 20, 28, 39, 46, 73, 92, 136n66, 136n68
Ghana, 1, 92
Gikandi, Simon, 88
Girls at War (Achebe), 41
global memory, 90, 92–93, 103, 116, 124
Glynn, Irial, 74
Gobodo-Madikizela, Pumla, 54–55, 151n67
God's Bit of Woods (Sembene), 16
Going Down Road (Mwangi), 17
Gowon, Yakubu, 23, 135n46
The Guardian (newspaper), 25
Gunning, Dave, 50
Gutman, Yifat, 91

Habila, Helon, 25
Habyarimana, Juvénal, 97
Halbwachs, Maurice, 7
Half of a Yellow Sun (Adichie), 3–4, 5, 14, 18–19, 23–47, 117–25; aesthetics of postmemory in, 31–35; Biafra, postmemory and the possibility of justice for, 43–45; Biafra, the shadow of, 23–26,

28; concatenated memories, ancestral memories, 45–47; film adaptation of, 26, 137n71; nexus between postmemory and postcolonialism in, 36–40; postmemory, 26–28; remediation of memory, 40–43; vicarious witness, Adichie as, 28–31
"Harold Wilson Syndrome" (Kwashiorkor), 42, 137n81
Hartman, Saidiya V., 22, 136n60
haunting, 10–11, 42–43, 51, 78–79, 81. *See also* mourning; spectrality; wake work
Hausa people, 23. *See also Half of a Yellow Sun* (Adichie); Nigeria
hegemonic memory, 13, 15
Herero people, 39
High Life music, 34
Hiroshima crisis, 73
Hirsch, Marianne, 26–27, 46, 133n12, 133n23, 134n35
historiography: fiction, historicity of, 31–33, 123; historiographic metafiction, 33; *History, Memory, and Migration* (Glynn and Kleist), 74; "A History of the Future" (Staley), 117; "people's history," 33, 135n50; progressive historicism, 4, 11
Hitchcott, Nicki, 98, 112
Hobsbawm, Eric, 90
Holocaust memory, 2–3, 7, 13, 20, 28, 39, 46, 73, 92, 136n66, 136n68
home country, 85
homogeneous empty time, 11
How to Read the Air (Mengestu), 75, 76, 80–81
human time, 72, 142n62
Hutcheon, Linda, 33, 135n48
Hut tax war, in Sierra Leone, 140n28
Hutus. *See The Shadow of Imana* (Tadjo)
Huyssen, Andreas, 6

identity categories, fixed, 97, 107, 147n3
Igbo people. *See* Biafra; *Half of a Yellow Sun* (Adichie)
Ike, Chukwuemeka, 40, 42

illocutionary silence, 52–54
imagination, 3–6, 14–16, 19, 27, 30, 33–35, 43, 90, 94, 110, 123
"Imagining the Future Is Just Another Kind of Memory" (Beck), 117
immigrant melancholia, 20–21, 74–83
implicated subject, 66
indigenous peoples, 144n31; Indigenous People of Biafra (IPOB) movement, 45
indirect witnessing. *See* secondary witnessing
individualism, mnemonic, 145n51
institutionalized amnesia, 2, 15, 24
intellectual witnessing. *See* secondary witnessing
interiority, 31, 110
internationalism, Black, 40
intertextuality, 14, 19, 41–42, 86, 145n40
investigative journalism, 109
involuntary memory, 71
Irele, F. Abiola, 17–18
Israel, role in Rwandan genocide, 97
Iweala, Uzodinma, 25
Iyayi, Festus, 17

Japan, Hiroshima crisis in, 73
Jews, European. *See* Holocaust memory
justice, 43–45, 119, 137n89. *See also* reconciliation; repair

Kenya, 21, 75, 77–78, 88, 94, 124, 148n14
King, Martin Luther, Jr., 83
Kleist, Olaf, 74
Kony, Joseph, 94
Kwashiorkor ("Harold Wilson Syndrome"), 42, 137n81

Labyrinths (Okigbo), 42
LaCapra, Dominick, 96, 111–12, 130n55, 139n22
Lachmann, Renate, 14
Landsberg, Alison, 76, 91, 102–4, 143n6, 150n44
The Land without Shadows (Waberi), 17
Lategan, Bernard, 10

178 • Index

Laub, Dori, 33, 106
Law of Historical Memory (2007), 58
Lawson, Rex, 34
lieux de memoire. See sites of memory linking objects, 44, 80, 138n95, 143n21
literary analysis, relationship to memory, 13–16, 117–25; extratextuality, 26; intertextuality, 14, 19, 41–42, 86, 145n40; *memory in literature*, 14–15; metatextuality, 14, 19, 33, 39, 135n48; textual mourning, 80, 122, 143n22; textual silence, 52–54, 139n13; transtextuality, 26. *See also* fiction of memory; frictions of memory
Loftus, Elizabeth, 19
Lule, Yusuf, 94
Lumumba, Patrice, 94

macro-ethics, 100
Madiebo, Alexander, 42
Mamdani, Mahmood, 9, 12, 44, 97; *Neither Settler nor Native*, 74; *When Victims Become Killers*, 147n2
Mandela, Winnie, 92
Manga Sewa and Mandinka army battle, in Sierra Leone, 140n28
"Mango Seedling" (Achebe), 41
Mani invasion, in Sierra Leone, 140n28
Mapanje, Jack, 16
Margalit, Avishai, 21, 146n58; *The Ethics of Memory*, 100, 149nn21–22
Mariam, Mengistu Haile, 94
mass media, 91; experiential museums, 104–6, 143n6; social media, 40, 92; Western biases in, 37–38
Mbembe, Achille, 5, 22, 37, 69, 88, 96
mediated witnessing. *See* secondary witnessing
melancholia, 31, 36, 60, 79, 122, 130n55; immigrant melancholia, 20–21, 74–83; melancholic subject, 139n10; "Melancholy and the Act" (Žižek), 79–80; melancholy of no return, 81–82, 144n25; "Melancholy/Postcoloniality" (Eng), 74; national melancholia, 50–51, 56, 69. *See also* mourning
Memory and the Postcolony (Werbner), 2–3, 16, 129n39, 146n56
memory contracts, 46
The Memory of Love (Forna), 3–4, 5, 19–20, 48–73, 117–25; complicity, silence of, 64–68; culture of silence, 57–58; oppression, silence of, 56; post-conflict timescapes in, 69–73; reading silence, 48–52; silent and silenced memories, 58–64; as textual silence, 52–54; trauma, silence of, 54–55. *See also* silence
Mende uprising, in Sierra Leone, 140n28
Mengestu, Dinaw, 3, 121; *All Our Names*, 75; *How to Read the Air*, 75, 76, 80–81. *See also Children of the Revolution* (Mengestu)
metatextuality, 14, 19, 33, 39, 135n48
meta-witnessing, 110, 150n57
methodological nationalism, 12, 91
micro-ethics, 100
micronational enclaves, 83–84
migration, 8, 20–21, 118, 129n37; African Memory Game, 147n73; immigrant melancholia, 20–21, 74–83; migrant double bind, 82–83; migrant memory-making, 88; translocalities, memory, and alternative practices of belonging, 83–88; transmigrants, 84–85. *See also* African transnational memory (ATM); *Children of the Revolution* (Mengestu); transnationalism
Minow, Martha, 26
mnemocide, 3, 127n3
mnemonic relationality, 152n7
Morrison, Toni, 15, 27–28, 34, 135n45
mourning, 10–11, 16, 22, 26, 31, 54, 99–100, 118, 124–25, 130n55; Freudian theory of, 78–79; minute of silence, to honor dead, 62; perennial mourning, 138n95; textual mourning, 80, 122, 143n22. *See also Children of the Revolution* (Mengestu); *Half of a Yellow Sun*

(Adichie); haunting; melancholia; *The Memory of Love* (Forna); wake work
Movement of the Actualization of the Sovereign State of Biafra (MASSOB), 45
Mukandori (Rwandan woman), 104–5
multidirectional memory, 7–8
multiperspectivity, 15, 118
Murambi, the Book of Bones (Diop), 104, 149n27
Murphy, Laura, 23, 46
Mwangi, Meja, 17, 148n14

Namibian genocide, 92
narrative truth, 135n45
narratology, 15
nationalism, 12–13, 50, 82, 85; African, 89, 92, 145n54; deterritorialized, 95; methodological, 12, 91; ultranationalism, 90. See also *The Memory of Love* (Forna); transnationalism
national melancholia, 50–51, 56, 69
national memory, 12, 83–88, 115, 151n73
Necropolitics (Mbembe), 96
Neither Settler nor Native (Mamdani), 74
Nelly (Rwandan genocide survivor), 111
neoliberalism, 2, 77, 79, 82, 90, 92, 119, 145n51
Never Again (Nwapa), 41, 42
Newton, Thandie, 26
New York Times (newspaper), 25
Nguyen, Viet Than, 23
Nietzsche, Friedrich, 19
Nigeria, 3; Nigerian Film and Censorship Board, 45; *The Nigerian Revolution and the Biafran War* (Madiebo), 42; third generation of Nigerian writing, 25. See also Biafra; *Half of a Yellow Sun* (Adichie)
Nkrumah, Kwame, 89
non-contemporaneous time, 11
non-redemptive narratives, 56, 121–22
Nora, Pierre, 7, 12
Norridge, Zoe, 50, 137n86
Nothing Ever Dies (Nguyen), 23

Ntarama Church memorial, 102, 104–6
Nünning, Ansgar, 14
Nwapa, Flora, 40, 41, 42
Nyamata Church memorial, 102, 104–6

objective response, 111
oblivion, 58, 140n33
Ojukwu, Chukwuemeka Odumegwu, 35, 135n46
Okello, Tito, 94
Okigbo, Christopher, 34, 41, 42
The Old Man and the Medal (Oyono), 16
Olick, Jeffrey, 6–7
1.5 generation, 49, 138n4
one world in relation, 87, 145n42
Opération Turquoise, 97
oppression, silence of, 56
Organization of African Unity, 97
Orientalism (Said), 8
oubli de reserve (forgetting as a reserve), 57, 140n34. See also forgetting
Ouma, Chris, 35, 41, 135n51
outsider within, 107, 150n48
Oyono, Ferdinand, 16

Pan-Africanism, 89–90, 100, 101, 145n54; PANAFEST, 92
Passerlini, Luisa, 58
past continuous, 2. See also present, continuity of the past in the
"people's history," 33, 135n50
Perceiving Pain in African Literature (Norridge), 50
periodization, 16–17
Petals of Blood (Thiong'o), 17
phallocentric narratives, 38
phenomenological time, 118–19, 142n56
philanthrocapitalism, 2
photographs, role in memory, 42–43, 137n82
"The Pitfall of National Consciousness" (Fanon), 89
placelessness, sense of, 87
plagiarism, allegations of, 41, 137n78
political exigency, 2

political reform, 44
The Politics of Friendship (Derrida), 48
polysemy, of silence, 19, 51–52
portable monument, 30
positionality, 4, 22, 118, 123–24; interiority, 31, 110; subalternity, 2. *See also* alterity; exteriority; secondary witnessing; subjectivity
postcolonialism, 6, 129n44; postcolonial disillusionment, 17; "The Postcolonial Flaneur" (Williams), 1; "Postcoloniality and the Artifice of History" (Chakraborty), 9; postcolonial memory studies, 6–13, 129n39; postcolonial studies, 8; postmemory and, in *Half of a Yellow Sun* (Adichie), 36–40. *See also* colonialism
post-conflict, terminology of, 5–6, 137n86
postmemory, 14, 18–19, 26–28, 133n23; aesthetics of, in *Half of a Yellow Sun* (Adichie), 31–35; "familial" *versus* "affiliative," 134n35; generation of, 25; possibility of justice for Biafra and, 43–45; postcolonialism and, in *Half of a Yellow Sun* (Adichie), 36–40. *See also* *Half of a Yellow Sun* (Adichie)
postmodernism, 109
postnational network of diasporas, 83–84
posttraumatic, postcolonial history as, 11
"poverty porn," 6
Prague school, 52, 139n13
precarity, 22, 77, 79, 82–83, 100
prememory, 39, 136n67
present, continuity of the past in the, 11–12, 22, 115, 117–25
privilege of distance, 35, 120. *See also* distance, relationship to memory
progressive historicism, 4, 11
prosthetic memory, 22, 100, 102–4, 107–8, 150n44
Proust, Marcel, 71
provincialism, 90, 92
public practice, memory as, 2, 121. *See also* national memory
Putuma, Koleka, 48

Radstone, Susannah, 92
Rauff, Ulrich, 14
reading silence, 48–52
realist fictions, 15
reconciliation, 44–45, 119, 120, 131n89, 137n89; Fambul Tok (family talk), 145n65. *See also* justice; repair
regional memories, 13. *See also* African transnational memory (ATM)
relational discourse, 94
remediation of memory, 40–43
remembering, 118, 124; empty remembering, 95; misremembering, 115; "re-membering," 13; "remembering back," 36–40; remembering to forget, 62, 140n25; "remembering together," 21, 88, 93–94; rememory, 27–28; "Rwanda: Writing as a Duty to Remember" project, 21, 98–101, 103, 114, 116, 120, 124, 148n14, 149n27; thick and thin relationships of, 90, 99–100, 107, 146n58, 149n21. *See also Children of the Revolution* (Mengestu); commemoration; forgetting; sites of memory
Renan, Ernest, 23
repair, 26, 43–45, 47, 120, 133n12, 137n89; reparative humanism, 113, 151n67. *See also* justice; reconciliation
responsibility-in-complicity, 67
Ricoeur, Paul, 19, 22, 57, 99, 140n34, 142n62; *Time and Narrative*, vol. 1, 142n56
Rigney, Ann, 30
Rogers, Juliet, 70–71
romanticizing memory, 35
Rothberg, Michael, 7–8, 39, 144n49
Rusen, Jorn, 10
Russia, role in Nigeria-Biafra War, 43
Rwanda, 3, 12; genocide museum, in Johannesburg, 92; Rwandan Patriotic Front (RPF), 112; "Rwanda: Writing as a Duty to Remember" project, 21, 98–101, 103, 114, 116, 120, 124, 148n14, 149n27. *See also The Shadow of Imana* (Tadjo)

Said, Edward, 8
Salih, Tayeb, 16
Sanders, Mark, 66, 67
Sankara, Thomas, 117
Sankofa bird, 120
Sanyal, Debarati, 66
Sarafina (film), 92
Scott, David, 11
Season of Migration to the North (Salih), 16
Sebald, W. G., 26
secondary witnessing, 4, 22, 42, 100, 101–2, 106, 109–16. *See also The Shadow of Imana* (Tadjo)
secondhand memories, 26
Second World War. *See* Holocaust memory
Seko, Mobutu Sese, 94
Selasi, Taiye, 88
Selassie, Haile, 75, 86
self-reflexivity, 110–11, 112, 113
Sembene, Ousmane, 16
"Seven Types of Forgetting" (Connerton), 48, 132n2
sex, as a synecdoche of violence, 50
sexual violence, 25, 104–5; female genital mutilation, 141n37
The Shadow of Imana (Tadjo), 3–4, 5, 21–22, 118–25; affective encounters, 103–8; African transnational memory and the genocide of the Tutsi, 96–103; secondary witnessing, aesthetics of, 109–16
shared memory, 149n22
Shaw, Rosalind, 57, 140n32
Sierra Leone, 3, 10, 140n28; Freetown, 72, 140; Sierra Leone Truth and Reconciliation Commission (SLTRC), 56, 57–58, 67–68, 140n32, 142n65. *See also The Memory of Love* (Forna)
silence, 19–20, 98, 117, 118, 139n14; collective silence, 61–62; complicity, silence of, 20, 62–63, 64–68; culture of silence, 57–58, 140n26, 141n37; illocutionary silence, 52–54; minute of silence, to honor dead, 62; oppression, silence of, 56; plurality, of silence, 73; polysemy of, 19, 51–52; reading silence, 48–52; silencescape, 72; *Silencing the Past* (Trouillot), 96; "silent" and "silenced" memories, 20, 24, 28–29, 58–64, 80; silent time, as chrono-trope, 52, 72–73, 139n12; Spain, pact of silence in, 20, 58; state repression of memory, 2–3, 5, 23–24, 45; textual silence, *The Memory of Love* (Forna) as, 52–54; trauma, silence of, 54–55. *See also* forgetting; *The Memory of Love* (Forna); state repression of memory
"single story" of Africa, 37
sites of memory, 4, 7, 12, 40, 102–8, 115–16, 118, 122–23, 150n48; portable monument, 30; "The Site of Memory" (Morrison), 135n45. *See also* commemoration
Sithole, Ndabaningi, 89
slavery: African American, 28; transatlantic slave trade, 36, 124, 136n60; Trans-Saharan, 140n28
social forgetting, 57–58, 140n32
social media, 40, 92
solidarity: anamnestic solidarity, with the dead, 10, 43, 104, 122; with the dead, 10, 104, 122; horizontal and vertical, 57, 100, 146n57; racial, 82, 87, 100, 124–25. *See also* transnationalism
Solomon Mahlangu College, in Tanzania, 92
Sons of Africa, 145n54
Sontag, Susan, 113
South Africa, 10, 54–55, 97
Soyinka, Wole, 1, 11–12, 23
Spain, pact of silence in, 20, 58
spectrality, 10–11, 28, 33, 41, 45, 51, 53, 79, 119–20, 122. *See also* haunting
Staley, David, 117
Stanley, Liz, 27
state repression of memory, 2–3, 5, 23–24, 45. *See also Half of a Yellow Sun* (Adichie); silence
Stevens, Siaka, 64–65

Stone, Charles B., 59, 62–63
"Stories of Africa" (Adichie), 28–30, 34, 40
Strasser, Valentine, 94
Sturken, Marita, 112, 151n65
subalternity, 2
subjectivity, 4, 69, 77, 79, 82, 101–2, 112, 113–14. *See also The Shadow of Imana* (Tadjo)
Suleiman, Susan, 49, 138n4
Sunset at Dawn (Ike), 42
surrogate victimhood, 111, 118
survival, 4, 56, 66–67, 119

Tadjo, Véronique, 3, 18, 148n14. *See also The Shadow of Imana* (Tadjo)
talking cure, 55
Tan, Kathy-Ann, 87–88
Taya, Ahmed, 94
Taylor, Charles, 64
temporality, 11–13, 22, 58, 80, 81–82; being-in-time, 70; chronotopes, 15, 72, 139n12; chrono-trope, silent time as, 52, 72–73, 139n12; cosmological and phenomenological times, 118–19, 142n56, 142n62; disjunctive temporality, 69–73; flattened time, 105, 150n44; futurity, 11–12, 22, 108, 119–20, 125; homogeneous empty time, 11; human time, 72, 142n62; minute of silence, to honor dead, 62; non-contemporaneous time, 11, 112, 118–19; silencescape, 72; *Time and Narrative*, vol. 1 (Ricoeur), 142n56; timeless present, 69; time of/in the wake, 125; timescapes, post-conflict, 69–73; victim time, 72
testimonies, collection of reported, 109
textual mourning, 80, 122, 143n22
textual silence, 52–54, 139n13
thanatourism, 112
There Was a Country (Achebe), 45
Things Fall Apart (Achebe), 16
Thiong'o, Ngugi wa, 16, 17
Thomas, Dominic, 17
Thomas Sankara Speaks (Sankara), 117

tourists of history, 112, 151n65
transculturality, 128n26
transferential spaces, 104–6
transgenerational memory narratives, 74–77. *See also Children of the Revolution* (Mengestu)
transgenerational trauma, 26–28, 36, 118. *See also Half of a Yellow Sun* (Adichie); postmemory; witnessing
translocalities, 83–88
transmigrants, 84–85
transnationalism, 8, 21–22; minor transnationalism, 147n74; transnational Black solidarity, 87; transnational memory studies, 8; transnational sites of memory, 38–40; transnational urbanism, 84. *See also* African transnational memory (ATM); migration; nationalism
transtextuality, 26
trauma, 50, 121, 123; posttraumatic, postcolonial history as, 11, 125; secondary, 106; silence of, 3, 54–55, 139n22; traumascape, 69–73, 104–6; trauma tourism, 112. *See also The Memory of Love* (Forna); mourning; postmemory; witnessing
trauma, transgenerational transmission of, 26–28, 36, 118. *See also Half of a Yellow Sun* (Adichie); postmemory; witnessing
trauma narratives, aesthetics of, 109–16, 118. *See also The Shadow of Imana* (Tadjo)
travelogue, 109, 112
T. Rex (band), 87
Trezise, Thomas, 110
Trouillot, Michel-Rolph, 96, 101, 139n14
Truth and Reconciliation Commission (TRC), 54–55; Sierra Leone Truth and Reconciliation Commission (SLTRC), 56, 57–58, 67–68, 140n32, 142n65
Tsing, Anna, 18
Tutsis, genocide against: African Transnational Memory and, 96–103. *See also The Shadow of Imana* (Tadjo)

Ubuntu, 100
ultimate witness, 43, 137n86
ultranationalism, 90
Under the Tongue (Vera), 16
Un di Velt Hot Geshvign (And the World Remained Silent) (Wiesel), 39
Unigwe, Chika, 25
United States of America, 43; African American slavery, 28; American dream, 78; exiles within, 86–87, 144n27; as "nation of immigrants," 83–84, 144n31; role in Rwandan genocide, 97–98; transatlantic slave trade, 36, 124, 136n60
United States of America, Ethiopian immigration to. *See Children of the Revolution* (Mengestu)
"Unpacking the Unspoken: Silence in Collective Memory and Forgetting" (Chana and Vinitzsky-Seroussi), 58–59
unreliable narrator, 66

van Gils, Martijn, 44
Vera, Yvonne, 16
vernacular intellectualism, 135n51
vicarity: vicarious response, 111; vicarious responsibility, 66; vicarious witnessing, 28–31. *See also* secondary witnessing
victimhood, 106; surrogate, 111, 118; vicarious, 100; victim time, 72
Vinitzsky-Seroussi, Vered, 58–59
Violence (Iyayi), 17
visiting witness-ing. *See* secondary witnessing

Waberi, Abdourahman, 17, 148n14
wake work, 10–11, 22, 125. *See also* anamnestic solidarity, with the dead; commemoration; haunting; mourning; sites of memory
war, terminology of, 1–2, 5–6. *See also* post-conflict, terminology of

Washington, DC, Ethiopian immigration to. *See Children of the Revolution* (Mengestu)
Weep Not, Child (Thiong'o), 16
Werbner, Richard: *Memory and the Postcolony*, 2–3, 16, 129n39, 146n56
"What Is a Nation?" (Renan), 23
Wiesel, Elie, 39, 137n86
Williams, Adebayo, 1
"will to forget," 16, 24
Winter, Jay, 19
witnessing, 122–24; "born-after" generation, 138n4; child witnesses, 49; co-witnessing, 113; meta-witnessing, 110, 150n57; 1.5 generation, 49, 138n4; ultimate witness, 43, 137n86; vicarious, 28–31; witnessing witnessing, 110. *See also* secondary witnessing; transgenerational trauma
women: burden of memory among, 125, 152n8; female genital mutilation, 141n37; feminism, 38; *Half of a Yellow Sun* (Adichie), centering women's experiences in, 38; outsider within, in academia, 150n48; sexual violence, 25, 104–5; white women, interracial relationships with, 75, 78, 79–81; women perpetrators, 112; Women's Prize for Fiction, 25. *See also* gender, memory and
The Wretched of the Earth (Fanon), 8
"writing back," 13, 36–40, 131n77
Writing History, Writing Trauma (LaCapra), 96
The Writing of History (de Certeau), 1

xenophobia, 82

Zaire, 21, 75, 77, 86, 88
Žižek, Slavoj, 79–80